Pro Python Best Practices

Debugging, Testing and Maintenance

Kristian Rother

apress®

Pro Python Best Practices: Debugging, Testing and Maintenance

Kristian Rother
Berlin, Germany

ISBN-13 (pbk): 978-1-4842-2240-9   ISBN-13 (electronic): 978-1-4842-2241-6
DOI 10.1007/978-1-4842-2241-6

Library of Congress Control Number: 2017936044

Managing Director: Welmoed Spahr
Editorial Director: Todd Green
Acquisitions Editor: Steve Anglin
Development Editor: Matthew Moodie
Technical Reviewer: Michael Thomas
Coordinating Editor: Mark Powers
Copy Editor: Brendan Frost
Compositor: SPi Global
Indexer: SPi Global
Artist: SPi Global
Cover image designed by Freepik

Distributed to the book trade worldwide by Springer Science+Business Media New York, 233 Spring Street, 6th Floor, New York, NY 10013. Phone 1-800-SPRINGER, fax (201) 348-4505, e-mail orders-ny@springer-sbm.com, or visit www.springeronline.com. Apress Media, LLC is a California LLC and the sole member (owner) is Springer Science + Business Media Finance Inc (SSBM Finance Inc). SSBM Finance Inc is a **Delaware** corporation.

For information on translations, please e-mail rights@apress.com, or visit http://www.apress.com/rights-permissions.

Apress titles may be purchased in bulk for academic, corporate, or promotional use. eBook versions and licenses are also available for most titles. For more information, reference our Print and eBook Bulk Sales web page at www.apress.com/bulk-sales.

Any source code or other supplementary material referenced by the author in this book is available to readers on GitHub via the book's product page, located at www.apress.com/9781484222409. For more detailed information, please visit http://www.apress.com/source-code.

Printed on acid-free paper

To my parents

Contents at a Glance

Contents

About the Author

Kristian Rother had his first contact with programming 30 years ago in the children's section of the local library. After reading all the books on computers there and writing programs on paper for a couple of months, his parents decided to buy a computer to prevent the kid from becoming crazy. Whether that helped is still being debated. Since then, he has written programs in Basic, Assembler, Pascal, Java, Perl, PHP (but with a very good excuse), C, C++, Fortran, Haskell, Ada, Bash, Cache, Brainf***, and, of course, Python.

Being enthusiastic about technology, Kristian decided to study biochemistry. After producing a lot of broken glassware and several gallons of obnoxious goo, he discovered his general ineptitude for work in a biochemical laboratory. Fortunately, he joined a bioinformatics research group where he could apply his programming abilities to the analysis of biological data. He spent the next decade as a researcher on protein and RNA 3D structures, which involved data analysis, database and software development, 3D algorithms, creating videos of molecules flying through space, and a lot of writing. He received a doctoral degree at the Humboldt University Berlin. In 2013, Allegra Via from Rome and Kristian teamed up to publish a book on biological data analysis with Python.

Over time, Kristian came to understand that learning programming is not easy. He started to help other people in that area. During many courses, he sharpened his teaching skills until he decided to make a career out of it. He is currently working in Berlin as a professional trainer with a strong focus on Python, but keeps an open mind for diverse topics. Besides conducting Python trainings, he is passionately teaching biochemistry, statistics, web testing, search engines, public speaking, and any combination of the aforementioned.

Kristian is convinced that everybody can program.

About the Technical Reviewer

Michael Thomas has worked in software development for more than 20 years as an individual contributor, team lead, program manager, and vice president of engineering. Michael has more than 10 years of experience working with mobile devices. His current focus is in the medical sector, using mobile devices to accelerate information transfer between patients and health care providers.

Acknowledgments

First of all, I would like to thank my mentors: Wolfgang Vahrson, who introduced me to Python; and Christoph Gille, Cornelius Frömmel, and Ulf Leser, whose guidance helped me to develop my programming skills. I am thankful for the Python projects I had the pleasure to work on with Kaja Milanowska, Anna Philipps, Joanna Kasprzak, Tomasz Puton, Justyna Wojtczak, Pawel Skiba, Marcin Feder, Michal Gajda, Staszek Dunin-Horkawicz, Michal Boniecki, Wojciech Potrzebowski, Natalia Szostak, Michal Pietal, Silke Trissl, Christian Tismer, and Raphael Bauer. Without these people, I would not be in the position to write anything about Python.

I am grateful for many opportunities to teach Python provided by Pedro Fernandes, Allegra Via, Jasmin Touati, Veit Schiele, Jose Quesada, Janick Mathys, Martin Hoste, Julia Rose, Eryk Hajecki, and Edward Jenkins. I recall many fruitful conversations inside and outside of training rooms with most of these people about learning programming skills.

Credit goes to Dinu Gherman, Sebastian Thieme, Daniel Godoy, and Markus Rother, who reviewed my early notes for the book and provided plenty of valuable feedback on the structure. An especially big "Thank You" is reserved for my Technical Reviewer, Michael Thomas, who undertook the ordeal of reading through the early drafts of all chapters and provided constructive reviews that motivated me to improve the material.

This book would not have been possible without the diligence and patience of my Coordinating Editor, Mark Powers, who displayed a great deal of professionalism dealing with both the ups and downs of a manuscript and whose merit it is that the book actually got finished. The support of Development Editor Matthew Moodie and Acquisitions Editor Stephen Anglin was equally indispensable during the last 12 months.

Finally, I would like to thank my family for the support that gave me the courage to finish the book. My wife Magdalena Rother, being a fabulous Python developer, gave me counsel throughout the writing process, including critically examining my code, testing Python tools with me, debating programming practices after midnight, and making every other moment with her a moment well spent.

Preface

Writing good Python programs is difficult. Once your programs grow past a few lines, they are inherently prone to errors of all kind. There are many pitfalls unknown to the apprentice developer, but not because Python as a language is difficult to use. To the contrary, the overabundant opportunities Python provides make it difficult to figure out what matters in your daily practice. Instead of trying to cover the entire world of Python, this book focuses on a few essential practices used by most professional Python programmers. These Best Practices will help you to debug programs, write automated tests for your software, and keep it in a state that can be maintained with reasonable effort. I have picked techniques useful for Python developers in data analysis, web development, and scientific software development alike. If you feel you have mastered the basics of Python and want to improve the way you write programs, this book is here to help you raise the bar.

CHAPTER 1

▓ ▓ ▓

Introduction

A Lesson in Humility

I started writing my first computer game when I was 16. It was a puzzle game where you had to move bricks and make them disappear. A couple of friends joined the project, and soon the game featured a detailed concept, graphics, levels, and even a penguin mascot (the Linux mascot was yet to be invented). Only the program had to be written. At that time, I was coding in the assembler language on a C64 computer. At first, programming was easy. In juvenile audacity I was convinced that programming meant throwing enough brain at writing code, until it worked. I had already written many small programs like this and everything had worked fine. But soon, programming the graphics and game mechanics turned out to be more difficult than I had thought. I was spending days trying to get small improvements to work, with little or no progress. My programming workflow was

1. Turn on the computer

2. Load the compiler

3. Load the program

4. Write a few lines of code

5. Run the program

6. Frequently, the program would crash and take down the operating system

7. Switch off the computer and return to step 1

Effectively, I was spending not more than a rough 10% of my time actually working on the code. It is not surprising that development slowed down and soon came to a halt completely. At the moment, the project is 23 years late. It took me very long to figure out what had happened. Any mentor (an experienced programmer or an older version of myself) would have insisted on finding a shortcut from step 5 to step 4. Such shortcuts existed at the time in the form of a cartridge you plugged into the back of the computer. Finding these shortcuts is not a trivial matter. Yet they make all the difference. We will call these shortcuts **Best Practices**.

The Case for Best Practices in Python

Today, 23 years later, we have **Python**, a language that makes many things easier. We don't have to restart the computer when the program contains an error. We have libraries like **Pygame** that help us to create nicer and faster graphics with very little code. Do we still need Best Practices for writing Python code? Although you will anticipate my point of view from the title of this book, I would like to start with a simple example that explains why it is still worth to think about Best Practices in Python. Suppose we want to create graphics for our own

K. Rother, *Pro Python Best Practices*, DOI 10.1007/978-1-4842-2241-6_1

small game using **Python** and **Pygame**. As a proof of concept, we will load two images, one with a level and one with the player figure, and combine them to a single image (Figure 1-1). The functions in the **Pygame** library do most of the work. To combine the images and save them to a new file, only five lines of code are needed:

```python
from pygame import image, Rect

maze = image.load('maze.png')
player = image.load('player.png')

maze.blit(player, Rect((32, 32, 64, 64)), Rect((0, 0, 32, 32)))
image.save(maze, 'merged.png')
```

Figure 1-1. *Two images to be combined with Pygame*

At first sight, the program looks dead simple. What is more, it works correctly and produces a merged image. The program is too short to fail... or is it? I took the time to enumerate ways in which this five-line program might fail:

- A typo in the program terminates Python with a `SyntaxError`

- Pygame is not installed, so Python exits with an ImportError

- An incompatible version of Pygame is installed, so Python terminates with an Exception

- One of the image files does not exist, so Python exits with an `IOError`

- There is no write permission for the output image, so Python terminates with an `IOError`

- One of the image files is corrupted, so Python terminates with an Exception

- One of the image files is distorted, so the output image will be distorted as well

- The program is incompatible with Python 3, so users are dependent on Python 2

- Generating the image is too slow, so the game becomes unplayable

- Image transparency is not handled correctly, so artifacts appear in the output image

- A wrong output file name is given, so an important file is overwritten

- Pygame contains malicious code, so system security becomes compromised

- The program is distributed with unlicensed images, so the authors have IP lawyers at their neck

- The program does not run on mobile phones, so nobody wants to use it

- There is no documentation, so potential users are unable to install or use the program

I am sure you can find even more potential problems. Even in a five-line program, many more than five things can go wrong. We can be sure that even more things can go wrong in a long program. When we look at the list of problems more closely, we see that some of the problems are clearly connected to the code itself (e.g., the wrong import). Others, like the lack of documentation or the legal issues) have nothing to do with the code itself, yet they have severe consequences.

▓ **Conclusion**   Some problems in programming can be solved by programming. Other problems in programming cannot be solved by programming. As programmers, we are responsible for both.

No matter what the problem is, we, the programmers, and our users will have to live with the consequences. I am frequently using my own five-line Python programs for small tasks (e.g., merging PDFs or shrinking digital camera images). As the only user, I can easily change the code or rewrite the program completely. But if we want to write bigger programs, programs with more users, and cooperate with other programmers, we need to prevent our projects from coming to a standstill. We need to prevent running into too many problems at the same time. We need techniques that keeps our program healthy and *easy* to work with. The premise of this book is to introduce you to established techniques or **Best Practices** to write better Python programs.

The Origin of Best Practices

How can we create well-written programs that solve or avoid the previously described problems? There are several schools of thought that have put a lot of energy into the subject. Here, we will explore whether they help us (see Figure 1-2).

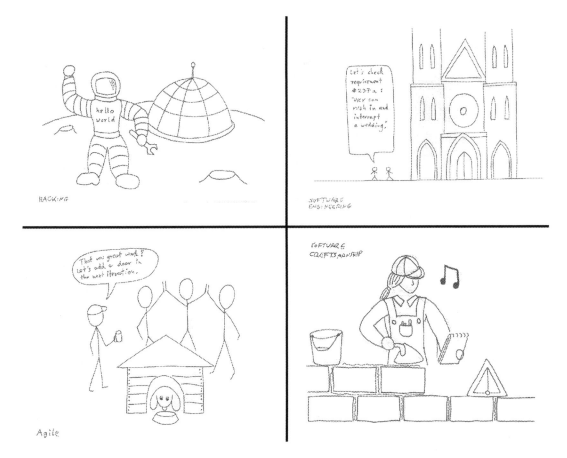

Figure 1-2. *Building a house as a metaphor for building software. Upper left: Hacking, love for the challenge of overcoming technical limitations. Upper right: Software engineering, a systematic approach found in large projects. Lower left: Agile, fast, iterative development. Note that the product is inhabited by the end user while development goes on. Lower right: Software craftsmanship, focusing on doing things right using a set of established tools.*

Hacking

According to Richard Stallman, **hackers** have *love of excellence and programming* in common (*Hackers: Wizards of the Electronic Age,* 1985, TV documentary). They enjoy the creative challenging to overcome technical limitations and achieve things not thought possible before. People who are good at hacking are indispensable in todays technology-driven society. Hacking is a key skill, and we need people who are good at it. Without doubt, hacking is a useful skill in programming. Python is an excellent language to hack things in.

However, I don't think hacking is a great approach to programming in general. I give three reasons for that. First, hacking focuses on novel, difficult, or otherwise challenging problems. By their very nature, the according solutions have a touch of genius and a touch of improvisation. This is a good combination, if you are solving problems at the frontier of what has been done before. But what if you just want to write *ordinary* programs? For many of us finding a working solution is sufficient, even if the solution will be boring.

Second, hacking has a strong connotation of excellence. Hackers are often considered an *elite*, a community that requires an unspoken skill level to belong to. But in programming, there are many problems that do not need an expert to solve. Often, an average programmer is sufficient, where a hacker might become bored. In business terms, a path that thousands of programmers have walked before is much less risky than a path that only a few chosen ones can take or is yet unknown.

Third, not everybody *wants* to devote themselves to hacking. Many of us have other things to do than figuring out in all details how computers work; we have data to understand, websites to create, a business to run, and families to take care of. In my opinion, programming is far too important to leave it to a small group of devoted experts. One reason why I wrote this book is that I want to push back the boundary and make programming accessible to more people. In my opinion, everybody can program, and everybody is able to do it well. There are other ways to program than hacking. There is a lot we can learn from the hacker culture, though: the tremendously useful technologies and tools it has produced and the *love for excellence and programming*.

Software Engineering

Opposed to hacking, we find s**oftware engineering**. Software engineering is concerned with a systematic approach to building software, usually in a corporate environment. Instead of focusing on the individual, software engineering is about *controlling the entire process of building programs*: its techniques cover finding out precisely what is to be built, designing a program with clearly defined components, verifying that the program actually works correctly and, finally, maintaining the program once it is being used. There is a lot we can learn from software engineering as well. For instance, background research has been done on the work caused by problems like the ones in the preceding list. Depending on which study you cite, we find that only one-third of the total cost of software is the initial development; the rest is maintenance. And of that initial third, only 25%–50% is for writing code; the rest is planning, debugging, testing, and maintenance.

The drawback of the software engineering approach is that it is too big for most Python projects. The typical project where software engineering methods become useful ranges in time from half a year to several years, sometimes even decades. Often, we chose Python because it is possible to achieve results within days, hours, sometimes minutes. Also, software engineering projects often involve dozens or hundreds of people, thousands to millions lines of code, and documentation covering thousands of pages. If your goals are more modest, we need to look for a lighter approach. If you feel that you would like more background information, the book *Software Engineering* by Ian Sommerville (Addison-Wesley, 2000) is a good starting point.

Agile

The notion that software engineering is a rather heavy methodology is not new. When asking for an alternative, the answer you will often hear in 2017 is **Agile**. Agile is a philosophy dedicated to improving the software development process. Its core values are *individuals and interactions, working software, customer collaboration*, and *responding to change* (also see `www.agilemanifesto.org/`). Agile (and its most prevalent manifestations, **Scrum** and **XP**) promotes rapid, evolutionary development of programs and working in short iterations (see Figure 1-2). Building a program in small working increments has had a huge positive impact on programmers around the world.

Knowing about Agile is useful, because it provides a philosophical foundation to efficient programming. It places the human factor in programming in the front row. Many of the tools described in this book have been developed with Agile principles and practices in mind. This brings us to the limitation of the Agile approach: Agile is a philosophy, not a set of tools. Agile tells us *why* we might want to program in a certain way (to create working software quickly and have satisfied customers), but it does not tell us *what* to do when in front of a keyboard. Also, Agile frameworks are often difficult to implement in practice. For instance, the Scrum framework is restricted to five to nine people and it requires a lot of commitment from an organization. In addition, Agile processes are sometimes adopted mainly for their fashionable names. In practice, there is a thin line between following a well-defined process and blindly following a rulebook, and it takes both experience and common sense to find the right balance.

Software Craftsmanship

Being a genius hacker helps. Having a well-engineered blueprint of your software helps. Having a dynamic customer-oriented process helps as well. But at the bottom of things is the work we do in front of the computer. Acknowledging this work is the basis of a discipline called s**oftware craftsmanship**. Software craftsmanship acknowledges that a big portion of programming consists of simple tasks that need to be done. To do it well, we need to have the right tools, we need to have the right skills, and we need to apply both in practice. Programming being a *craft* like masonry, carpentry, or confectionery suggests that

- Purpose matters. We are creating programs as a means to an end. Programming is not an art; we want to write programs that are used.

- Planning matters. It is a helpful and necessary part of the work (*measure twice, cut once*).

- Tools matter. We need to take care of our tool set and keep our workplace in a good shape. The craft helps us to pick the right tools.

- Skills matter. We are continuously working on improving our craft. We strive to program as well as we can, and at the same time acknowledge that our skills are not perfect.

- Community matters. There is a big community of likeminded people who honor the craft. The community is a place for apprentices and for masters alike.

- Size does not matter. We do not restrict ourselves to a certain type of project. The craft is needed whether we write a five-line program or contribute to a huge project.

- Practice matters. We cannot solve programming problems on a whiteboard or a spreadsheet alone. To program successfully, we need to get our hands dirty.

Software craftsmanship is a useful metaphor for Python programmers. Therefore, this book is built upon the idea of software craftsmanship. The Best Practices we will see in this book have been tried, tested, and found useful by many software craftspeople before us.

Who This Book Is For

You have mastered the basics of Python and written Python programs on your own for some time. You apply data structures like lists, dictionaries, and sets securely and are able to write your own functions. Maybe you have started writing object-oriented programs using Python classes and programs consisting of multiple modules. With improving programming skills, your programs are growing bigger and bigger. You find that bigger programs are harder to debug and test, and have a general tendency to fall apart. In order to write reliable Python programs between 100 and 10,000 lines, techniques that counter these problems might be useful. You may have realized that programming is more than just writing code. Knowing all the commands is not enough to make programs work. You may also have realized that the world of Python is huge. There is an overabundant number of tools and libraries that might help you. Finding out which of them is worth trying is hard, though. This book has been written to help you find out what to do next.

This book is for people who are programming frequently, but are not full-time software developers. You could be a biologist who has data for a few million DNA sequences to analyze. You could be a journalist using Python to harvest information from the web automatically. You could be using Python to boost your work as a system administrator managing a big network. You could run programming classes where you are building an interactive website. Whatever you do, you are an expert in your own domain and have relevant problems to solve. This book has been written to improve your Python projects without having to study computer science first. You want to write Python code that not only *somehow works* but is also *well-written*. In that case, this book on Best Practices on **debugging**, **automated testing**, and **maintenance** will help you to develop your Python skills further.

What This Book Is About

Python is not a new language. It has been around for more than 25 years now. During that time, a huge number of techniques and tools that help writing better Python programs has emerged, and new tools are constantly being developed. For someone relatively new to Python these huge numbers can easily become overwhelming. To offer some guidance, this book will focus on three questions:

- How can we make our code work?

- How can we check whether our code works?

- How can we make sure that our code will work in the future?

I have found these three problems central to my own programming practice in Python, and I have seen many emerging Python programmers struggle with these areas. The next 16 chapters of this book are grouped into three parts, each of them presenting Best Practices answering one of these three questions.

Part 1: Debugging

Our first priority as programmers is to get a program running. And the first thing that gets in the way are bugs. In the first part of the book we will examine what types of bugs or, more precisely, *Exceptions* and *semantic errors* occur in Python and how to eliminate them. Instead of guessing wildly, we will use the *scientific method*, a systematic thought process. The Best Practices for debugging include tools like `print`, *introspection* to produce diagnostic information, and an *interactive debugger* for tracing the execution of code line by line. These Best Practices for debugging are useful regardless of the type and size of program you are writing.

Part 2: Automated Testing

Once we have written a program, how do we know that it works? Of course we can run it ourselves manually, but with frequent changes manual testing gets error-prone and tedious. Fortunately, testing in Python is easy to automate. Starting from simple *test functions*, we will add *test data* to test our program under various conditions. We will assemble our tests for the program into a *test suite*. We will look at Best Practices of testing: What kinds of tests exist? In what situations are they useful? Finally, we will examine strengths and weaknesses of automated testing. Automated testing will help you to check whether bugs are present in your program, and thus prevent them from reappearing once you fixed them.

Part 3: Maintenance

Writing a program is one thing. Keeping it working is another. Maintaining software is a wide field, and Python offers a plethora of great support tools. We start our tour of Best Practices for maintenance with *Version Control*, which is considered a must-have by any professional programmer. We will see how *files and folders* are structured in a well-kept Python project. Two chapters deal with *cleaning up code* and *decomposing a programming problem* into smaller parts to make it easier to manage. Next, we take a closer look at *typing* in Python and what options we have to make our data types more reliable. In the final chapter, we will use the Sphinx tool to write *documentation*. All things combined create an healthy ecosystem in which your program can thrive.

Further Benefits

The benefit of reading about Best Practices from these three areas is twofold: First, you will learn the tools and techniques themselves, so that you can apply them in your everyday programming practice. Second, you will get an overview of Best Practices that are considered important by many experienced Python programmers. Knowing them will help you understand what other developers do. It will also help you to assess, on your own, what practical problems might be solved by *other* techniques not covered in this book and whether they might be useful for you.

The MazeRun Game

Many years after the traumatic experience with my first game programming project, programming has become a lot easier. On an operating system with multitasking, a single crashed program does not require us to reboot everything. We have comfortable programming languages and powerful libraries that handle graphics, input devices, and sound effects. On the web, we have an ubiquitous, practically infinite stream of information at our fingertips. Over the past years, I have taken advantage of that situation and successfully written many minigames in Python (mostly for my own pleasure). In this book, we are going to write the game **MazeRun** in Python. The game shall feature a figure eating its way through a maze. The player moves the figure remotely resembling a wheel of cheese through a landscape built from square tiles, devouring dots and trying to avoid ghosts that roam around the maze. The idea of the game can be sketched on a napkin quickly (see Figure 1-3).

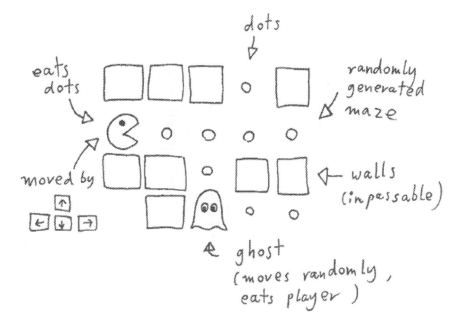

Figure 1-3. Sketch of the MazeRun game—the Python example we will use throughout this book

There are a number of reasons why I am convinced that **MazeRun** is a great example for a book on Best Practices:

1. The game is easy to understand. Most of you probably have played a dot-eating game before.

2. We can implement the game as a short Python program and won't need thousands of lines of code.

3. Writing a game gets complex quickly. We need to organize data, graphics, user interfaces, performance, concurrent events, and so on.

4. Details matter. Small glitches impede the gameplay or even make the game unplayable.

5. Writing computer games is a common denominator among software developers. Even if you haven't written any games yet, you probably have played some. For sure you know enough about the subject to assess whether a game works or not. With other favorite topics of mine (e.g., *"algorithms to model 3D structures of RNA"*) this might not be the case.

6. You can use the code examples to create your own games.

7. The two-dimensional levels are apt to create illustrative figures, which can be placed in a book (I also would have liked to create a game about traveling the space-time continuum, but the four-dimensional images are too difficult to print).

We are going to approach writing **MazeRun** in small steps, a few lines of Python code at a time. Therefore, the game is going to improve from chapter to chapter. Before we are ready to start, though, we need to prepare a few technical things in the next section.

How to Use This Book?

To make best use of the explanations and code examples in this book, I highly recommend that you download and execute the code yourself. To do so, you need to take care of four things:

1. Install Python 3

2. Install the Pygame library

3. Install a text editor

4. Download the source code examples

All chapters assume that you are working on an **Ubuntu Linux** system. With a few exceptions, the tools in this book should work on MacOS and Windows as well. However, I haven't tested these operating systems and there won't be any specific installation instructions for these operating systems. In the following you will find detailed hints for each of the four points.

Install Python 3

To execute the program, you need **Python 3.5** or higher. On Ubuntu, Python 2 is installed by default. Some examples will fail on earlier Python versions, and I won't tell you which. To avoid frustration later, I recommend you to install a recent Python version with

```
sudo apt-get install python3
```

If this method fails for whatever reason, please download and install a current Python interpreter from www.python.org. I encourage you to install the **IPython** shell as well with

```
sudo pip install ipython
```

IPython will make your life easier in many ways. In many of the chapters, we will install additional Python libraries and a few extra tools. Most of them can be comfortably installed using **pip** and **apt-get**. Precise instructions are given in the respective chapters.

Install the Pygame Library

Because the MazeRun game will be built on top of the **Pygame library** (www.pygame.org), you will also need to install it. Installing Pygame is less convenient than other Python libraries. You will need to download the right file for your system from https://bitbucket.org/pygame/pygame/overview, unzip the file, and install it from the unpacked directory with

```
python setup.py install
```

Install a Text Editor

To view or edit Python source code, you will need a text editor with syntax highlighting for Python. You can use your favorite text editor. For instance, **Sublime, PyCharm, Anaconda Spyder, Emacs,** and even **vim** will be perfect. If you are working on Windows, the **IDLE** editor or **Notepad++** are good editors for Python. Please **do not** use **gedit** or even **notepad** to view Python code, because the capabilities to edit source code are very limited in both.

Download the Source Code Examples

The source code used in this book is completely available on **Github**. Usually, there are separate files for each chapter plus a complete version for each part. You can download the source code from its GitHub repository:

```
https://github.com/krother/maze_run
```

On the right side, there is a button for downloading the entire source code as a `.zip` file. The more elegant method using the `git` program will be introduced in Chapter 12. The files contain one main folder, `maze_run,` that contains the entire game, as well as several examples for individual `chapters` in the chapters folder. The code is released under the conditions of the **MIT License**, which gives you a lot of freedom to reuse the code. It is therefore compatible with most other licenses, and there are no restrictions on private or educational use of the code, including redistribution. Note that neither the author or the publisher of the book takes any warranty for whatever you do with the code. Please see the **LICENSE.TXT** file on the GitHub repository for the exact legal terms.

With these steps done, we are ready to start. Let's dive into **Python Best Practices!**

PART I

Debugging

CHAPTER 2

▨ ▨ ▨

Exceptions in Python

Once we accidentally inserted an extra zero in the headline: '2000 tanks destroyed.' The authorities were quite angry.

—memories of my grandfather while working in a printing press in 1941

As soon as a program contains a single line of program code, that line could contain a defect—and sooner or later it will. If **defects** are when our code does not do what it is expected to do, **debugging** is fixing those defects. This is more complicated than it sounds. Debugging implies a couple of things:

- We know what a *correct* program is supposed to do.

- We know that there is a defect in our program.

- We acknowledge that the defect needs to be fixed.

- We know how to fix it.

For many subtle bugs, the first three points are not trivial. However, when an Exception occurs in a Python program, the situation is rather obvious: *we want the Exception to disappear*. In this chapter, we will therefore concentrate on the last point: *how to fix a defect we know about*. We will deal with the other problems in later chapters.

Exceptions Are Defects We Know About

Few programs work smoothly at the first attempt. Normally, we will see at least one error message before things start to work. When we see an error message or **Exception** in Python, we know something is wrong with our code. To reuse the metaphor from Chapter 1, if our program were a building, an Exception would mean the house is on fire (Figure 2-1). Because Python Exceptions usually occur because of a defect, there is little doubt *whether* there is a bug or not. Therefore, this kind of defect is relatively easy to debug.

As an example, we will prepare graphics for the MazeRun game. We will use Pygame to construct an image from graphical tiles. The tiles are 32 × 32 pixels large and we can combine them neatly to build levels and moving objects. All tiles are in an image file like the one in Figure 2-2. We need to read the image file and store all square-shaped tiles in a Python dictionary so that we can access them easily, for instance using characters as keys:

```
tiles = {
    '#': wall_tile_object,
    ' ': floor_tile_object,
    '*': player_object,
}
```

© Kristian Rother 2017
K. Rother, *Pro Python Best Practices*, DOI 10.1007/978-1-4842-2241-6_2

While writing the code for creating the dictionary, we will see typical Exceptions in Python. In this chapter, we will examine three straightforward strategies for debugging Exceptions:

1. Reading the code at the error location

2. Understanding the error message

3. Catching Exceptions

While doing so, we will hopefully learn something about the nature of defects in general.

Figure 2-1. *If a program were a building, an Exception would be a fire. There is no reason to run away from an Exception. At least we know it's there.*

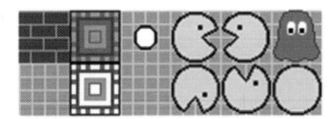

Figure 2-2. *Tiles we will use to create graphics for MazeRun. We want to create a dictionary, from which we can access tiles by single characters (e.g., represent the wall tile in the top-left corner with a #). The image itself is in the XPM format (tiles.xpm. The format allows Pygame to handle transparency easily, although other formats may work equally well.*

Reading the Code

Generally, Exceptions in Python fall into two categories: Exceptions raised *before executing code* (SyntaxErrors), and Exceptions raised *while executing code* (all others). Only if Python does not find any SyntaxError, it starts to interpret and execute the code line by line. From that point on, other types of Exceptions can occur.

SyntaxError

The Python Exceptions that are easiest to fix are SyntaxError and its subtype IndentationError. In both, Python fails to interpret or *tokenize* a Python command correctly, because it was badly written. The tokenization is done before any code is executed. Therefore, a SyntaxError is always the first error to appear. The reasons for a SyntaxError are mostly typos of different kinds: forgotten characters, extra characters, special characters in the wrong place, and so on. Let's look at an example. We start to prepare our tile set by importing Pygame:

```
imprt pygame
```

This fails with an annoying message, which I have seen on my first day of programming, and which I will probably see on my last day as well:

```
File "load_tiles.py", line 2
    imprt pygame
              ^
SyntaxError: invalid syntax
```

There is a misspelled import command that Python did not understand. This probably has happened to you as well. In this case it is enough to read the code in the error message and see what the problem is. Can we determine a defect from reading the code indicated in the error message *all the time*? To find out, we will need to look at more Exceptions. A second common SyntaxError is caused by missing brackets. Suppose we try to define a list of tiles and their x/y indices in the image:

```
TILE_POSITIONS = [
    ('#', 0, 0), # wall
    (' ', 0, 1), # floor
    ('.', 2, 0), # dot
    ('*', 3, 0), # player
```

This code blows up the moment you feed it into Python:

```
SyntaxError: unexpected EOF while parsing
```

In the error message, Python doesn't give us much of a clue that the closing square bracket is missing. It reaches the end of the file and quits. However, if we append another line to the file, for example, the size of tiles in pixels:

```
SIZE = 32
```

15

The error message changes to

```
File "load_tiles.py", line 11
    SIZE = 32
```

```
SyntaxError: invalid syntax
```

Note that the traceback indicates the line *after* the list, which has nothing to do with the missing bracket. It just happened to get in the way. A Python programmer needs to learn to recognize symptoms of missing brackets quickly. Also, a good editor counts brackets for us and gently indicates when one seems to be missing. We can identify the defect from a `SyntaxError`, but the description is often not accurate. A more unsettling aspect of missing brackets is that if we forget the opening bracket instead, we get a completely different type of Exception:

```
TILE_POSITIONS = ('#', 0, 0), # wall
                 (' ', 0, 1), # floor
                 ('.', 2, 0), # dot
                 ('*', 3, 0), # player
                 ]
```

This line fails with

```
IndentationError: unexpected indent
```

Python is lacking a clue why the second line is indented here. Note that we only get an `IndentationError` if the first list item starts in the line with the assignment; otherwise, it will be a `SyntaxError` again. These kinds of defects are very frequent, but usually the easiest to fix.

▦ **Conclusion**   Similar defects in Python code can lead to different error messages.

Apart from a missing bracket, an `IndentationError` is also caused by wrong indentation. Wrong indentation occurs if we indicate a new code block by a colon (:) but forget to indent. Wrong indentation occurs if we use a whitespace more or one whitespace less than in the line before. The worst case of wrong indentation occurs if we have tabs instead of spaces somewhere in our file, because we cannot tell them apart visually. This can be avoided by using an editor designed for writing Python code. Fortunately, the symptoms of wrong indentation are often obvious (see Figure 2-3), and we can identify the location of an `IndentationError` by checking the line number in the error message.

Best Practices for Debugging SyntaxErrors

A `SyntaxError` or its subtype `IndentationError` can frequently be fixed by reading the code line indicated in the error message carefully. The strategy is a bit similar to the famous *"veni-vidi-vici"* of Julius Caesar: We first *go* to the line indicated in the code (*veni*), then we *look* at the line(s) at that location (*vidi*) and fix the problem (*vici*). In practice, many Exceptions can be solved with this strategy in very short time. The most common fixes for a `SyntaxError` are the following:

- Look at the line specified in the error message first.

- Look at the line right above it.

- Cut and paste the code block with the error to a separate file. Does the SyntaxError persist in what remains? (Other errors are OK.)

- Check for missing colons after commands like `if`, `for`, `def`, or `class`.

- Check for missing brackets. They are easy to find with a good editor.

- Check for incomplete quotes, especially in multiline strings.

- Comment the line indicated in the error message. Does the error change?

- Check your Python version. (Are you using `print` without brackets in Python 3?)

- Use an editor that inserts four spaces whenever you press Tab.

- Make sure your code conforms to PEP8 (see Chapter 14).

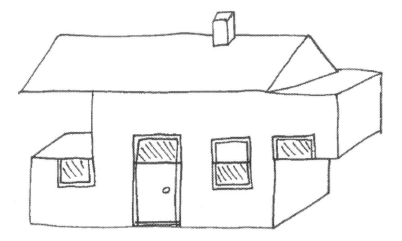

Figure 2-3. *An IndentationError if programs were buildings*

Examining the Error Message

In the previous section we used the "*veni-vidi-vici*" strategy to fix `SyntaxErrors`, Essentially we looked hard enough at the line in the error message. Does this strategy work for all bugs? Given that we have five more chapters about debugging ahead of us, probably not. Let us look at a slightly more complex example. To create an image we will create a dictionary to look up rectangles for the tiles to copy. These rectangles are **pygame.Rect** objects. We create the rectangles in a helper function `get_tile_rect()`, and the tile dictionary in the function `load_tiles()`. Here is a first implementation:

```
from pygame import image, Rect, Surface

def get_tile_rect(x, y):
    """Converts tile indices to a pygame.Rect"""
    return Rect(x * SIZE, y * SIZE, SIZE, SIZE)

def load_tiles():
    """Returns a dictionary of tile rectangles"""
    tiles = {}
```

```
for symbol, x, y in TILE_POSITIONS:
    tiles[x] = get_tile_rect(x, y)
return tiles
```

Now we can call the function and attempt to extract the wall tile (abbreviated by '#') from our dictionary:

```
tiles = load_tiles()
r = get_tile_rect(0, 0)
wall = tiles['#']
```

However, executing this code results in a KeyError:

```
Traceback (most recent call last):
  File "load_tiles.py", line 32, in <module>
    wall = tiles['#']
KeyError: '#'
```

However hard we gaze at line 32, we do not find anything wrong with requesting a '#' from tiles. This is how our dictionary is supposed to work. And if the defect is not in line 32, we can logically conclude that it must be *somewhere else.*

▓ **Conclusion**   The location given in an error message is not necessarily the location of the defect.

How can we find the defect? To obtain more information, we will take a closer look at the error message. Reading an error message produced by Python is not very difficult. An error message in Python contains three relevant pieces of information: The **error type**, the **error description,** and the **traceback**. Let's go through them:

The Error Type

Technically, an error message means that Python has raised an Exception. The error type indicates which Exception class was raised. All Exceptions are subclasses of the Exception class. In Python 3.5, there is a total of 47 different Exception types. You can see the full list of Exceptions with

```
[x for x in dir(__builtins__) if 'Error' in x]
```

The diagram in Figure 2-4 shows the hierarchical relationships between these classes. You can see that many error types are related to input/output. What is also intriguing is that there are four separate categories related to Unicode.

Since Python 3, *Unicode* has enhanced the possibilities by which characters can be misspelled by a few orders of magnitude. Knowing what Exception types are possible—and their meaning—is solid background knowledge for experienced Python programmers. In our case, the KeyError is a clear hint that we tried to look up something in a dictionary that was not there.

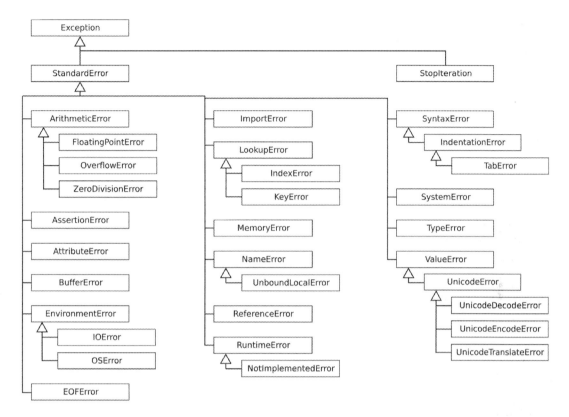

Figure 2-4. *Hierarchy of Python Exceptions. The figure shows the inheritance for 34 of the 47 Exceptions in Python 3.5. Fine-grained types, mostly subclasses of IOError, were left out for clarity.*

The Error Description

The text right after the error type gives us a description what exactly the problem was. These descriptions are sometimes very accurate, sometimes not. For instance, when calling functions with too many or too few arguments, the error message give us the exact numbers:

```
TypeError: get_tile_rect() takes 2 positional arguments but 3 were given
```

The same applies when unpacking tuples fails. In other cases, Python is politely telling us that it has no clue what went wrong. Most `NameErrors` fall in this category. With our `KeyError`, the only information we get is the character `'#'`. The inner voice of an experienced developer quickly auto-completes this to

> Dear User,
>
> Thank you for your recent command. I tried to extract the value '#' from the `tiles` dictionary as you instructed. But after looking through it, I could not find it. I have looked everywhere and it's not there. Are you sure you didn't put the entry somewhere else? I'm really sorry and hope to do better next time.
>
> Forever Yours, Python

The Traceback

The traceback contains accurate information *where* in the code an Exception happened. It contains the following:

1. A copy of the code executed. Sometimes we spot the defect here immediately. Not this time.

2. The line number executed when the error occurred. The defect **must** be in the line itself or in a line executed earlier.

3. The function calls leading to the error. You can read our traceback like a chain of events: "*The module called function X, which called Y which in turn failed with an Exception.*" You see both events in separate lines of the traceback. When reading a longer traceback, **start reading from the bottom**. This does not mean that the cause of the error is always at the bottom. But often enough it gives us a hint where to look for the problem.

Deduction

To track down our KeyError, we can **deduce**: If the key '#' is not in the dictionary, was a key written at all? In which line was the key written? Was that line reached? There are several places in the code where the data flows into the tiles dictionary could be interrupted. When examining the load_tiles function, you may notice that the wrong keys are assigned. The command doing the assignment is

```
tiles[x] = get_tile_rect(x, y)
```

while it should be

```
tiles[symbol] = get_tile_rect(x, y)
```

Reading and understanding the error message was helpful to identify the defect. Even if the defect is more complicated, the error message usually gives us a starting point to look for the source of the problem. We notice however, that some deduction was necessary, because the Exception occurred in a different line than the one with the defect. There are many possible defects that could have led to the same symptom. Sometimes we need to check several locations. In a short code fragment, we can apply deduction intuitively and check multiple candidate locations for defects. In Chapter 4 we will see a more systematic approach.

Catching Exceptions

Once we get the import and the tiles dictionary working, we can try to load the image with tiles:

```
from pygame import image, Rect

tile_file = open('tiless.xpm', 'rb')
```

which fails with the following unspectacular message:

```
FileNotFoundError: [Errno 2] No such file or directory: 'tiless.xpm'
```

The defect is a misspelled filename. A `FileNotFoundError` is a subclass of `IOError`. All siblings of `FileNotFoundError` are very common errors when processing data. In some projects it seemed that half of my errors were `IOError`s. Fortunately, this is a precise error message with little room for interpretation. This error can be fixed by checking the path and filename in our code diligently. To fix the defect we need to find out where the file really is, then recheck the spelling in our code. Sometimes we will need a couple of attempts because of nasty details: absolute and relative paths, missing underscores, dashes, and, last but not least, backslashes on Windows that need to be expressed as double backslashes (\\) in Python strings. **The defect resulting in an `IOError` is almost exclusively a wrong file name.**

It is clear that we cannot prevent every Python Exception. What else can we do? One possibility is **reacting to Exceptions** inside the program. We try to perform an operation, being aware that it may fail. If it fails, Python will raise an Exception. With the `try.. except` construct, we can react specifically. A typical situation where catching Exceptions is useful are file names entered by a user:

```python
filename = input("Enter the file name: ")
try:
    tiles = load_tile_file(filename)
except IOError:
    print("File not found: {}".format(filename))
```

With the except statement, we react to specific types of Exceptions accordingly. This strategy has been termed **EAFP**, *"Easier to Ask Forgiveness than Permission."* *"Asking Forgiveness"* means reacting to the Exception, *"Asking Permission"* means checking whether the file is there before trying to open it. Easier, because checking every possible thing in advance that *might* go wrong is neither possible nor desirable. Python developer *Alex Martelli* states that catching Exceptions is a great strategy for reacting to invalid input or configuration settings and to hide Exceptions from users. Catching Exceptions is also useful for saving important data before terminating a program. But catching Exceptions has also received considerable criticism. Joel Spolsky, a well-known authority in software development, states:

> The reasoning is that I consider Exceptions to be no better than "goto's," considered harmful since the 1960s, in that they create an abrupt jump from one point of code to another.

In fact, the path Exceptions take through a program is *invisible* in the code. By looking at a Python function, we do not see what Exceptions might be raised inside it, or where any raised Exceptions are brought to a halt. Therefore, it becomes very difficult to take all possible execution paths into account, which makes it easier to introduce additional defects. Also, we need to be careful deciding *which* Exceptions to catch. For sure, the following usage of `try.. except` is a terrible idea:

```python
try:
    call_some_functions()
except:
    pass
```

This construct is known as the *diaper pattern*. It catches everything, but after a while you don't want to look inside. It makes the Exception disappear, but creates a worse problem instead: the Exceptions are covered, but so are our possibilities do diagnose what is going on (compare Figure 2-5). A Best Practice is to use `try.. except` only for well-defined situations instead, and to always catch a specific Exception type.

Best Practices for Debugging IOErrors

Because IOErrors are frequent and often very annoying for beginners, it can't hurt to enumerate the most common counter-strategies here:

- Find the exact location of the file in the terminal or a file browser.

- Print the path and filename used in your program. Compare it to the real one.

- Check the current working directory (`import os; print(os.getcwd ())`).

- Replace relative by absolute paths.

- **On Unix**: Make sure you have access permissions to the file in question.

- Use the `os.path` module to handle paths and directories for you.

- Watch out for backslashes in your path! You need to replace them by forward slashes (`/`) or double backslashes (`\\`) to obtain the correct separator.

Figure 2-5. *If Exceptions were a fire in the building, this is what* `except: pass` *would look like. We extinguish the Exception for sure, but is that really what we want?*

Errors and Defects

In this chapter we have seen three strategies to handle **defects** that cause an Exception: debugging it by looking at the code, debugging it by looking at the error message, and catching the Exception. Let us summarize our observations: Sometimes the error message points directly at the defect (e.g., a SyntaxError). There are also many examples where the error message is precise enough to narrow down the defect to a few possibilities (e.g., an IOError). Other error messages are more obscure, and it requires experience to see what is meant. You may find the exemplary counterstrategies given in this chapter helpful. But we also saw how a defect was far away from the location in the error message. In such a situation the error message is not that helpful. Like an oracle, it provides a hint, but it is impossible to locate the defect by looking at the error message alone. In Python, there are usually many possible defects that can lead to the same error, a situation very common for TypeError, ValueError, AttributeError, and IndexError. Another tricky situation occurs if we feed the wrong data into a library function like pygame.Rect; as a result we will get an Exception from within the library, even though the defect is in our own code. In these situations, we need to take all information from the error message into account: **the location in the code**, **the error type**, and **the traceback**. There are many cases where this information is sufficient to locate the defect, making this a good *intuitive* debugging strategy.

What about silencing Exceptions with `try.. except`? Catching Exceptions is a great strategy to deal with *exceptional* situations that are beyond our control: for example, invalid input data or wrong file names. But Exception handling is insufficient to fix the defects that are already *inside* our program. A program will not work better just because it pretends everything is correct. But `try.. except` shows us that we can manage errors a program throws, even if we are unaware of the underlying defect. One conclusion we will explore further in the next chapter is that **errors and defects are distinct**. The error is something we observe, a symptom that something has gone wrong. The defect, on the other hand, is hidden somewhere in the code. To fix the code, we need to find the underlying defect first. Finding the defect becomes a **deduction problem**.

Where Do Defects Come From?

Why do we introduce defects in the first place? The reasons that defects occur in our programs are manifold. To debug successfully, it is worth knowing where defects come from. Here is how I produced most of my Python bugs:

- First, **mistakes during the implementation** occurred. The code was right in my head, but something went wrong on the way to the text editor: a missing colon, a misspelled variable, a forgotten parameter. Or I forgot how exactly to use a function and add the wrong parameters. Most of these defects will fail early, often with an Exception.

- Second, **bad planning** produced more subtle defects. The code was incorrect in my head already: I picked an inappropriate approach, forgot about an important detail so that I ended up solving a different problem than I initially meant to. This kind of defect is harder to recognize. The usual result is that I can start writing a code section all over again. **Testing** is a good strategy to bring bad planning to light early.

- Third, **bad design** lead to defects indirectly. Whenever I wrote redundant code, paid little attention to cleaning up my code, or didn't document what I was doing, *later modifications* of the program were more likely to produce incorrect programs. To avoid such problems, we need Best Practices for **maintaining a software project**.

- Finally, there were underlying **human factors**. When using a language feature or library for the first time, when communication with other programmers was difficult and when writing programs in a hurry or being tired, defects were flocking in. Apart from the practices mentioned in the preceding, a modest attitude toward your own abilities helps a lot. Do not trust your code blindly, because it will contain defects more than occasionally.

Python is not the easiest language to debug. The dynamic typing in Python results in very general error messages that require interpretation. In other languages, the compiler provides more precise messages (and more errors) that help us to produce *executable* code. On the other hand, Python gives us many possibilities to interact with our code closely, examine the defects from a close distance. That allows us to *fight one fire at a time*, and eliminate Exceptions as they occur. We need to use this as a strength if we want our programs to run correctly. Because looking at the error message alone is not sufficient, we will need to look at other debugging techniques to debug or even find the more challenging defects. We will examine the nature of defects further in the next chapter before moving to methods to debug systematically.

The Correct Code

Before we depart to the next chapter, it is worth completing the code for loading tiles. With the import, the list of tiles, and the `load_tiles` function debugged, we can add a few lines to compose an image of three tiles. The following is the complete code:

```python
from pygame import image, Rect, Surface

TILE_POSITIONS = [
    ('#', 0, 0), # wall
    (' ', 0, 1), # floor
    ('.', 2, 0), # dot
    ('*', 3, 0), # player
]

SIZE = 32

def get_tile_rect(x, y):
    """Converts tile indices to a pygame.Rect"""
    return Rect(x * SIZE, y * SIZE, SIZE, SIZE)

def load_tiles():
    """Returns a dictionary of tile rectangles"""
    tile_image = image.load('tiles.xpm')
    tiles = {}
    for symbol, x, y in TILE_POSITIONS:
        tiles[symbol] = get_tile_rect(x, y)
    return tile_image, tiles

if __name__ == '__main__':
    tile_img, tiles = load_tiles()
    m = Surface((96, 32))
    m.blit(tile_img, get_tile_rect(0, 0), tiles['#'])
    m.blit(tile_img, get_tile_rect(1, 0), tiles[' '])
    m.blit(tile_img, get_tile_rect(2, 0), tiles['*'])
    image.save(m, 'tile_combo.png')
```

The code results in an image we can take as a proof of concept that we can now compose bigger graphics from tiles (see Figure 2-6). Maybe the tile example has already encouraged you to try things on your own, so that you will have plenty of opportunities to debug your own error messages soon. The code is stored in the file maze_run/load_tiles.py available from https://github.com/krother/maze_run.

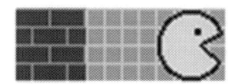

Figure 2-6. *Successfully composed tiles*

Best Practices

- Wrong code, leading to an error, is called a **defect**.

- Some Exceptions have precise error messages that can be fixed by examining the code.

- Some defects are found at the location indicated by the error message.

- Some defects are far away from the location given in the error message.

- Error messages consist of an error type, a description, and a traceback.

- **Deduction** is a strategy to determine the root cause of an error.

- **Catching Exceptions** with `try..` except is a strategy to deal with specific situations and error types.

- **Always** use except with a specific Exception type.

- **Never** use except with `pass` inside.

- **Errors** and **defects** are distinct.

CHAPTER 3

■ ■ ■

Semantic Errors in Python

Have you tried turning it off and on again?

—The IT Crowd, *Helpdesk message on an answering machine*

For the MazeRun game to become interesting, we will need mazes. The player figure shall move around these mazes, eat dots, and be chased by monsters. In this chapter, we will write a program that produces such mazes. When implementing that program, we will reach a point where the program is *almost working*. Probably, you are familiar with the phenomenon: You have taken care of all Exceptions that occurred in the first test runs. However, the program still does not do what it is supposed to do. It may still be full of **semantic errors**.

A semantic error occurs when a program works without raising an Exception, but gives a different than the expected result. The underlying defects are usually more difficult to eliminate than defects that result in error messages. The information provided by Python Exceptions may not be great, but at least it gives you a starting point. With a semantic error, we frequently start with less information. Nevertheless, the reasons for semantic errors are sometimes very simple: typos, omitted lines, statements in the wrong order, and so on (also see Figure 3-1).

© Kristian Rother 2017
K. Rother, *Pro Python Best Practices*, DOI 10.1007/978-1-4842-2241-6_3

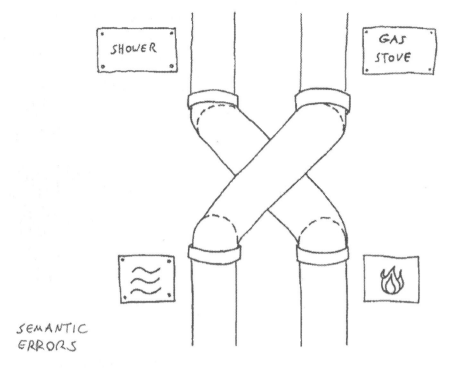

Figure 3-1. *Semantic errors can be hard to spot at first glance but have severe consequences*

In this chapter, we will examine semantic errors in Python. To do so, we will deliberately introduce defects into code and see what happens. By doing so, we will try to understand what causes semantic errors and how they behave. Any attempt to list all possible semantic errors is futile. There exists no classification like there is for Exceptions. Instead, we are going to abstract from recurring defects and see what we can learn on the way.

Comparing Expected and Factual Output

In the previous chapter it was easy for us to determine whether a program produces an error: there was either an error message or not. The Python interpreter *tells* us there is an error. With semantic errors the situation is less obvious. We perceive an error, because the program does something different than we had *anticipated*, but Python thinks everything is working. The first place where the problem might start are our expectations: they may simply not be *clear enough*. Sometimes, expectations are obvious: if we write a program to add two numbers and enter 1 and 1, we anticipate to see 2 as a result. There is not much room for discussion. Let us consider a more challenging example.

What is our program for generating mazes going to do exactly? It shall produce a rectangular grid of wall tiles (#) and corridors filled with dots (.) constituting a maze. Now you may already have a clear image how a maze should look. Given this description, a team of software developers might come up with the mazes shown in Figure 3-2.

Figure 3-2. *Four possible outputs of an imprecisely described maze generator*

Which of these mazes match your anticipation and which don't? Which did you not even think of before? It is very common that the same description of a programming problem leads to very different outcomes for different programmers. Understandably, all of them will believe their solution is *correct*. And all of them are, because the preceding description is imprecise!

To tell apart what is a semantic error and what is not, we need to describe *precisely* what kind of output we expect for a given input. Computers need the precision, but we need the precision as well, because if we change our opinion about what the program should be doing too frequently, it will be impossible to ever finish it.

An easy way to make our expectations more precise is to write down a sample **input** and the **expected output** up front. This can be done in a table listing input/output values. Let's determine both in our program:

> **Input:** Two integer values x and y, specifying the size of the resulting maze in grid tiles.

> **Output:** A random maze consisting of a grid of x * y tiles. The maze is surrounded by a frame of wall tiles (#). It contains an interconnected network of connected corridors separated by walls and filled up with dots (.). No room should be wasted by filling it up with walls. A 12 x 7 maze could look like the one in Figure 3-3.

Figure 3-3. *Example output of a more precisely described maze. Although small, this is what we really need.*

It is generally a good idea to write down the input and expected output before starting to program. There are more sophisticated methods for planning larger software, but starting with a simple table on a piece of paper is sufficient to get started.

▓ **Warning** It may happen that your project is not specified accurately enough to write down the input and expected output. This is a very serious obstacle, because it is likely that whatever you program will turn out to solve the wrong problem. When this happens to you, you have two alternatives: First, *stop programming immediately* and find out what exactly you are supposed to do (more thorough planning). Second, *work toward a minimal solution* with the least possible effort, expose it to reality, and be prepared to throw everything away (prototyping). Python is good for both.

Defects

Identifying an input and the expected output allows us to identify *semantic errors* by comparing the expected and factual output. Finding an error is the starting point for searching the cause of the error or the *defect*. Searching for defects is what debugging is mostly about. Finding a defect through *deduction* is often difficult. To learn about the nature of defects and semantic errors, we will approach the problem from the other end: we will introduce typical defects in the code and see what happens. What are typical defects in Python? What are the according errors we observe? How do defects lead to errors?

Defects in Variable Assignments

We start our consideration with a function producing the final maze. As an input, this create_grid_string() function uses a Python set with positions of dots and the *x, y* size of the grid. As an output it returns the maze as a string. By using a set we make sure each position occurs only once. When we call the function with a sample set of dot positions:

```
dots = set(((1,1), (1,2), (1,3), (2,2), (3,1), (3,2), (3,3)))
create_grid_string(dots, 5, 5)
```

we expect the following grid:

```
#####
#.#.#
#...#
#.#.#
#####
```

Here is one possible implementation of the `create_grid_string()` function:

```python
def create_grid_string(dots, xsize, ysize):
    grid = ""
    for y in range(ysize):
        for x in range(xsize):
            grid += "." if (x, y) in dots else "#"
        grid += "\n"
    return grid
```

As you can see, there are three variable assignments in the function (lines 2, 5, and 6). Let us consider what happens when these variable assignments contain a defect.

Multiple Initialization

The first variable assignment sets `grid` to an empty string. There are a few ways to do this wrong. If we omit the line entirely, we will get a `UnboundLocalError` because of the undefined variable only a few lines later. But we also could, for example, initialize `grid` just one line later inside the `for` loop:

```python
for y in range(ysize):
    grid = ""
...
```

And instead of the expected output we get only

```
#####
```

What happened when we initialized the variable within the loop? The variable is *initialized multiple times*, once in each round of the loop. Initialization means that we **overwrite** whatever `grid` contained previously. Thus, the five hashes we see are actually the *last* row of the grid. Multiple initialization is a very common semantic error, and it usually occurs in conjunction with `for` or `while` loops.

Accidental Assignment

A similar semantic error occurs if we create a variable assignment by accident. Imagine we replace one of the `+=` operators by `=`. Let's consider the second occurrence of `+=` first:

```python
grid = "\n"
```

Most likely, this line is the result of a typo. The result is that our output is a newline character, and as a result we see an empty output. This is a more disturbing kind of bug than the previous one, because programmers start to imagine monstrous possibilities of what went wrong when they see an empty output. Fortunately, the brevity of the line makes this defect easier to find.

Let's consider what happens if we replace += by = in the ternary expression as well:

```
grid = "." if (x, y) in dots else "#"
```

Again, the `grid` variable is reinitialized in each iteration of the loop. The result of this defect is that the output string only contains a single hash (#). The reason of this defect is likely to be a typo (the += was in the programmer's head but didn't reach the finger) or a logical omission while thinking the problem through (the += didn't emerge in the programmer's head in the first place).

Whether you easily spot this kind of defect or not varies a lot with experience. This is the reason why some beginners prefer the more verbose addition operator:

```
grid = grid + "." if (x, y) in dots else "#"
```

until they are more comfortable with spotting a += with the same precision.

Accidental Comparison

A less common defect is introducing a comparison operator by accident:

```
grid == "\n"
```

This defect is more difficult to spot because of the similarity of == and +=. This is with a high probability the result of a typo as well. What is annoying about this line (and the reason we declinate this defect here) is that it is a valid Python expression, even though it does nothing. As a result of the defect, our output will not contain any line breaks.

```
######.#.##...##.#.######
```

Seeing this output, we need to deduce the defect in two steps. First, we need to *recognize that the line breaks are missing.* Second, we need to examine *why the line breaks got lost.* This two-step deduction is conceptually new compared to the previous defects. Fortunately, a defect caused by a rogue == is easy to fix once we find it.

Wrong Variables in an Expression

Whenever we use a variable, there is a probability that we accidentally use the wrong one. This kind of defect may be hard to deduce as well. Imagine we use the grid size (`xsize, ysize`) instead of the grid position (`x, y`) in the following ternary expression:

```
grid += "." if (xsize, ysize) in dots else "#"
```

We search the set for a tuple with the grid size instead of the loop indices (`x, y`). As a result, the `if` condition never evaluates to `True` and the expression never returns a "." When we execute this code, we observe a solid brick wall without any floor tiles:

```
#####
#####
#####
#####
#####
```

The grid size and line breaks are correct; only the dots are missing. The key question for deducing this semantic error is: **In which line has the dot character not been introduced properly?**

To figure out what is happening, we need to be aware of what (xsize, ysize) *means* while checking the ternary expression. Otherwise the line looks fine. This defect is potentially hard to spot. Imagine we named the parameters of the function xs and ys. It is much harder to tell (xs, ys) apart from (x, y) than from (xsize, ysize). One reason the parameters are named xsize and ysize is that they have a large **psychological distance** to the other variables used in the function (also see the book *Code Complete* by Steve McConnell [2nd ed., Microsoft Press, 2004]).

Swapped Literals in Expression

The final defect that we will probe in the create_grid_string() function is swapping the two strings in the ternary expression. Instead of the correct one, we write

```
grid += "#" if (x, y) in dots else "."
```

It is not surprising that we obtain the inverted output. This output looks more like a helicopter landing site than a maze:

```
.....
.#.#.
.###.
.#.#.
.....
```

Defects that involve swapping, exchanging, and inversion of values are very common. We can have similar effects in ternary expressions, conditional blocks, or simple boolean operators. Please note that this kind of defect easily overlaps with other defects. In a simple scenario, we could invert the if condition as well by adding an additional not operator:

```
grid += "#" if not (xsize, ysize) in dots else "."
```

after which the output is correct again. When we have more than two values that can be swapped, or we are making more than one decision in the code, this kind of defect becomes a real challenge to deduce.

All defects we found in the preceding variable assignments affected the data returned by the function. This is at the same time the main output of our program. The path from the defect to the output is rather short. In some defects, the defect could be spotted directly, but in others a bit of deduction was involved. In all cases, we observed the error directly by matching the factual output with our expected one.

Defects in Indexing

Indices of lists, tuples, sets, and dictionaries provide ample opportunities for defects other than *IndexErrors*. Here, we look at just two representative examples. To create a maze, we need to generate all positions in which dots could possibly occur, except the border of the grid. When carving out a 5 × 5 grid with these positions, the expected output is the following grid:

```
#####
#...#
#...#
#...#
#####
```

This can be implemented using a **list comprehension**. We define the according function for generating the positions:

```
def get_all_dot_positions(xsize, ysize):
    return [(x,y) for x in range(1, xsize-1) for y in range(1, ysize-1)]
```

We use the resulting list as an input for the `create_grid_string()` function, which generates the correct expected output:

```
positions = get_all_dot_positions(5, 5) print(create_grid_string(positions, 5, 5))
```

Creating Wrong Indices

There are uncounted possibilities in which we can mess up the indices of lists by one position. In our example, it comes down to setting the right parameters for the `range()` function. We could set both the start and end indices by one too high or too low. Table 3-1 contains four defects and the resulting grids.

Table 3-1. *Wrong Start and End Indices for Range*

range(0, xsize)	range(1, xsize)	range(0, xsize-1)	range(2, xsize+2)
.....	#####	....#	#####
.....	#....	....#	#####
.....	#....	....#	##.##
.....	#....	....#	#####
.....	#....	#####	#####

Python counts indices in a different way than humans do. This is why indices are often counterintuitive. All four possibilities—and more—occur commonly whenever we create or slice lists with numerical indices. What we do not always have is a visual representation of the data. In fact, it is worth pointing out that the **error** we observe here is the grid produced by `create_grid_string()`. The **defect** however is in `get_all_dot_positions()`.

How are the two connected? Of course, the error **must have been** in the variable `positions` we used to create the grid - The set contained the wrong indices. That means, the error was first caused by the defect in `range`, it then traveled invisibly through the program, and finally it caused an error in the output. We can say the error has **propagated** through our program. In our case, the error propagated from the `get_all_dot_positions()` function to the main program and from there to the `create_grid_string()` function.

Using Wrong Indices

To create a maze with connected paths, we will need to identify neighboring positions in the grid. In a 2D grid, each position has exactly eight neighbor positions. For a given position x, y, we can define a function `get_neighbors()` that returns a list of eight neighbor positions:

```
def get_neighbors(x, y):
    return [
        (x, y-1), (x, y+1), (x-1, y), (x+1, y),
        (x-1, y-1), (x+1, y-1), (x-1, y+1), (x+1, y+1)
        ]
```

This function returns a list of *indices* that can be used by create_grid_string(). We can use the output of the function to generate a grid:

```
neighbors = get_neighbors(2, 2)
print(create_grid_string(neighbors, 5, 5))
```

The expected output for the neighbors of position 2, 2 is a donut-like shape:

```
#####
#...#
#.#.#
#...#
#####
```

Does this code example convince you? In the preceding code, there are a few serious **design flaws**. Let us consider things that could go wrong:

First, a defect might increase or decrease any of the indices in get_neighbors() by one like in the previous example. This inevitably destroys the donut shape. We know this defect already, and could deduce it in a similar way.

A second kind of defect is that in one of the tuples x and y could be swapped, so that instead of (x, y+1) we would obtain (y, x+1). When we introduce this defect, however, we do not see *any* effect. The donut is still complete. But let us try instead to calculate the neighbors of a different position, for instance 3, 2:

```
neighbors = get_neighbors(3, 2)
```

Instead of the donut, we obtain the neutrino signature of a Romulan warship:

```
#####
##...
##.#.
##.#.
##.##
```

This is very, very bad news! By swapping an x for a y, we have introduced a defect that sometimes causes an error and sometimes doesn't. Of course, the code example we examined was badly designed itself: when we place a square shape in the center of another square, we shouldn't be too surprised that it does not matter whether we insert x or y. Nevertheless, we need to remember the *quality* of this bug: we will see more defects that sometimes propagate into an error and sometimes don't. It is very difficult to identify all possible parameter combinations of a program a priori in order to exclude errors.

What is more, the code itself is prone to errors of this kind as well. The get_neighbors() function is very hard to read; the meaning of the list elements are not clear, and it is difficult to see whether all the commas, minuses, and parentheses are in the right place, and whether the elements of the list are in the right order. For instance, the following version of the list *does not contain even a single correct entry*:

```
def get_neighbors(x, y):
    return [
        (x, -1), (y, x+1), (x-(1), y), (x+1), y,
        (x,(-1, y)), (x+1, y, 1), (x-1, y+1, x+1, y+1)
        ]
```

The code still executes. Of course, the result is a disaster:

```
#####
#####
##.##
#####
##.##
```

This is an example of a **design weakness**. Even if the code works correctly, defects can find their way in very easily. Therefore, in addition to debugging, we will need to think about how to make code more robust (and readable), so that the defects become easier to find.

Defects in Control Flow Statements

What happens if we write a control flow statement wrong? In control flow statements like if, for, and while, we encounter diverse interesting defects. We will examine them in the maze generation algorithm. A straightforward algorithm for maze generation could work as follows:

1. create a list of all positions in the grid.

2. pick a random position from the list.

3. if the position has up to four adjacent dots as neighbors, mark the position as a dot.

4. otherwise, mark the position as a wall.

5. repeat steps 1-4 until the list of positions is empty.

With a value of 5, this algorithm constructs balanced mazes that contain very few open areas, and all corridors are connected with each other. In addition, it leaves a circular path at the outer wall which is great for running away from ghosts.

An implementation could look like this:

```python
def generate_dot_positions(xsize, ysize):
    positions = get_all_dot_positions(xsize, ysize)
    dots = set()
    while positions != []:
        x, y = random.choice(positions)
        neighbors = get_neighbors(x, y)
        free = [nb in dots for nb in neighbors]
        if free.count(True) < 5:
            dots.add((x, y))
        positions.remove((x, y))
    return dots
```

▓ **Tip**   The algorithm is not perfect. If you try the algorithm by yourself you may notice that it occasionally produces inaccessible areas. This is another kind of design weakness, because it occurs irregularly. For our purpose the procedure is good enough, but if you want to develop a more robust maze generator, give it a try. That is a good debugging exercise as well.

Defects in Boolean Expressions

Both if and while contain boolean expressions. In both cases, defects in the expression change which commands are executed next. For instance, we could accidentally use a *greater than* symbol (>) instead of a *less than* (<) when comparing the number of adjacent dots:

```
if free.count(True) > 5:
```

The boolean expression never evaluates to True. As the error propagates, no position gets marked as a dot, and we obtain a wall-only grid as a result.

A defect with the same outcome is to omit the function call in free.count. Unfortunately for many programming apprentices, the following is a legal expression in Python 2.7:

```
if free.count < 5:
```

Although the preceding expression raises an Exception in Python 3.5, similar defects exist there as well. For example

```
if "ABC".lower == 5:
```

A bit of care is required when designing explicit conditions like in the while statement:

```
while positions != []:
```

This is not the same as the simplified version of the preceding statement:

```
while positions:
```

Both expressions work. However, the former is prone to changes in the type of positions (e.g., to a set or dictionary). Generally, all kinds of defects in boolean expressions in control flow statements change the order of execution and potentially create unreachable code.

Defects with Indentation

In Python, indentation changes the meaning of the code. Therefore we can create semantic errors by wrong indentation. A very common case is found in while loops. Consider we dedent the line calling positions. remove by four spaces, so that it is on the same level with the return statement:

```
    ...
    if free.count(True) < 5:
        dots.add((x, y))
positions.remove((x, y))
return dots
```

As a consequence of the defect, the list positions never run empty, and the while loop never finishes. We have created an *endless loop* by removing four spaces. This is a new quality of semantic error, because the program never reaches the output stage. The error propagates infinitely. This leads to a number of interesting theoretical questions (can we prove that the program really contains a defect?) and practical issues (how long do we need to wait until we know something went wrong?). In this example, we terminate both these questions and the program by pressing Ctrl+C.

You can build endless loops with for as well. This happens if we iterate over a list and append to that list in the loop. A much more common defect is that a line is dedented, even though it should be within a for loop or vice versa. Such a for loop usually finishes, but produces a wrong result. The effects of such a defect are often more subtle.

Defects in Using Functions

In the final section of this chapter we will look at three defects related to functions. For the advanced programmer, these are trivial defects, but I have seen so many beginners struggle with them (in particular if they knew functions only from calculus) that I feel the necessity to illustrate them briefly. To complete our program, we write a short function create_maze that uses the code written so far to generate a maze:

```python
def create_maze(xsize, ysize):
    """Returns a xsize*ysize maze as a string"""
    dots = generate_dot_positions(xsize, ysize)
    maze = create_grid_string(dots, xsize, ysize)
    return maze

maze = create_maze(12, 7)
print(maze)
```

Let's see how we can break this code!

Omitting a Function Call

First, we could write the name of the function but forget to call it by omitting the parentheses:

```python
maze = create_maze
```

This is more likely to happen when using functions without arguments, for example, str.upper(). The effect is that we end up with the function itself in our result variable. In maze we end up with something like:

```
<function create_maze at 0x7efdf7427598>
```

Missing Return Statement

Second, the return statement return maze could be missing. As a consequence of the defect, the function does not deliver its result to the main program. It returns None instead, which is what we see in the output as well:

```
None
```

Forgetting a return is a defect that does not necessarily produce an Exception. Often the default return value None lets the program finish gracefully (e.g., when you interpret the result as a boolean). As a result, the error continues to propagate.

Not Storing the Return Value

Third, we could call the function but not do anything with the result (e.g., storing it in a variable). The call would look like this:

```
create_maze(12, 7)
```

At this point beginners usually get confused. If they see no output and figure out they should print something, the first attempt could be

```
create_maze(12, 7)
print(maze)
```

Which of course raises a `NameError`. The problem gets worse if a variable `maze` occurs both in the function and in the main program. The `maze` within the function expires as soon as the function terminates. This is a good example why using the same variable name in different places is a bad idea. I believe the proper way to deal with this kind of defect is to play through a simple code example like this one yourself and see different ways of getting the code to work. I hope that after trying these examples on your own keyboard you will have one problem less to deal with.

The example illustrates three common problems beginners face when getting familiar with functions. In addition to that, all the issues enumerated in the previous sections may occur in functions, too. In particular, indentation and namespace defects are more likely to be found. Even if you write everything well and the function produces the correct result, the bigger question remains *how to design functions well*. This is a wonderful question indeed, and therefore we will save it up until Chapter 15.

Error Propagation

While declinating through common semantic errors, we have made a couple of observations. First, semantic errors and the underlying defects are distinct. They may or may not be found in the same location. This is in accord with what we found for defects when looking at Exceptions in Chapter 2.

Second, defects **propagate** through the program. What does that mean? In Figure 3-4 we see the chain of events in error propagation drawn schematically. A defect in the code causes a part of the data to be wrong, or the wrong function being called. The program continues to function. However, the error introduced by the defect travels through the program. Depending on the defect, it eventually spreads or disappears completely. If and only if something caused by the defect reaches the output, we have a chance to observe it as a semantic error. Error propagation can lead to Exceptions as well. In that case, the chain of events does not need to reach the output.

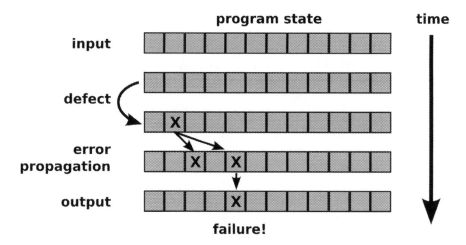

Figure 3-4. *Error propagation. A defect causes a chain of events that travels through the program execution. If the chain manifests in the output, we can observe the error. Note that multiple propagation paths can exist, including such that never lead to an observable error. The figure was inspired by the work of Andreas Zeller. Image covered by the CC-BY-SA License 4.0.*

Andreas Zeller has developed a very clear and accurate description of defects and error propagation that goes far beyond the one in this chapter. You can find it explained in the software debugging course on Udacity (`https://www.udacity.com/course/softwaredebugging-cs259`) and described in his book *Why Programs Fail: A Guide to Systematic Debugging* (Dpunkt Verlag, 2006).

What conclusion can we draw when we have found a defect? Ideally, the defect is a single line of code that is simply written in the wrong way. Then we fix that line of code and the program works. But there are a number of other possibilities:

- We have to write a bigger portion of code to fix the defect.

- We know what is wrong, but the solution is incompatible with the way the program is written. We need to reorganize the code first.

- Several defects in different places overlap, and we only observe one of them. Fixing a defect only leads us to the next error. And the next.

- The defect is caused by two lines that propagate into an error in combination. Either of them could be fixed.

- Two defects compensate each other partially. Fixing one of them seems to make the problem worse.

- The input is a special case we didn't think of before. We need to decide whether the special case needs to be covered by the program.

There are many different kinds of semantic errors. They range from ones that are easy to find and easy to fix, to real brain-twisters that can take hour or days to debug. And then there are the real bad ones, defects that point out a major weakness in our algorithmic approach, our data structure, or the architecture of our program. The worst kind are the defects that reveal that we have not understood the problem we are solving properly. In the latter case we can code as much as we like, and it won't help at all.

The further away from the output a defect is (in execution time, operations processed or code lines), the more difficult it is to find. Much of our debugging efforts aims at slicing the space in Figure 3-4 into smaller chunks. We can either slice *data* by trying a smaller input. This is why we started with a 5 × 5 maze, not a bigger one. Or we can slice *operations processed* by examining smaller portions of the program. An approach to decide what to try first is the topic of the next chapter.

Best Practices

- Defects not resulting in an error message are called **semantic errors.**

- To determine whether a semantic error exists in the first place, it helps to write down the **expected output** for a given input first.

- Some defects resulting in semantic errors can be identified directly by looking at the output, then looking at the code.

- Some defects require **deduction** to figure out what caused a semantic error.

- Some defects do not cause an error in the output directly. They **propagate** through the program, until they cause an error in the output.

- In addition to defects, code also may contain **design weaknesses** that make the code more prone to adding errors or existing errors harder to find.

CHAPTER 4

■ ■ ■

Debugging with the Scientific Method

I have a background in IT. I don't take anything for granted.

—Anonymous

In the previous two chapters, we have seen a few frequently occurring defects in Python. Not only does that help us to recognize and fix similar defects, we also know that defects may *propagate* through a program, and the diagnosis may not be obvious. It is time we turn our attention to fixing more difficult bugs. How can we fix an error we have never seen before? In this chapter, we will analyze a bug in the game controls of MazeRun systematically.

In any game, there is a mechanism by which the player controls what is happening. In our case, the controls will be very simple: the player moves a figure using the arrow keys. Because many prospective game programmers had the same idea long ago, it is no surprise that Pygame provides infrastructure for handling keyboard and mouse events. We will use that infrastructure to write an **event loop**. The event loop shall check continuously for new key events. Pygame uses the function pygame.event.pump() to prepare events internally and pygame.event.poll() to retrieve an event. The event loop then sends the pressed key to a custom function that performs an action (e.g., moving a figure). The code for the event loop looks like this:

```python
from pygame.locals import KEYDOWN
import pygame

def event_loop(handle_key, delay=10):
    """Processes events and updates callbacks."""
    while True:
        pygame.event.pump()
        event = pygame.event.poll()
        if event.type == KEYDOWN:
            handle_key(event.key)
        pygame.time.delay(delay)

if __name__ == '__main__':
    pygame.init()
    event_loop(print)
```

We pass print as a callback function to event loop, so that we can directly see the keys entered by the *player*. Because the callback function is passed as a parameter, we can replace it by a different function later easily. When we run this code, however, *nothing happens*. There is no keyboard output at all. We have

© Kristian Rother 2017
K. Rother, *Pro Python Best Practices*, DOI 10.1007/978-1-4842-2241-6_4

discovered another *semantic error*. In this chapter we will use a systematic approach, the **scientific method**, to track down the underlying defect. The scientific method is a key Best Practice in programming, first because it provides a conceptual framework where other debugging techniques fit in, second, because it perfectly complements the Best Practices for testing and maintenance we will see later in the book.

Applying the Scientific Method

In Chapter 2 we were able to track down the reasons for errors by looking at the generated error messages. In these error messages, the line where the error occurred and the location of the defect were often different. However, these were relatively simple defects. Such defects can often be solved by unsystematic *guessing*: You look at the symptom, look at your code, try out a few possible solutions, and (hopefully) solve the problem.

With the semantic errors in Chapter 3 we learned that a defect *propagates* through the program, eventually leading to an error. When the nature of the error propagation or the defect itself becomes more complicated (complicated for the person who has to fix the bug, not by absolute terms), the guessing strategy will utterly fail. In a complicated defect, the symptoms and the underlying defect(s) are connected by a long cause-effect chain. Simply looking harder at the code and trying more guesses will quickly wear out the programmer (see Figure 4-1a). The main problem why the guessing strategy fails is that we obtain little, if any, new information about the defect.

The *scientific method* is a Best Practice to solve problems of unknown origin. In a nutshell, instead of focusing on the solution alone, we try to identify the origin of the defect first by collecting hard evidence. It is in many aspects superior to the intuitive idea of looking at the code. Similar to what you find in a textbook on science, the scientific method consists of five steps (also see Figure 4-1b):

1. **Observe**: We start with an observation of a programs behavior we want to change.

2. **Hypothesize**: We express an idea, a *hypothesis*, why the observed behavior occurs.

3. **Predict**: Based on our hypothesis, we make a testable prediction *what else* our program would do if the hypothesis is correct.

4. **Test**: We examine our prediction by exposing our program to an experimental condition and observe the outcome.

5. **Conclude**: Finally, we accept or reject our hypothesis, based on the result. Unless we have found the cause of the defect, we return to the second step and refine our hypothesis further – or come up with a completely new one.

The scientific method turns a guessing problem into a deduction problem. Followed rigorously, the scientific method is well apt to track down even complicated defects. It is superior to guessing also because it leads to cleaner solutions and code that is easier to maintain. There are four techniques worth knowing that will help us to apply the scientific method effectively to debugging in practice. These are

- reproducing the defect

- automating the defect

- isolating the defect

- getting help

We will meet all four while tracing the bug in our event loop.

▓ **Tip** Set yourself a time limit for quick fixes. There are many defects to which you do not need to apply the scientific method. If you see an error and know after a few simple tests what is going on, you can probably fix the defect right away. As a rule of thumb, if you have not found the defect after 10–15 minutes, it is time to switch to a systematic approach.

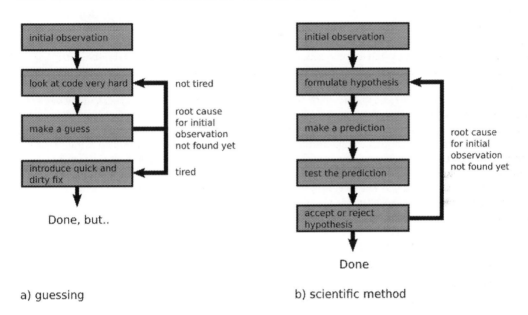

Figure 4-1. *Suggestive comparison of a) trying to guess the source of the defect and b) systematically testing hypotheses with the scientific method*

Reproducing the Error

We start with the observation that our event loop does not produce any output at all (if you see some weird characters on the console, these originate from Unix, not from our program, because print should produce a line break after each key). Before formulating any hypothesis, we need to make sure that this is a persistent problem and not a temporary or random condition. To collect evidence, we at least need to run the program a second time and check whether we get the same observation (we do).

Reproducibility is a prerequisite for successful debugging. If we can reproduce a defect, we can find it. If we can find it, we can fix it. If we cannot reproduce the error, we are chasing ghosts—a bug hunt that never ends. Therefore, reproducing errors is the most essential Best Practice in debugging. In some situations errors can be hard to reproduce. Naturally, programs involving random numbers produce unpredictable results. For instance, the maze generator in Chapter 3 creates a different maze every time. About one in five mazes contains inaccessible areas (e.g., a single dot enclosed by walls). If we wanted to eliminate these, it would be cumbersome to rerun the program several times and scan the output. With the default random number generator, this is fortunately easy to fix. To make the mazes produced by our generator reproducible, we need to initialize the random number generator with a seed value. Try running the following program with and without calling random.seed a couple of times:

```
import random
random.seed(0)
print(create_maze(12,    7))
```

It is perfectly fine to use seed values to make the behavior of our program predictable for the sole purpose of better debugging. When a system gets more complex, errors become generally less reproducible. This is a common situation when two or more computers talk to each other. In web and server programming there is a plethora of devices and protocols involved, resulting in many possible reasons for a failure. A defect might appear because of a HTTP timeout one time but not the other time. A defect might appear on a production server but not on a test server. A defect might appear when there is a lot of web traffic, when there is little memory available, when a user clicks a web page superquickly, only on Wednesdays, and so on. The worst such errors alter their behavior when being examined and have consequently been termed *Heisenbugs*, borrowing their name from quantum mechanics. Expect to collect a lot of information on the ecosystem of your program from log files and monitoring tools before finding the defect leading to a Heisenbug (which may turn out to be annoyingly simple).

Even though the event loop does not seem to have any issues with reproducibility, we are not sure whether all the keys are affected. To make our initial observation more precise, we formulate a **first hypothesis:** *none of the keys on the keyboard produces an output*. The hypothesis allows a straightforward **prediction**: *if we press each key once, we still see no output*. The **test** for this hypothesis can be performed with one finger. In fact, we still don't observe any output from `print` and consequently **accept the hypothesis**. Our more precise, reproducible observation becomes: *none of the keys on our keyboard produces an output in the callback function*.

▓ **Tip**   One of the most common nonreproducible bug many beginners face is that they are maintaining two versions of the same program on their computer and inadvertently run the wrong one. The same happens when running the same program with two different Python versions (this is likely if you are using an IDE like Anaconda or Canopy and a manually installed Python in parallel). If you experience an irreproducible bug in a simple program, check the location of your Python file (and your Python interpreter) first.

Automating the Error

Sometimes it is difficult to reproduce a bug, because we need to enter lots of information manually. Rigorously speaking, "lots of information" means "*we need to press more than one button to see whether the problem is still there.*" Automating things early saves a lot of time debugging later. Automation also helps with reproducibility. If, for example, our event loop responds only if we type at a certain speed, we might see a different outcome every time. Automation eliminates a potential source of uncertainty from our observation.

Let's formulate a **second hypothesis** for the event loop: *the event handling in our program is generally broken*. To **test** this hypothesis *by automation,* we create an artificial keyboard event. If the hypothesis is true, we **predict** that *we will still see nothing*. In Pygame, it is very straightforward to generate artificial events using the `pygame.event.post()` function. We insert the following code at the beginning of our event loop:

```
eve = pygame.event.Event(KEYDOWN, key=42)
pygame.event.post(eve)
```

When we rerun the program, we observe that it prints

```
42
42
42
..
```

We observe that our program is able to process our artificial key events perfectly. It is only the physical keys that get ignored. Therefore, we **reject the hypothesis**. It turns out the automation is not suitable to find our defect, but it provided us with new information: *everything else seems to work correctly*. We will therefore stick to the manual input for the time being. There is a lot more to say about automation (for instance, we could create an automatic test function, but will save that up until Chapter 8).

Isolating the Defect

The more code we are analyzing, the more places there are where a defect could hide. A crucial task in debugging is to make the amount of code to debug as small as possible, or to *isolate the defect*. We can view much of this book as different techniques to isolate defects, or to make isolating them easier. We will stick to one example here: The fact that pressed keys do not reach our program code can still be explained in a couple of alternative ways. We can formulate them as **alternative hypotheses:**

- Pygame is not properly installed, so that Pygame and the physical keyboard are unable to communicate.

- We are using Pygame the wrong way, so that it does not produce a key event.

- Pygame produces the event but we don't display it correctly.

Let's check these hypotheses one by one. When faced with multiple alternatives, the Best Practice is to check the *simpler* options first. On one hand, the simpler alternatives are *easier to test,* and on the other hand they are usually *more likely*. Of the three alternative hypotheses, the first one is *unlikely* (after all, our artificial event worked well, and the examples in the first two chapters worked, too). It is, however, easy to test. To be 100% sure that Pygame is properly installed, you can execute another Pygame-based game on the same Python installation (I recommend *Bub-n-Bros,* see http://bub-n-bros.sourceforge.net/, although it can be distracting). This works, so we can **reject the first hypothesis** and focus on the two remaining hypotheses. The second alternative seems likely, but difficult to test. The third alternative is easier to test. Looking at the code, we see the if conditional only checks for events labeled as KEYDOWN and discards all other events. It could be that the keyboard events we are looking for have a different type. We can formulate another **prediction:** *If we print all events regardless of their type, we should see the pressed keys.*

The Strip-Down Strategy

To **test** our prediction and look at all produced events without the conditional, we need to simplify the code. We want to find the minimal lines necessary to reproduce the error. One way to do this is to execute code in the Python shell. Another is to copy the function to a test script and successively remove lines (which should be named test_event_loop.py). A worse way is to copy-paste the entire script or to comment out half of the lines in your code. Both methods would mess up our entire workplace quickly.

With a test script, we can remove lines in multiple iterations, trying to find a point where either the error disappears or there are only few lines left. With the `if` and the callback function removed, the minimized event loop looks like this:

```python
import pygame

pygame.init()
while True:
    pygame.event.pump()
    event = pygame.event.poll()
    print(event)
```

The resulting code is much shorter and easier to read. When running this code, we see an infinite output of messages, all identical to

```
<Event(0-NoEvent {})>
```

Nothing we do (pressing keys, clicking, moving the mouse, making faces to your webcam) will change this message. We observe that apparently no Pygame events reach our code and therefore **reject the third alternative hypothesis**. By shrinking our program to six lines, three of which are trivial (the `import, while,` and `print` statements), there are very few potential points of failure left. **We have isolated the defect**. The only remaining explanation at the moment is that *we are using Pygame the wrong way*.

▓ **Tip**   It is worth keeping such short test scripts for later. Often, they can be developed into **test functions** that we will see in later chapters.

The Binary Search Strategy

An alternative strategy to narrow down the location of a defect is to use *binary search* (see Figure 4-2). This technique is very useful if we have a lot of code where the defect could hide. To perform a binary search, we divide the code in two portions of similar size (e.g., major modules or functions). Then we check in which portion the defect propagates. We then partition that portion a second time and so on (see Figure 4-3). This is a potent isolation strategy, because the size of the remaining code is cut by half in each iteration. With ten partitions we can narrow down the source of a defect from thousands of lines of code to a single function or less. The only prerequisite for using the binary search strategy is that the defect must be relatively easy to identify along the way. In the event loop example, this is not easy, because there we are tracking something *that is not there*. To some extent, the binary search and the strip-down search strategy are complementary.

Figure 4-2. *Looking for defects using binary search if your program were a building*

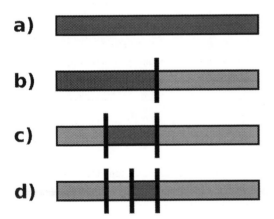

Figure 4-3. *Binary search for isolating bugs: a) initially, the bug can be everywhere; b) code to examine after a first division; c) code remaining after a second division; d) isolated bug location after a third division.*

Getting Help

At this point in the debugging process we might become tired (at least I was after struggling with the issue for 15 minutes). It seems likely that the solution to the problem cannot be found *in* our code. Our most recent conclusion (*we are using Pygame the wrong way*) does not tell us *how to use Pygame right*. **We need help.** This is a very powerful yet often underestimated debugging strategy. Admitting that throwing more time/ willpower/coffee at the problem won't help is often the key to constructive problem-solving. There are at least five ways to get help. All five are Best Practices every programmer ought to remember, *especially* when under pressure.

Taking a Break

Sometimes, we stop seeing a solution because we are tired. This is normal. A fresh pair of eyes might as well be your own. So getting off the problem for a while by taking a walk, a nap, a lunch, a workout, might do wonders and bring us closer to the solution. If the problem we are working on feels intense enough, sleeping over it helps as well. Our subconscious will continue working for us. I have experienced it many times that a problem that seemed tiresome and overwhelming one afternoon disappeared within five minutes in the light of a new day.

Explain the Problem to Someone Else

Explaining the problem to a colleague or another programmer can help a lot. Often, we will get fresh ideas that we didn't think of before. Explaining the problem does not require looking at the code. In fact, when we are forced to formulate our line of thought understandably, we may discover new aspects by ourselves in the process. Surprisingly, this technique works equally well if we explain the problem to junior developers or nonprogrammers. I have often seen people stopping halfway through a sentence while explaining a bug to me, having realized the solution themselves. There are even reports that programmers talk to a duck or a teddy bear to find a solution. Personally, I prefer talking to people, but in case you are programming in seclusion and people are a luxury, talking to a bear sounds like a reasonable alternative.

Pair Programming

Pair programming means that two people sit at the computer and work on a problem together. I find working in a team of two especially valuable in debugging. It is much harder to overlook things if there is a second pair of eyes. In addition it usually helps to avoid dirty fixes. There are controversial opinions on whether pair programming is generally more efficient than programming separately. I won't take any sides on that topic, but I am convinced that solving a problem in a pair is a great way to debug code.

Code Reviews

A code review is having another person read our code. Often, reviewers ask naive questions that point to things we did not think of before. Even though a code review does not include editing or modifying the code, we can learn a lot: A skilled reviewer will point out actual defects, but also ambiguously written statements or even larger architectural weaknesses. We may also find out more efficient ways to use a library or learn about new technologies worth knowing after a code review, or simply decide to update the documentation to make the code easier to understand. One possible activity during a review is to *walk through* the code line by line. Check for each line what the line does and which line is executed next. If you do this alone, it requires very high concentration and is tiresome. If you do it in a team of two or three people, it becomes a superior debugging technique.

Formal code reviews (where a meeting time is set and a protocol written afterward) are an established technique for building software that has to meet the highest quality standards. There is some research evidence that code reviews are superior in finding defects even to automated testing (however, the according research is more than 10 years old and does not include Python, so it falls a bit out of our scope; for details, see Ian Sommerville, *Software Engineering* 9th ed., Pearson, 2011). All kinds of code reviews serve the purpose of revealing the blind spots a programmer creates during development.

Reading

Sometimes we need to take a step back and read background information. That means, if we are implementing an algorithm, we need to understand its theory thoroughly. If we are working with a database, we need to know the database architecture and interface in detail. If we are debugging data records, a good understanding of what the data is about helps. With any library, we need to know its basics. Many debugging problems can be solved simply by doing our homework. Reading won't give us quick results, especially not if we want to fix a bug *right now* (type import this in the Python console to see what Guido van Rossum recommends on *right now*). But reading certainly pays off in the long run.

In our event loop, the most likely hypothesis was *we are using Pygame the wrong way*. What is the right way, then? The Pygame documentation is a good place to investigate that question. When we check the documentation of the pygame.event module on www.pygame.org/docs/ref/event.html, we will find a list of functions and classes within the module. After that, the first text paragraph reads:

> *Pygame handles all its event messaging through an event queue. The routines in this module help you manage that event queue. The input queue is heavily dependent on the Pygame display module.* ***If the display has not been initialized and a video mode not set, the event queue will not really work.***

Gotcha! We have initialized the display with pygame.init() but we have not set the video mode. Reading a bit more about the pygame.display module on www.pygame.org/docs/ref/display.html quickly leads to the pygame.display.set mode() function. We can incorporate it into the main part of our program:

```
pygame.init()
pygame.display.set_mode((640, 400))
event_loop(print)
```

And, marvelously, the program starts to work. An extra window with a black background appears (the Pygame display), and our keyboard input appears on the console (see Figure 4-4). Note that the Pygame window needs to be selected (active). We have successfully found the source of the defect and eliminated it.

▒ **Reality Check**   How realistic is this example? Would someone really miss out an essential command that is clearly written in the first paragraph of the module's documentation? First, it is a real bug that happened to me. For a moment, I was proud enough to think that after writing half a dozen minigames using Pygame I wouldn't need the documentation any more. Second, I believe the same happens to other people as well. Third, the knowledge about libraries and tools of every programmer is finite. Sometimes we realize soon enough that we are approaching the boundaries of our knowledge, but sometimes we choose to go a bit further anyway. When facing a decision whether to read stuff or to write code, many of us prefer writing code. I assume this is why we became programmers in the first place.

Please note that the error was mostly based on a **wrong assumption**. When writing the buggy version, the assumption was: *We don't need to create a window to read from the keyboard*. This assumption turned out to be wrong. We realized in the end that the Pygame library requires its own window to read keyboard events. Lesson learned! When debugging, it is a good idea to keep a notepad nearby. Taking notes about the hypotheses we are considering helps to stay focused as we follow them through. Also, in a tough debugging session crossing out the hypotheses we already rejected may be the only satisfaction we get for some time (see Figure 4-5). In my opinion, paper for taking notes beats electronic notepads by far. I am even keeping a scrapbook on my desk to keep track of bugs I introduced on purpose while writing this book.

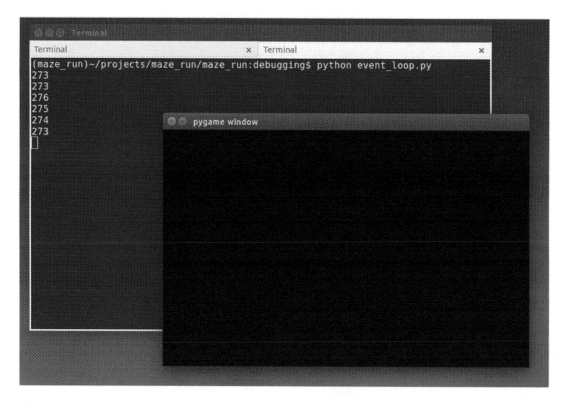

Figure 4-4. Working event loop. The Pygame window, although empty, is essential to make the program work.

Cleaning Up

Even though the program is in a working condition now, we are not done yet. We still need to clean up our construction site. This means removing any commented or extra lines that we introduced in the process, as well as additional files we created. We may decide to keep our test script and place it next to other test code we wrote earlier. Afterward, we need to check again, whether the event loop is still working. In a more complex project, the cleanup work involves many other things. Do we need to reorganize our code to make the fix for the defect fit cleanly to the existing code? Do we need to rewrite code to have a consistent style? Do we need to write additional automatic tests? Are there other components of the software affected by the fix? How soon do we need to incorporate the fix in the final product? Do we need to update any documentation? Do we need to inform team members or even customers? Et cetera.

Cleaning up sounds like a boring duty, but it is imperative not to postpone it. Taking care of these and similar issues diligently is key to keeping our program in a healthy state. Continuously ignoring the cleanup leads straight to a nasty phenomenon called *technical debt*, the official term for software that is slowly deteriorating. After we finish the cleanup, we can finally run the program and identify the codes for the arrow keys we will use for game controls (see Figure 4-6).

Hypotheses

1) none of the keys on the
keyboard produces an output. **OK**

~~2) event handling in Pygame is
generally broken.~~

~~3) key handling in Pygame is
broken.~~

4) we are using Pygame the
wrong way. *got it!*

~~5) Pygame produces events but
we don't display them correctly.~~

Figure 4-5. *Notepad with hypotheses tested on the event loop*

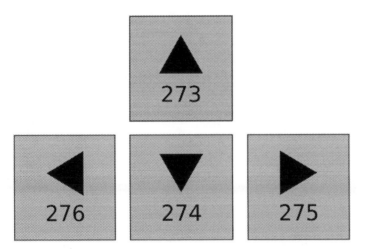

Figure 4-6. *Arrow keys and their key codes produced by Pygame*

The Scientific Method and Other Best Practices

Applying the scientific method during debugging is a general Best Practice for debugging programs. While applying the method, we may use multiple debugging tools, like the ones in the three next chapters: using `print` in Chapter 5, introspection functions in Chapter 6, and an interactive debugger in Chapter 7. Once we discovered a defect, several Best Practices complement the scientific method while fixing it: in Part II on **automated testing,** we will use techniques that prove that, once fixed, a defect does not come back. In Part III on **maintenance**, we will learn support structures that help us to integrate the fix of a defect with the rest of the program cleanly. The lesson for us to learn is that debugging is much more than looking at code. To build reliable software, we need to consequently apply a systematic approach.

Best Practices

- Debugging by unsystematic **guessing** works for minor defects only.

- In the **scientific method**, you formulate **hypotheses** about a defect, make **predictions**, and subsequently **test** them.

- Depending on the observed outcome of the test, you accept or reject the hypothesis.

- Iteratively **refine a hypothesis** until you found the underlying reason for an error.

- **Reproducing** an error is an essential prerequisite for successful debugging.

- **Automatically reproducing** a defect helps you to iterate faster.

- Defects can be **isolated** by **stripping down code** or **binary search in the code**.

- When nothing else works, **getting help** is a natural part of the debugging process.

- **Explaining the problem** to someone else helps, too.

- **Cleaning up** after debugging keeps **technical debt** low.

CHAPTER 5

Debugging with print Statements

I see a darkness.

—Will Oldham, also performed by Johnny Cash

In the previous three chapters, we have seen a zoo of program errors and the defects causing them. We have learned about error propagation and the scientific method as a general approach to eliminate bugs. How can we put this knowledge into practice? In this and the following chapters, we will gather tools to **diagnose** programs in order to find defects. In this chapter, we start with a very simple yet powerful diagnostic tool: print.

The code we will diagnose is drawing the in-game graphics. We will draw the mazes we generated as images on the screen. As input data, we will use the string-based representation from Chapter 3. This means we will recalculate the image every time something in the game changes (for a fast game, this is not a great approach, but sufficient for now). In this chapter, we will write a function to compose an image for the entire maze from X * Y individual tiles. We will start with a few imports and a string representing a random maze:

```
from pygame import image, Rect, Surface
from load_tiles import load_tiles, get_tile_rect, SIZE
from generate_maze import create_maze

level = """
       ############
       #...#.##.#.#
       #.##.......#
       #....##.##.#
       #.#.##...#.#
       #......#...#
       ############"""
```

We first convert the maze data into a list by splitting the string into separate rows. For easier reuse, we wrap the code in a function:

```
def parse_grid(data):
    """Parses the string representation into a nested list"""
    return [list(row) for row  in data.strip().split("\n")]
```

In the resulting nested list, we can address tiles by their row and column indices (i.e., level[y][x]). Next, we implement the function to draw the grid itself. We use the Surface.blit method from Pygame to copy parts of the image from one rectangular area to another:

© Kristian Rother 2017

K. Rother, *Pro Python Best Practices*, DOI 10.1007/978-1-4842-2241-6_5

```
def draw_grid(data, tile_img, tiles):
    """Returns an image of a tile-based grid"""
    xs = len(data[0]) * SIZE
    ys = len(data) * SIZE
    img = Surface((xs, ys))
    for y, row in enumerate(data):
        for x, char in enumerate(row):
            img.blit(tile_img, tiles[char], get_tile_rect(xs, ys))
        return img
```

Using the load_tiles function from Chapter 2, we can attempt to draw a level in just three lines. For clarity and better testability, we will write the image to a file:

```
If __name__ == '__main__':
    tile_img, tiles = load_tiles()
    level = create_maze(12, 7)
    level = parse_grid(level)
    maze = draw_grid(level, tile_img, tiles)
    image.save(maze, 'maze.png')
```

When we execute this code, we observe that the program finishes without an error. It also writes an image file. But when we look at the image maze.png itself, it just shows 384 x 224 pixels of darkness (Figure 5-1).

Figure 5-1. *Output of the buggy function draw grid(). To find out why we see darkness, we need to generate diagnostic information.*

The program finishes, but does not do what we expected. We have just discovered another *semantic error*. In this chapter, we are going to diagnose our code by adding print statements. For many Python programmers, print is their number one debugging tool. print solves one major problem in debugging semantic errors: the lack of information.

print is a very straightforward, crude tool for collecting observations. Nevertheless, it is not without perils: It is easy to overuse print and mess up your entire code with diagnostic statements. In order to avoid such pitfalls, we will continue to use the scientific method from Chapter 4 rigorously. Throughout the chapter, we will state hypotheses that can be answered by adding print statements to our code.

Diagnose Whether Code Was Executed

The simplest usage of print is to check whether a piece of code has been executed or not. In our example, one reason could be that the for loop was not reached. Accordingly, we formulate the following **hypothesis:** *The for loop is not executed.* To **test** the hypothesis, we add a single print statement right after the first for, whose job is to give us a sign of life. We **predict** that we won't see the message if our hypothesis is true:

```
for y, row in enumerate(data):
    print("I'm stuck in Folsom prison.")
    for x, char in enumerate(row):
        ...
```

In practice, most programmers don't quote Johnny Cash in their diagnostic print statements. The following is quicker to write and easier to spot on the screen:

```
print("A" * 40)
```

Which gives you an output you might also hear at a laryngologist's:

```
AAAAAAAAAAAAAAAAAAAAAAAAAAAAAAAAAAAAAAAA
```

Whichever print you used after the for, you will see the message in the output. The print statement has given a sign of life from within the loop. Code within the for loop is executed. We therefore need to **reject our hypothesis.**

Print the Content of Variables

Nevertheless, you may notice something peculiar. We would expect a printed line for each row of the maze, but we observe only one. We need more information on that. Let's formulate a new **hypothesis:** *Only the first row of the maze is processed.* We **predict** that y would take the value 0 and x loops through 0 to 11 (the width of the maze). We will use print to display the value of these variables and **test** the hypothesis. This time, we insert a print statement in the inner loop to watch it at work:

```
for y, row in enumerate(data):
    for x, char in enumerate(row):
        print("x={} \t y={} \t {}".format(x,y,char))
```

Which gives us the output:

```
x=0      y=0      #
x=1      y=0      #
x=2      y=0      #
x=3      y=0      #
..
x=10     y=0      #
x=11     y=0      #
```

We have found evidence that the inner loop is executed 12 times, the outer one only once. Therefore we **accept the hypothesis**. Printing information from variables is a very powerful diagnostic tool, because it is easy to use. However, you need to select the information to be printed carefully. Imagine we would be processing a much bigger maze (or more generally, a huge data table). The output would litter many screen pages and we would still see nothing. To use `print` effectively, knowing *format strings* and *string methods* in Python well is a must.

Pretty-Printing Data Structures

Looking for the reason why only the first row is printed, we can refine the hypothesis further. One thing we should check is whether there is anything wrong with the maze data itself. One possible explanation is that there is only one row in the maze (and the others somehow got lost). Our refined **hypothesis** becomes: *There is only one row in the maze*. We can **test** the integrity of our maze by printing `data` in the beginning of the function. However, the output of `print(data)` is potentially long and hard to read, because the line breaks do not correspond with the rows of the list. String formatting does not help much here. A better alternative is to use the `pprint` module from the Python Standard Library:

```python
def draw_grid(data, tile_img, tiles):
    """Returns an image of a tile-based grid"""
    from pprint import pprint
    pprint(data)
    ...
```

which gives us a nicely formatted maze:

```
['############',
 '#...#.##.#.#',
 '#.##.......#',
 '#....##.##.#',
 '#.#.##...#.#',
 '#......#...#',
 '############']
```

Pretty-printing works well for lists, dictionaries, sets, tuples, and any data composed of the former. There are a few options, the most important settings being the *line width* and the *depth* of nested data structures to be displayed.

For instance, we could force the maze to be printed on a single extralong line with `pprint(data, depth=1, width=500)`. The `pprint` module is useful both for diagnosis and to produce regular program output.

As we can see, the maze data is correct and contains more than one row. Again, we **reject the hypothesis**. Looking for alternative explanations, we sooner or later end up with a **hypothesis** similar to the following: **the outer for loop is exited too early**. By stripping, tracing, or simply reviewing the program code, we sooner or later stumble upon the innocent-looking line

```python
        return img
```

The line is aligned with the inner for loop. That means, the function returns as soon as the first line is finished. Unindenting the statement by one level

```python
    return img
```

lets both loops iterate the correct number of times (one of the earlier `print` statements will confirm that). At this point we have corrected at least one defect in the code—and produced a lot of console output. This is a good moment to clean the print statements from the code before moving on.

Simplify Input Data

Even though we have just fixed a defect, we still don't see anything in the output image. Apparently there are more defects to fix. Since the image itself is created and written in the correct size, the most probable source of the defect are the lines

```
rect = get_tile_rect(xs, ys)
img.blit(tile_img, tiles[char], rect)
```

Our follow-up **hypothesis** is: *the line with* `blit` *uses the wrong coordinates*. At this point, using the scientific method *rigorously* saves us from getting lost in the details. It is very tempting to simply print the coordinates of all tiles inside the loop:

```
rect = Rect((xs, ys, SIZE, SIZE))
print(tiles[char], rect)
img.blit(tile_img, tiles[char], rect)
```

which results in a long list of Pygame rectangle objects as an output:

```
<rect(0, 0, 32, 32)> <rect(...)>
<rect(0, 0, 32, 32)> <rect(...)>
<rect(0, 0, 32, 32)> <rect(...)>
...
```

As long as we don't know the **expected** coordinates, this information is close to useless. The amount of output produced by `print` becomes overwhelming. We don't know which rectangle to check first. Calculating the expected output for each rectangle manually is not a good idea either. We need another debugging strategy: **simplifying the input data**.

▧ **How exactly does blit work?** Before **testing** our hypothesis, we need to predict the expected coordinates. This time I have learned from my mistake in the previous chapter and read a little about `blit` *before* writing the code. The Pygame method `blit` copies a rectangular area from one image (`img`) to a second rectangular area in a second image (`map_img`). The method requires three parameters: the copied image `img`, the destination rectangle on `map_img`, and a rectangle specifying which part of the source image should be copied. The `Rect` objects themselves contain four values: the x and y coordinates of the top left corner and the width and height of the rectangle.

Start with Minimal Input

Getting the coordinates of rectangles right is a recurring problem when using Pygame. I keep messing them up all the time. Dealing with a persistent problem (it has persisted for four pages already), we would be happy to see at least a single tile drawn correctly instead of the blank image. We scale down our problem, because a maze consisting of a single tile is all we need:

```
level = ['#']
```

When we calculate which coordinates we would expect, the rectangle on the destination image should be at (0, 0, 32, 32) and the source rectangle at (0, 0, 32, 32) as well, because the wall tile is in the top-left corner of tiles.png. Using minimal input reduces the amount of information produced by the preceding print statement to a single line:

```
(<rect(0, 0, 32, 32)>, <rect(1024, 1024, 32, 32)>)
```

The produced image is still black, only much smaller. When we compare the printed coordinates to our expected value, it turns out that the second rectangle rect is incorrect. We have enough evidence to **accept the hypothesis**. Where do the wrong coordinates come from? When we double-check the get_tile_rect function from Chapter 2, we see that it calculates a rectangle from *tile indices*; for example, (0, 0) for the tile in the top left corner, (1, 0) for the second tile from the left, and so on. The parameters xs and ys therefore need to be checked. A refined **hypothesis** is: *xs and ys are the wrong tile indices*. We would expect the indices to be (0, 0) in any case. We can **test** the hypothesis with a single print statement:

```
print("xs={} \t ys={}".format(xs, ys))
```

This results in the following output:

```
xs=32        ys=32
```

This is far away from the expected 0, 0. We thus **accept the hypothesis**. It turns out that we have mixed up the *size* of the image xs with the loop index x. Using similar names for the two variables was probably not a good idea. We need to use the loop indices x and y for calculating the rectangle instead:

```
rect = get_tile_rect(x, y)
```

Not only do we observe the correct rectangles:

```
(<rect(0, 0, 32, 32)>, <rect(0, 0, 32, 32)>)
```

We also see a single wall tile on the produced image (see Figure 5-2). We have fixed another defect. Yay!

Figure 5-2. *Single wall tile*

Gradually Add More Input Data

Now that we got the program working for minimal data, we can try to generate the full maze again. But if we replace the microlevel by the original variable and rerun the program, everything is entirely black again. We are literally back to square one! Our **hypothesis** still is: the line with blit *uses the wrong coordinates*. Again, we need more diagnostic data. Again, it is very tempting to start inspecting single positions in the big output (e.g., using a conditional phrase):

```
# check bottom right tile
if x == 11 and y == 6:
    print(tiles[char], rect)
```

This is a bad idea! Why is combining an if conditional with print a bad idea? First, it makes our code harder to read by adding a code block. Because we may need to test more than one condition, conditional prints tend to proliferate quickly. Second, with a conditional print we are probing only a small portion of our data. This makes it harder to spot the big picture. Occasionally I use a conditional print to limit the size of my output. However, I prefer the (also dirty) strategy to exit the program altogether by introducing a ZeroDivisionError:

```
print(tiles[char], rect)
1/0
```

Albeit weird, I prefer this phrase over both sys.exit(0) and assert False, because it is faster to write and obviously wrong. Both conditional prints and premature exits tend to mutilate our program during debugging. Please consider these tools a last resort. We will see a more elegant way to probe single values in Chapter 7.

Before poking in a huge maze with conditionals, we will examine an *almost* minimal input. What is a bit more complicated than a single tile? *Two tiles!*

```
level = ['##']
```

As an expected output we **predict** the four rectangles:

```
(<rect(0, 0, 32, 32)>, <rect(0, 0, 32, 32)>)
(<rect(32, 0, 32, 32)>, <rect(0, 0, 32, 32)>)
```

And we observe the following:

```
(<rect(0, 0, 32, 32)>, <rect(0, 0, 32, 32)>)
(<rect(0, 0, 32, 32)>, <rect(32, 0, 32, 32)>)
```

The output shows a strange nonwall tile besides an empty tile. What is more, the console output indicates that the rectangles are in the wrong order. We thus **accept the hypothesis** and inspect the code. It turns out that the *order of parameters* to blit is wrong. It is tiles[char], rect while it should be rect, tiles[char]. We can fully explain our observation: the first of the two tiles gets drawn correctly, because both rectangles are identical. The second tile overwrites the first with the tile in position (1, 0) (also see Figure 5-3). We can fix the defect by swapping the two parameters:

```
map_img.blit(img, get_tile_rect(x, y), tiles[char])
```

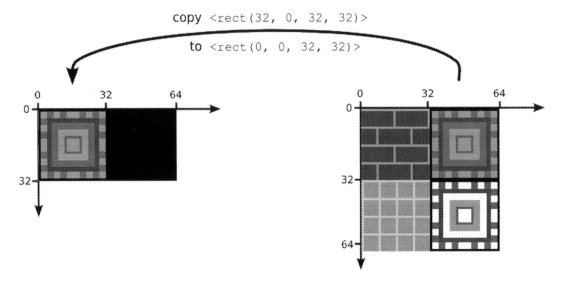

Figure 5-3. *Full diagnosis of the defect with rectangle coordinates*

Running the program results in two correctly drawn wall tiles. *It gets more exciting*: we can now switch to the full maze again, rerun the program, keep our fingers crossed... and finally see the full maze in all its beauty (see Figure 5-4)!

Figure 5-4. *Generated maze image*

▓ **Tip**   If you feel writing your own small games is a good programming exercise, but still feel programming graphics is a bit scary, simply leave the graphics out! Many successful games in computing history were entirely based on text or graphics built from ASCII characters. The graphics are here mainly because they look much better in a book than tons of character graphics.

Switching print Output On and Off

Throughout our debugging session we introduced several lines that produce diagnostic information. In my copy, I now have 12 commented lines in a 40-line program. To clean up everything properly, we have to remove the diagnostic code. However, what do we do if we know that we will *probably* need to diagnose this part of the program again? Rewrite the same print statements over and over? Editing our code back and forth carries a severe risk of introducing new errors. Isn't there a possibility to switch print statements on and off?

We could start by defining a constant for debugging:

```
DEBUG = True
```

We can then use the DEBUG variable to decide whether information should be printed or not. But as said previously, littering our code with diagnostic conditional prints is not the best idea. Imagine every print statement in our code inflated to something like this:

```
if DEBUG:
    print(rect)
```

A better alternative is to replace print by a debug_print function that takes care of checking the DEBUG variable and passes arguments to the regular print function:

```
def debug_print(*args):
    if DEBUG:
        print(*args)
```

We can even combine this with a conditional term:

```
def debug_print(*args, **kwargs):
    condition = kwargs.get('condition', True)
    if DEBUG and condition:

        print(*args)

debug_print(rect, tiles[char], condition=(x==0))
```

Still, we have to edit the DEBUG variable in our code every time we want to toggle debugging on or off. We could add a simple command-line option:

```
import sys

DEBUG = "-d" in sys.argv
```

and now we can run the program in debugging mode with

```
python draw_maze.py -d
```

The treatment of diagnostic output and command-line options can be further extended as your program grows. The standard modules logging and argparse provide a more robust implementation for the same purpose.

Complete Code

The complete, working code including imports and an optional diagnostic statement is given here:

```
from pygame import image, Rect, Surface
from load_tiles import load_tiles, get_tile_rect,  SIZE
from generate_maze import create_maze
from util import debug_print
```

```python
def parse_grid(data):
    """Parses the string representation into a nested list"""
    return [list(row) for row in data.strip().split("\n")]

def draw_grid(data, tile_img, tiles):
    """Returns an image of a tile-based grid"""
    debug_print("drawing level", data)
    xsize = len(data[0]) * SIZE ysize = len(data) * SIZE
    img = Surface((xsize, ysize))
    for y, row in enumerate(data):
        for x, char in enumerate(row):
            rect = get_tile_rect(x, y)
            img.blit(tile_img, rect, tiles[char])
    return img

if __name__ == '__main__':
    tile_img, tiles = load_tiles()
    level = create_maze(12, 7)
    level = parse_grid(level)
    maze = draw_grid(level, tile_img, tiles)
    image.save(maze, 'maze.png')
```

Pros and Cons of Using print Statements

Using print to diagnose our code is easy. It is a debugging strategy that even Python beginners can apply after one or two lessons. print allows us to observe our program at work, collect information, and narrow down the source of a bug. There are many defects that can be discovered this way. Printing goes together well with the scientific method and with the binary search strategy described in Chapter 4. So does simplifying input data, a general debugging strategy not limited to the combination with print. You could argue that we should turn to minimized input data as soon as we find the first semantic error, or even before we start writing any code. This is a great idea; please go for it! In general, print is a powerful diagnostic tool.

From an engineering point of view, adding print statements to our code is not an elegant way to debug, though. First, we make the program do additional things it was not intended for. In a sense, we make the code more wrong in order to fix it. Imagine shooting holes into a wall to check whether there is a fire in the building (see Figure 5-5). Second, print statements make the code we are debugging harder to read, and the output gets harder to read (when the printed output mixes with the regular output of a program). Third, we need to remove every print afterward, which makes the debugging process tedious and more error-prone, especially if we reinsert them for the next bug. Finally, adding print statements does not help much with complex bugs. There are many defects where printing the value of variables is not very useful.

Figure 5-5. *Debugging with print is a bit like shooting holes into a wall to see what is inside*

Nevertheless, print is a very effective and widely used diagnostic tool. Combined with a systematic approach like the scientific method, you will be fine using print to collect data from small and medium-sized programs. For bigger programs you may need more sophisticated *logging* or other diagnostic infrastructure. Simply be aware that print is not the only debugging tool and that it requires a bit of discipline to use it cleanly.

Best Practices

- print is a powerful diagnostic tool in Python.

- print lets you observe whether a given line has been executed.

- print lets you observe the values within variables.

- print output is easier to interpret if you limit the input data.

- Start with minimal input, then gradually increase the input size.

- Consider conditional print statements a last resort.

- A DEBUG variable allows switching printed messages on and off.

- Using print statements is not a very clean way to write programs. It should be used with caution and is generally less suitable for larger programs.

- print combines well with a rigid methodology like the scientific method or binary search.

CHAPTER 6

■ ■ ■

Debugging with Introspection Functions

Insufficient facts always invite danger.

—Leonard Nimoy as Spock, *Star Trek*, season 1, episode 24

Over the first few chapters we have written a lot of functions that we can now start assembling. When using Python functions or modules, we are frequently faced with questions like *"Where did I put the function for ..?", "What does that function return?", or "What is in this module?"* All these questions can be answered with **Introspection**. Introspection in Python refers to a group of powerful functions that allow you to examine objects in detail. The detailed information provided makes introspection a powerful diagnostic tool for both debugging and writing code.

In this chapter we will use several introspection functions to look inside Python objects. As an example, we will make the player figure move around. The figure shall be blocked by walls and eat dots on its way. All we need is a function move(grid, direction) that uses the two-dimensional maze, and a direction out of (LEFT, RIGHT, UP, DOWN). Let's implement the movement as a random walk (so that we don't need to plug in the event loop yet):

```python
if __name__ == '__main__':
    tile_img, tiles = load_tiles()
    maze = create_maze(12, 7)
    maze = parse_grid(maze)
    maze[1][1] = '*'
    for i in range(100):
        direction = random.choice([LEFT, RIGHT, UP, DOWN])
        move(maze, direction)
    img = draw_grid(maze, tile_img, tiles)
    image.save(img, 'moved.png')
```

The result of the program should be a path similar to the one in Figure 6-1. Instead of throwing another buggy program at you, we will build the code for the move function step by step. We start our tour by using the introspection functions in the **IPython** shell. On the way, we will encounter **namespaces, docstrings,** and **types** in our program.

© Kristian Rother 2017

K. Rother, *Pro Python Best Practices*, DOI 10.1007/978-1-4842-2241-6_6

Figure 6-1. *Result of the random walk of the player figure. The arrow has been added to the figure for clarity.*

Explorative Coding in IPython

You are probably already familiar with **IPython**, the improved Python shell. IPython is a great tool for **explorative coding**. Explorative coding means trying out commands in a sandbox or using parts of existing Python programs. It is useful while writing and debugging programs. There are many IPython functions that support explorative coding (e.g., executing code, autocompleting with Tab, running shell commands, and browsing namespaces). Consequent use of IPython instead of the regular Python shell is a Best Practice recommended by most experienced Python developers, either as a standalone console or built into development environments like **Anaconda** (https://www.continuum.io/) or **Enthought Canopy** (https://www.enthought.com/products/canopy/). All three flavors of IPython work in the same way, which is why we will take a small tour of IPython commands here.

We start by writing a few lines in IPython interactively to define a set of movement vectors (as (x, y) tuples):

```
In [1]: LEFT = (-1, 0)
```

```
In [2]: RIGHT = (1, 0)
```

```
In [3]: UP = (0, -1)
```

```
In [4]: DOWN  = (0, 1)
```

The commands are executed immediately like in the standard Python prompt (>>>). What is new is that IPython provides us with many so-called *magic functions* that make our life easier. For instance, we can obtain a list of all commands we have written so far by writing %hist:

```
In [5]: %hist
LEFT  = (-1, 0)
RIGHT = (1, 0)
UP    = (0, -1)
DOWN  = (0, 1)
```

The %hist command allows us to copy-paste our explorative code to a regular Python file. This is a good strategy to write a program *incrementally,* saving our progress every time we have found a working piece of code. We can reverse this approach as well. If we already have these four lines in a Python script, we can execute them in IPython by copying the lines and insert them using the *magic function* %paste. This way we can examine pieces of code without executing the entire module or creating a script with copied pieces of code. The %paste function is superior to the regular Ctrl+V because it handles indentation smarter.

We can use %paste to examine our program by executing the code in small portions. Having an interactive environment makes it easy to test functions one by one, replacing them when code changes and examining the contents of variables. Alternatively, we could execute a Python module using the *magic function* %run <module name>. The outcome is the same as if we would execute the program with python <program name> from the operating system. Running a program from IPython has the advantage that all variables and functions created by the program are kept, making it easier to examine them after the program has finished.

Exploring Files and Directories

We can use Unix commands such as ls, cd, and pwd inside IPython directly. This way we can explore files and directories without leaving Python (or using the more verbose functions from the os module). Using shell commands facilitates identifying wrong filenames and paths tremendously. It also helps us to find out what Python modules we could import. Here, we use ls to list Python files created in previous chapters.

```
In [6]: ls *.py
load_tiles.py
generate_maze.py
event_loop.py
draw_maze.py
util.py
```

From this list, we will need to import the modules load_tiles from Chapter 2, generate_maze from Chapter 3, and draw_maze from Chapter 5 in order to perform a move in a maze and display the outcome. Before writing the according import statements, we will need to find out which objects we need to import from these modules.

▒ **Hint**   In case you have defined a Python variable named ls, the preceding command to list Python files will fail. In that case you will need to write !ls to indicate you mean the Unix command. In fact, you can run any Unix command by adding a preceding exclamation mark:

```
In [7]: !echo "Hello World"
Hello World
```

With IPython, we effectively have two interactive environments in one: a Python shell and a Unix terminal. If you are still learning both, focusing on IPython may be less confusing than switching terminals while programming (and remembering which command to write in which window).

Overview of IPython Commands

Like Python, IPython is a flexible tool for experimenting with Python code, executing small programs and running shell commands. It combines the advantages of the Python shell with those of a regular Unix terminal. This combination makes IPython a strong base for debugging as well.

The capabilities of IPython go beyond the preceding examples. Table 6-1 gives an overview of the most important IPython commands. An excellent comprehensive IPython tutorial can be found in Wes McKinney's book *Python for Data Analysis* (O'Reilly, 2013) and at `http://ipython.readthedocs.io/en/stable/interactive/magics.html`. If you like to use IPython for solving small problems or documenting your efforts, you might also consider **Jupyter notebooks** (`http://jupyter.org/`). The notebooks use IPython to execute Python code from a web browser, allow you to supplement your code with formatted text, and may contain dynamically generated plots, images, or even rotating 3D molecules (see `http://github.com/arose/nglview`). Besides debugging, IPython with or without notebooks is widely used for interactive data analysis.

Exploring Namespaces

We now have found out what modules are there to import. What functions or variables are defined in these modules? Recalling that in Python *everything is an object,* we can generalize this question from modules to all objects. In this section, we will use introspection to *look inside* Python objects. Finding out what is inside a given object is a frequent question during debugging. Instead of browsing the source code or scrolling up endlessly in a IPython session, it is a Best Practice to use Python's own introspection functions. The question *"What is inside an object"* is closely related to the concept of **namespaces**. What is a namespace? In Python, objects are bound to names, for example, by defining a variable:

```
In [8]: LEFT = (-1, 0)
```

The command creates an object (the tuple containing –1 and 0) and binds it to the name LEFT. The name is used as the key of a dictionary that Python uses internally to find the tuple whenever we use LEFT. This dictionary is called a *namespace*. Because Python does not distinguish at all between the types of the objects stored, a namespace is, sloppily speaking, a big bag of names connected to objects.

Table 6-1. *Useful IPython Commands That Supplement Introspection*

Command	Description
?name	display basic information about name
?nam*	list all objects starting with nam
Tab	autocomplete
pwd	print working directory (same as the Unix command)
cd name	change working directory (same as the Unix command)
ls	list working directory (same as the Unix command)
%run name.py	execute a Python module
%paste	execute code from the clipboard
%debug name.py	run debugger on a Python module
%reset	clear the namespace of the IPython session
%env	list environment variables

There are many namespaces in a Python program. For instance, if we use the name LEFT in another module, that module does not know how we defined LEFT in our IPython session and either will stop with an error message or will find a different object (if LEFT is assigned there, too). We can also say the module has a different **namespace**. A namespace is simply a bag of names attached to a Python object. Each module, each function, and every Python object has its own namespace. IPython has a namespace of its own, too. The components of a namespace are referred to as **attributes**. By the preceding assignment, LEFT became an attribute of the IPython namespace. Let's see how we can examine namespaces and attributes.

Exploring Namespaces with dir()

How can we *look inside* a namespace and see what names it contains? Namespaces can be easily explored with the dir function. By using dir without arguments we can see the contents of Ipython's main namespace:

```
In [9]: dir()
['DOWN', 'In', 'LEFT', 'Out', 'RIGHT', 'UP', '_', '__',
'___', '__builtin__', '__builtins__', '__doc__',
'__loader__', '__name__', '__package__', '__spec__', '_dh',
'_i', '_i1', '_i2', '_i3', '_i4', '_i5', '_i6', '_i7',
'_i8', '_ih', '_ii', '_iii', '_oh', '_sh', 'exit',
'get_ipython', 'quit']
```

This look behind the scenes of Python may require a bit of explanation if you haven't seen it before. dir() returns a list of the names of objects in a namespace in alphabetical order: first, names starting with capital letters; next, names starting with underscores; and finally, names starting with lowercase letters. Let's go through the items one by one:

- LEFT, RIGHT, UP, and DOWN are the tuples we previously defined further.
- In is created by IPython automatically. It contains a list of all commands we entered in IPython so far.
- Out is created by IPython as well. It is a dictionary of all outputs that IPython sent to the standard output.
- __builtin__ and __builtins__ refer to the module with standard Python functions like print. It gets imported automatically whenever you start Python.
- __doc__ is the documentation string of the current namespace.
- __name__ is the name of the current namespace.
- exit and quit are functions that terminate IPython.
- the remaining ones are other internal shortcuts used by IPython.

We can type each of these names at the IPython prompt to see what the according objects contain. Let's check how the namespace we obtain with dir changes when we import our own modules.

```
In [10]: import draw_maze
```

```
In [11]: import generate_maze
```

```
In [12]: import load_tiles
```

```
In [13]: dir()
['DOWN', 'In', 'LEFT', 'Out', 'RIGHT', 'UP', '_', '_9', '__',
 '___', '__builtin__', '__builtins__', '__doc__',
 '__loader__', '__name__', '__package__', '__spec__', '_dh',
 '_i', '_i1', '_i2', '_i3', '_i4', '_i5', '_i6', '_i7',
 '_i8', '_ih', '_ii', '_iii', '_oh', '_sh', 'draw_maze',
 'exit', 'generate_maze', 'get_ipython', 'load_tiles', 'quit']
```

When we invoke dir() again, we see the same names as previously plus the three imported modules. The *names* of all three modules have become part of the namespace. During debugging, it is very practical to use dir to find out what modules, functions, and variables are defined at a given moment. Some typos are easy to discover that way. In a sense, using dir is like opening the hood of a car and looking at the engine. dir shows us a complete list of parts.

Exploring Namespaces of Objects

Using introspection, we have found our own modules, imported them, and seen them in the IPython namespace. Still, we don't know what each module contains. We can use dir on a module and take a look at the namespace of these modules, *their own* list of parts, as well:

```
In [14]: dir(draw_maze)
```

This results in:

```
['Rect', 'SIZE', 'TILE_POSITIONS', 'Surface', '__builtins__',
 '__cached__', '__doc__', '__file__', '__loader__',
 '__name__', '__package__', '__spec__', 'create_maze',
 'debug_print', 'draw_grid', 'get_tile_rect', 'image',
 'load_tiles', 'parse_grid']
```

Now we see the functions and variables we defined in the draw_maze module. We also see objects that draw_maze imported into its namespace (e.g., Rect and debug_print). Additionally, we see a few names starting with underscores that Python uses internally. We can use dir on any Python object, not just on modules. For instance, we could inspect the attributes of the TILE POSITIONS object (a Python list):

```
In [15]: dir(draw_maze.TILE_POSITIONS)
```

As a result, we see a *long* list of items, at the end of which we find list methods that you might be familiar with, such as pop and sort.

When introspecting Python objects, the output of dir is sometimes hard to read because the underscore-prefixed attributes seem to be all over the place. Most of the time, we can ignore them. There are three attributes starting with underscores that I find useful frequently:

- _file_ – contains the physical location of a module. If we suspect we imported a module from the wrong location, __file_ contains the information to save the day.

- __name__ – helps us to find out the name of functions, classes, and modules, if we have been munging with them (e.g., using import .. as or using functions as parameters for another function).

- *magic methods* like __add__ and __len__ that map to operators or standard functions in Python. For instance, if we see the __add__ attribute in a namespace, we know that the + operator is supposed to work with that object. If we see the __getitem__ attribute in a namespace, we know that we can index it using square brackets. Keeping all the names of these *magic methods* in mind is not a piece of cake. Fortunately, the Python reference on them is exhaustingly accurate. See https://docs.python.org/3/reference/datamodel.html.

Using dir we can inspect the namespace of every Python object. In a debugging session, this helps us to find out whether we imported the right modules and spelled the names of objects and their attributes correctly. We have also seen that Python namespaces are nested: every Python object in our namespace has a namespace of its own. An example for namespaces in namespaces is illustrated in Figure 6-2. dir is a powerful tool to navigate this network of namespaces.

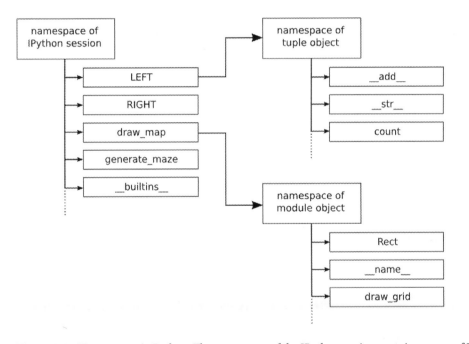

***Figure 6-2.** Namespaces in Python. The namespace of the IPython session contains names of Python objects we created directly, of modules we imported, and of IPython's own objects. Each of these objects has a namespace of its own. Two of these namespaces are indicated, each depicted with a small fraction of the names contained.*

Exploring Attributes in a Python Program

The contents of a namespace are also called *attributes*. dir only gives us the names of these attributes as a list of strings. If we want to access the real objects, we can use the dot (.) operator. For instance with draw_maze.SIZE we access the SIZE attribute of the draw_maze module. At runtime we don't always know an attribute name in advance. Then it is more convenient to use two other introspection functions, hasattr() and getattr(). Suppose we want to access the object draw_maze.SIZE in our program. Using getattr on the draw_maze function returns the according Python object:

```
In [16]: size = getattr(draw_maze, 'SIZE')
```

With `hasattr(x, name)` we can check whether a given object exists (like `dir`, but it returns a boolean). A typical example would be that we read a list of modules or functions from a configuration file and dynamically access them in our program. `getattr` and `hasattr` are sometimes useful during debugging, but most of the time we rather will find them in a program that dynamically adds modules and functions to itself (e.g., Django does this a lot).

Alternatives to dir in IPython

`dir()` is not our only option to list the parts of a Python object. In IPython we can explore namespaces quickly, because names of variables, functions, and modules are autocompleted by pressing `Tab`. We can also search namespaces using wildcards (`*`), for instance by typing

```
In [17]: ?dra*
```

You should see that `draw_maze` comes up in the results. If you don't care about seeing the namespace as a Python list, this method may be more efficient than `dir`.

The information produced by `dir` helps us to find out what to import. In addition to our own functions, we will also need `pygame.image` and two modules from the standard library, `random` and `sys`. The complete import block is

```
from load_tiles import load_tiles
from generate_maze import create_maze
from draw_maze import draw_grid, parse_grid
from pygame import image
import random
import sys
```

Namespace Mechanics

By examining namespaces, we can learn a lot about how Python works. In this section, we look at three special aspects connected to namespaces.

Python Uses Namespaces for Its Own Functions

Namespaces are ubiquitous. Even the regular Python functions are organized in the same way. A good example is the `__builtins__` module:

```
In [18]: dir(__builtins__)
```

We see a long list containing all the standard Python functions (and some you might want to read about). Every function in the `__builtins__` module is usable in every namespace by default as if it were a part of that namespace. A good reason for grouping the standard functions in their own module is that the output of `dir()` without parameters becomes a lot shorter.

Modifying a Namespace

How do namespaces change in a program? There are actually only a few Python commands that change a namespace *directly*. These are as follows:

- *a variable assignment* with = adds a new name to the namespace or replaces an existing one.

- the del instruction removes a name from the namespace.

- a function definition with def, which adds the function to the namespace. The function itself is a Python object having its own namespace; an additional local namespace or *scope* is created when the function is executed.

- a class definition adds the class to the namespace. The class and each instance of that class, when created, have a namespace of their own as well.

- every import adds a module or some of its components to a namespace.

- for and with statements create new variables similar to =.

- *comprehensions* create temporary variables that disappear as soon as the comprehension finishes.

Specifically looking for commands that modify a namespace helps to identify defects leading to a NameError. Let's examine how the namespace changes in a function for finding the position of a player in the maze. Let us consider the following piece of code (if you find it tedious to enter it line by line in IPython, use %paste).

```python
def get_player_pos(level, player_char='*'):
    """Returns a (x, y) tuple of player char on the level"""
    for y, row in enumerate(level):
        for x, char in enumerate(row):
            if char == player_char:
                return x, y
```

When we call dir() after entering the function, we will see that get_player_pos appeared in the namespace. However, we do not see any of the variables defined inside the function (level, y, row, etc.). We don't see any of them when examining the namespace of the function with dir(get_player_pos) either. These variables are only created dynamically when *executing* the function. As soon as we call get_player_pos and the code within the function is executed, the parameters level, player_char are added to the namespace. When the respective for loops are entered, the respective variables y, row, x, and char appear as well. All names added to the namespace inside the function will disappear when the function terminates. The reason is that the namespace had a *local scope*. In the next section, we will look at a few interesting effects that local scope has.

Namespaces and Local Scope

A practical consequence of having multiple namespaces and scopes is that two variables are not necessarily the same, even if they have the same name. The following example has driven many beginners into desperation:

```python
def f():
    a = 2

a = 1
f()
print(a)
```

If you are in the process of discovering namespaces for yourself, you may be wondering why the output of this program is 1. Of course, there are two separate namespaces at work: one for the function, one for the main program. A namespace in whose context code is being executed is also called *scope*. Both namespaces define the variable a. If Python cannot find a name in the local scope, it starts looking one level above (i.e., first inside the function, then in the main program). This is called moving from a local to a more global *scope*. This explains why the following example works as well:

```
a = 1

def f():
    print(a)

f()
```

The result of this code is 1. However, when a name is defined in a local scope, the local name is preferred over the global one:

```
a = 1

def f():
    a = 2
    print(a)

f()
```

The result of this example is of course 2. The following example terminates with an UnboundLocalError, because Python decides that a belongs to the local namespace during parsing the function:

```
a = 1

def f():
    print(a)
    a = 2

f()
```

Hopefully this example illustrates that keeping names cleanly separated (e.g., not using the same name inside and outside a function) is a Best Practice.

Namespaces Are a Core Feature of Python

Namespaces are a central feature of Python. We have seen that all Python objects have a namespace. Everything we see in any of those namespaces is also a Python object that in turn has its own namespace. In brief, Python consists of namespaces in namespaces in namespaces (see Figure 6-2). We have also seen that namespaces change frequently while a program runs.

This has a couple of deeper nontrivial implications for debugging. First, there is no real distinction between functions, methods of classes, and objects containing data. Python does not prevent us from mixing up these categories. Second, namespaces can be modified and recombined creatively (function decorators are a good example of this; metaclasses are a worse one). Third, there is no strict *encapsulation* in Python, meaning that every part of a program may modify the namespace of every other. While this is convenient, it also means that it is hard to keep things strictly separated; we cannot *prevent* other code from modifying a particular namespace. The lack of encapsulation makes writing short Python programs easier, but tends to fall on one's feet when writing large software.

As a consequence, keeping namespaces well-organized is a must. Organizing namespaces is up to the programmer, because Python does not care what we put in a namespace. This is why naming conventions and descriptive variable and function names are more important in Python than in other languages. Whether we decide to organize namespaces using functions, classes, modules, packages, or standard dictionaries is up to us. In a sense, all of these language features are solutions to the same abstract problem: *how to organize namespaces*. Knowing their strengths and weaknesses, we can choose which feature helps us to organize best at a given moment: If we want to organize units of code, functions are a good tool to organize our namespace. If we want to organize a few data objects, a simple list may be sufficient. If we need both, classes may be the right option. Functions, classes, and modules are there to make managing namespaces more convenient. In this, Python differs a lot from other programming languages internally, although the actual code may look similar.

Using Self-Documenting Objects

When we used dir, we could see what parts (functions, modules, other attributes) are there, but not how they work. Instead of reading the source code, we will use the documentation strings to find out. Instead of browsing the Internet, often we can find a quicker answer locally.

Accessing Docstrings with help()

A Best Practice is to examine a Python object briefly using the introspection function help(). The help() function displays docstrings of Python objects, which is very useful if we want to check what a given function does:

```
In [19]: help(draw_maze.draw_grid)
```

This command brings up a separate screen page with a help text:

```
Help on function draw_grid in module draw_maze:


draw_grid(data, tile_img, tiles)
    Returns an image of a tile-based grid
```

By pressing 'q' we can leave the help page again. Using help is useful to get quick hints for using a function or module (e.g., we could check the order of parameters with it easily). To gain deeper understanding, help is less appropriate, so it is insufficient as our only source of documentation while programming. But help does a decent job in supporting our memory of things *we did before*.

▨ **Hint** Sometimes the information displayed by help is not helpful at all. If you find the documentation too cryptic, or (worse) it is empty, leave the help screen immediately and look somewhere else.

---

help also lists the contents of **packages**. Sometimes dir does not work on a package very well (i.e., if the __init__.py file is empty). In that case, help() comes to the rescue:

```
In [20]: import pygame
In [21]: help(pygame)
```

The documentation contains an automatically generated section called **PACKAGE CONTENTS**, where all modules in the package are listed. In the case of Pygame, we can see the contents with dir, too; try import xml if you would like to see a package where dir doesn't help much.

Object Summaries in IPython

The IPython command ? symbol with an object name gives us a summary of the object type, contents, and description (a bit like the functions type, print, and help combined):

```
In [3]: ?maze
Type:        list
String form: [['#', '#', '#', '#', '#', '#', '#'],
              ['#', '.', '.', '.', '.', '.', '#'],
              ['#', '.', '.', '.', ' <...> ', '.', '.', '.', '#'],
              ['#', '.', '.', '.', '.', 'x', '#'],
              ['#', '#', '#', '#', '#', '#', '#']]
Length:      7
Docstring:
list() -> new empty list
list(iterable) -> new list initialized from iterable's items
```

Analyzing Object Types

With the four directional vectors (LEFT, RIGHT, UP, DOWN) and the get_player_pos function, we can implement the function for moving the player (or copy it with %paste to IPython). We simply add the movement vector to the player's position and modify the map accordingly:

```
def move(level, direction):
    """Handles moves on the level"""
    oldx, oldy = get_player_pos(level)
    newx = oldx + direction[0]
    newy = oldy + direction[1]
    if level[newy][newx] == 'x':
        sys.exit(0)
    if level[newy][newx] != '#':
        level[oldy][oldx] = ' '
        level[newy][newx] = '*'
```

Before we can call move, we need to set the starting position of the player. Let's start in the top-left corner of the maze, using an asterisk (*) as the player symbol:

```
In [22]: maze = create_maze(12, 7)

In [23]: maze[1][1] = '*'
```

Alas, we get another error message:

```
TypeError
Traceback (most recent call last)
<ipython-input-5-b9a7a1b90faf> in <module>()
----> 1 maze[1][1] = "*"

TypeError: 'str' object does not support item assignment
```

We probably need to take a closer look at the maze object. Instead of the somewhat crude print we will examine it with type(), another introspection function:

```
In [24]: type(maze)
str
```

The type function returns the object type (the class from which maze is derived). It works for any built-in or user-defined type. It turns out that our maze is a single string that cannot be modified. To modify the string, we need to convert it to a two-dimensional list. We have written code for that earlier in the draw_maze.parse_grid() function:

```
In [25]: maze = draw_maze.parse_grid(maze)
```

Now the type of maze is a list that of course is mutable:

```
In [26]: type(maze)
list
```

With that problem out of the way, we can finally assemble the preceding commands to a program that performs a random walk along the maze:

```
If __name__ == '__main__':
    tile_img, tiles = load_tiles()
    maze = create_maze(12, 7)

    maze = parse_grid(maze)
    maze[1][1]  =  '*'
    for i in range(100):
        direction = random.choice([LEFT, RIGHT, UP, DOWN])
        move(maze, direction)
    img = draw_grid(maze, tile_img, tiles)
    image.save(img, 'moved.png')
```

Checking Object Identity

There are a few more introspection functions that examine objects in detail: sometimes it is important to check whether two objects are really identical and not just containing the same data. This can be done with the is operator, whereas == only compares the content. The following example illustrates the difference:

```
In [17]: a = [1, 2, 3]
In [18]: b = [1, 2, 3]

In [19]: a == b
Out[19]: True

In [20]: a is b
Out[20]: False
```

Here, a and b are distinct objects, because modifying one list leaves the other unaffected. The same is true for dictionaries, sets, and, interestingly, tuples. For immutable basic types like strings and integers, the outcomes of both is and == are the same.

Checking Instances and Subclasses

With isinstance, we can check whether a given object is an instance of a given class:

```
isinstance("abc", str)
True
```

And with issubclass, we can check whether a given class is a descendant of another:

```
issubclass(str, object)
True
```

This works because every Python object is a descendant of object. Both isinstance and issubclass are essential for debugging code that uses a complex class hierarchy.

Practical Use of Introspection

To successfully debug Python programs, we need to know how to navigate and examine the namespaces in a program. Introspection is a powerful tool to analyze the *namespaces* in your Python program. We have a set of analytic functions like dir, help, and type that provide rich information about the contents, documentation, and types of any given Python object. You find a summary of introspection functions in Table 6-2.

Table 6-2. *Introspection Functions in Python*

Function	Description
l (list)	lists a few lines around the one executed next
dir()	returns a list of names in the current namespace
dir(x)	lists the contents of the namespace in x
help(x)	shows the docstring of a Python object
x is y	checks identity of two objects (as opposed to ==)
type(x)	returns the type of an object
hasattr(x, s)	returns True if the namespace of x contains the name s
getattr(x, s)	returns an attribute with name s from the namespace of x
issubclass(x, y)	returns True if x is a subclass of y
isinstance(x, y)	returns True if x is an instance of class y
callable(x)	returns True if x can be called
globals(x)	returns a dictionary of objects in the global scope
locals(x)	returns a dictionary of objects in the local scope (e.g., inside a function)

Together with the shortcuts in IPython (e.g., for checking file names or listing names with a wildcard) we can find out a lot about our program. Situations where introspection is useful include

- exploring a library

- experimenting with code fragments

- using print() to output information about your namespace or types from a program

- exploring the type of objects during debugging

- examining objects after running your program in IPython

- identifying overlapping namespaces

Most frequently, it is used in debugging, where it helps us to find even simple defects like typos.

Finding Typos with Introspection

Using introspection to analyze the contents of a namespace sometimes helps to identify typos. Consider the following instructions:

```
In [16]: player_pos = 7
In [17]: playr_pos = player_pos + 1
```

There is a defect that is easy to overlook in the code. However, after running `dir` we will see immediately that something is wrong:

```
..
'player_pos',
'playr_pos',
..
```

Looking into the namespace reveals a defect that might hide in the code for quite a while otherwise.

Combining Introspection Functions

To demonstrate the analytic power of introspection functions, we will look at one more example. In Chapter 2 we identified all Python errors with the instruction

```
[x for x in dir(__builtin__) if 'Error' in x]
```

The command works, but it is imprecise. We cannot be sure that all builtin Exceptions have `Error` in their name. A more correct approach would be to find all objects from the `__builtins__` module that are descendants of the base class `Exception`:

```
for name for name in dir(__builtins__):
    obj = getattr(__builtin__, name)
    if obj.__class__ == type \
        and issubclass(obj, Exception):
        print(obj)
```

We first loop through all objects in the `__builtins__` module. We use `getattr` to retrieve the object using its name. The first condition checks whether the object is a class (using a property called *metaclass*, in this case is `type`). The second condition checks whether the object is a subclass of `Exception`.

This is not how you would use introspection functions on an everyday basis. In particular, metaclasses in my opinion belong in the book *Pro Python: Black Magic* (if it ever were to be written). Like most dangerous Kung-Fu techniques, it is good to know about them but never to use them at all. However, writing expressions like the preceding helps us to achieve a deeper understanding of Python's internal mechanics.

Introspection in Big and Small Programs

Spending time in the interactive environment diagnosing Python objects with introspection is a Best Practice when writing both big and small Python programs. The main difference is that when writing small programs, introspection often happens in parallel to **explorative coding**, trying lines one by one and preserving those that work well, whereas in big programs introspection is rather found during a debugging session aiming to resolve one particular issue. Introspection is meant to *examine* Python programs. Sometimes you will find introspection functions used inside a program as part of its functionality. Although it may be useful if a program examines itself, it may feel a bit awkward (see Figure 6-3). I recommend using introspection at runtime sparingly, and only if you understand namespaces and introspection functions thoroughly.

Observing Python at work with introspection functions
seemed like a good idea. Sometimes, I had
a strange feeling about it though ...

Figure 6-3. Introspection functions

In brief, introspection is a tool that gives us detailed answers to the question *What objects **exist** in my program at a given moment and what are their properties?* Introspection allows us to analyze the **state** of our program, as opposed to the **dynamics** of code execution. The latter is the main limitation of introspection, because with introspection *alone* we will never see what the state of a namespace or object was *earlier* nor how it changes *later* in a program. We will overcome that limitation in the next chapter. Apart from this limitation, all introspection functions deserve a place in the toolkit of any Python programmer.

Best Practices

- **Introspection** is a set of accurate diagnostic tools to examine Python objects.

- **IPython** is an excellent environment to use **introspection functions** and **magic functions.**

- Every Python object has a **namespace** containing attributes.

- `dir()` lists the contents of a namespace.

- Namespaces are a core feature of Python. Namespaces may contain anything; thus, it is important to keep your namespaces well-organized.

- `help()` displays the docstring of a Python function, class, or module.

- `type()` shows the type of a Python object.

- Other introspection functions help to analyze types, classes, and attributes more precisely.

- During debugging, introspection allows you to diagnose the *state* of your program.

■ ■ ■

## CHAPTER 7

Using an Interactive Debugger

A debugger is like doing a full-body scan on a sick person.

—Zed Shaw, *Learn Python the Hard Way*
www.learnpythonthehardway.org

We now have all the parts in place to get the first version of our game running. We only need to combine the functions of drawing the map, moving the player, and running the event loop. Thus, we will import the modules written so far, add some code to glue them together, run the program, and play! Well, at least this is the theory. Do you think the components will cooperate smoothly at the first attempt? I don't want to disappoint you at the beginning of the chapter, but it is not very likely—at least not in my code. Of course, there is plenty of software that *must* work the first time it is used in a production environment (for instance, programs controlling aircraft, medical devices, elections, etc.). Such software is developed using a different process than *"let's crawl from one bug to the next."* When writing a game, we can afford the luxury to fix issues as they emerge.

In Chapter 6, we used introspection to examine the **state** of a program. In this chapter, we will examine its **dynamics**, how one state of a program transitions to the next. By using one more debugging tool, the **interactive debugger**, we will watch the program in slow motion, with the option to interact with it.

Before we can see the game in action, we have a bit of preparation to make. Let's start by importing everything we created so far. Because we already have a considerable number of imports, I placed them in ascending order:

```
from load_tiles import load_tiles
from generate_maze import create_maze
from event_loop import event_loop
from draw_maze import draw_grid, parse_grid
from moves import move, LEFT, RIGHT, UP, DOWN
from pygame import Rect
import pygame
```

We also need to initialize a Pygame display in order to handle events and draw graphics interactively. Because we will need the display later in other functions, this code needs to be executed first:

```
pygame.init()
pygame.display.set_mode((800, 600))
display = pygame.display.get_surface()
```

Next, we create a maze and add a player (*) and an exit (x) in opposite corners:

```
maze = parse_grid(create_maze(12, 7))
maze[1][1] = '*'
maze[5][10] = 'x'
```

© Kristian Rother 2017
K. Rother, *Pro Python Best Practices*, DOI 10.1007/978-1-4842-2241-6_7

Finally, we display the map right before the game starts (it would be awkward to make your first move with a black screen).

```
tile_img, tiles = load_tiles()
img = draw_grid(maze, tile_img, tiles)
display.blit(img, Rect((0, 0, 384, 224)), Rect((0, 0, 384, 224)))
pygame.display.update()
```

This is a good moment to execute the code. After five chapters on bugs you shouldn't be too surprised that the program fails:

```
Traceback (most recent call last):
  File "maze_run.py", line 22, in <module>
    img = draw_grid(maze, tile_img, tiles)
  File "/home/krother/projects/maze_run/maze_run/draw_maze.py", line 25, in draw_grid
    img.blit(tile_img, rect, tiles[char])
KeyError: 'x'
```

When combining a program from various pieces of code, we cannot expect everything to work smoothly right away. At the same time, the complexity of our program has grown (it should contain more than 100 lines and at least 10 functions by now). Whatever the underlying defect is, we can expect to jump around between various functions (as our code does) in order to identify the defect. In such a situation, the scientific method still fully applies. But to make precise observations on the executing program, we need an additional tool: An **interactive debugger**.

The Interactive Debugger ipdb

An interactive debugger like `ipdb` allows us to trace the execution of the program line by line and watch it execute in slow motion. Using an interactive debugger to track down defects is an essential Best Practice in most programming languages, including Python. There are a couple of things an interactive debugger allows us to do:

- inspect the content of variables.

- use introspection functions.

- evaluate regular Python instructions.

- examine the state of our program *right before* an Exception occurred.

- step through our code instruction by instruction. We need to press a key to execute the next instruction.

- continue or terminate the execution of our program.

- set *breakpoints*, locations in our code where normal execution is halted and the interactive debugging mode is entered.

In contrast to the *program state* we analyzed with `print` and introspection in Chapters 5 and 6, the strength of an interactive debugger is to analyze the **dynamics** of program execution: how one state transitions to the next, and, accordingly, how defects propagate. In Python, the interactive debugger of choice is **ipdb**.

Installing ipdb

ipdb is an extended version of the standard Python debugger pdb. Like IPython, it provides syntax highlighting and completion of names with [TAB]. The Traceback of Python Exceptions is more informative. The magic functions in IPython described in Chapter 6 (everything starting with %) don't work in ipdb, but neither do they in the debugger pdb in Python.

Using pip, ipdb is straightforward to install:

```
pip install ipdb
```

▓ **Note** If your installation fails for whatever reason, you can do most of the examples in this chapter using the built-in debugger pdb. Just replace ipdb with pdb.

Starting the Debugger

When using ipdb, we have three possibilities to start: at the beginning of program execution, at the end, and in the middle.

Running ipdb from the Command Line

We can start debugging our code by specifying ipdb as an extra module to the Python interpreter:

```
python -m ipdb maze_run.py
```

Alternatively, we can execute the program from within IPython with the -d option:

```
%run -d maze_run.py
```

In both cases, the program is executed in the debugger from the first line. You should see an output like this:

```
> /home/krother/Desktop/python_maze_game/maze_run/maze_run.py(1)<module>()
----> 1 from draw_map import draw_grid, parse_grid
      2 from event_loop import event_loop
      3 from generate_maze import create_maze
ipdb>
```

The arrow indicates the line the debugger is going to execute next (i.e., the first import has not been executed yet). After the code excerpt there is a prompt ipdb> at which we can enter commands. The most important command in idpb is **q**, which terminates the debugger. After all, the first line of maze_run.py is quite far away from the location of the traceback, so we will try a different way to invoke ipdb.

Starting ipdb from a Program

Alternatively, we can start the debugger at an arbitrary place within the program. To do so, we need to insert the following code fragment at the place from which we want to start the debugging session. For instance, we could call the debugger before line 22 in maze_run.py that raised an Exception:

```
..
tile_img, tiles = load_tiles()
import ipdb; ipdb.set trace()
img = draw_grid(maze, tile_img, tiles)

..
```

▓ **Hint**   This is one of the very few cases where placing two Python commands in the same line is appropriate. *"Appropriate"* as in *"at this particular party it is appropriate to have more than one drink."* You may conclude that it is still not a good idea.

When we execute the program, we see the ipdb prompt again. This time, the location in the code is where set_trace() was called. Now we can inspect variables. Looking at the KeyError when calling img. blit in the preceding, we hypothesize something is wrong with the tiles dictionary. We use the debugging session to print tiles with the pp shortcut:

```
ipdb> pp tiles
{' ': <rect(0, 32, 32, 32)>,
 '#': <rect(0, 0, 32, 32)>,
 '*': <rect(96, 0, 32, 32)>,
 '.': <rect(64, 0, 32, 32)>}
```

We observe that we forgot to add the exit tile to the dictionary. Our hypothesis is confirmed.

▓ **Hint**   If your program contains lists, dictionaries, or sets (which Python program doesn't?) using pprint is a Best Practice that makes screen output easier to read. Fortunately for us, the pp shortcut in ipdb saves us the trouble of importing the module.

We can attempt to fix the defect immediately. ipdb accepts any Python command, so we can simply add the missing entry. The top-left corner of the exit tile is position (32, 32). Afterward, we use the c command to continue program execution:

```
ipdb> tiles['x'] = Rect((32, 32, 32, 32))
ipdb> c
```

After adding the missing entry, the program runs flawlessly. We see the level, at least for a short moment before the window closes. Hotfixing our program is not a very clean or elegant strategy, but sometimes it is the fastest way to check whether an assumption is correct. Let's remove the call to ipdb.set_trace() from our code in order to try another debugging strategy.

Postmortem Debugging

The trouble for most crime scene investigators is that they notoriously arrive too late. The crime is over, the suspect ran, and the investigators need to reconstruct the event from various clues. Not so ipdb: In **postmortem debugging** we arrive at the crime scene the moment an Exception occurred, as if time froze. We can examine our program *right before* it crashed. This is possible because Python memorizes a lot of information about the last Exception (available via `sys.exc_info()`). Of course, the Python interpreter must still be running. Fortunately, IPython keeps the Python objects around when we start a program from the interactive prompt, so that we can start the postmortem debugger using the function `ipdb.pm()`:

```
In [1]: %run maze_run.py

    .. Traceback

KeyError: 'x'

In [2]: import ipdb

In [3]: ipdb.pm()

ipdb>
```

An annoying thing about this command is that if we mistype `ipdb` we need to start all over again (Python only memorizes one Exception and any newly created error on the console discards the previous one). Fortunately, IPython provides the `%debug` magic function that replaces the preceding sequence:

```
In [1]: %run maze_run.py

    .. Traceback

KeyError: 'x'

In [2]: %debug

ipdb>
```

Like with `ipdb.set_trace()`, we can examine the content of variables and modify them. The main difference is that you cannot continue execution (the program is already dead). Pressing c terminates the debugger session and returns to the IPython prompt. **Postmortem debugging** is an exciting alternative to stepping into the debugger during the lifetime of the program.

▓ **Postmortem Analysis**   The term *postmortem* is also used as a term to describe after-project meetings or retrospectives. This is not what is meant here. I think they also do postmortem analyses at the morgue, but this is far from what we are doing here.

Launching the Debugger on Exceptions

There are situations in which we need to enter the debugger by default whenever an Exception occurs. For instance, we have a program that we need to keep alive at any costs (a production web server). Or we have data we don't want to lose. Or we are field-testing our program and are curious what kind of problems occur. In such situations we could wrap our entire program in a big `try` block and start `ipdb.pm()` in the `except` block. The code for that is so ugly and un-Pythonic that I don't want to show it here. The proper way to achieve this in Python is using a Context Manager and `with`.

```
from ipdb import launch_ipdb_on_exception

with launch_ipdb_on_exception():
    # your code
```

This expression smoothly integrates with existing code, is easy to read, and we can choose which parts of the program ipdb shall examine. All three modes of starting the interactive debugger (beginning of the program, during execution, or after it terminated with an Exception) are Best Practices. Like with print, having a hypothesis helps to decide which of the three to use in a given situation and usually prevents you from searching *everywhere* in the code.

Fixing the Defect

Of course, we still need to add the extra entry to the dictionary in the program in load_tiles.py:

```
TILE_POSITIONS = [
    ('#', 0, 0), # wall
    ('␣', 0, 1), # floor
    ('x', 1, 1), # exit
    ('', 2, 0), # dot
    ('*', 3, 0), # player
    ]
```

With the addition of a single line, our program sets up the graphics correctly. We can continue adding the game mechanics.

Commands at the Debugger Prompt

Before we look at the more sophisticated functions of a debugger, let's summarize the basic options we have once we reach the ipdb prompt:

Inspect Variables

We can check the contents of any variable from the ipdb prompt. This is done by typing their name (as you would in the Python shell) or with p name. The main advantage of inspecting variables with ipdb is that we can examine the program state without littering our code with calls to print and introspection functions.

▓ **Tip** There are escapes for one-character variables: Most of the debugger commands have names that some programmers like to use as variable names. If you have such a name, you can still access your variable by escaping it with an exclamation mark (!):

ipdb> !p = 3

ipdb> p p

Evaluate Python Expressions

We can write Python expressions to change values of variables (e.g., to check whether we found the reason for a bug by correcting it manually). To do so, simply type a Python command and see what happens. This way, we can test hypotheses about what *fixes* a defect immediately. The latter doesn't work all the time; when fixing the preceding KeyError, we were a bit lucky.

Stepping Through Our Code

To get to the site of the problem, we can execute the next line in the debugger with n. If we need to dive into a function and observe it from the inside, use s instead of n. With s we can essentially climb up the entire *call* stack inside our code (and back). With l and ll we display the line executed next and a few around it. In general, a combination of the debugger commands l, n, and s allows us to efficiently navigate our program step by step. Shortly, in the section "Example ipdb Session", we will look at a detailed example for an interactive session.

Start Over

As soon as we have seen enough, we may simply hit c and continue execution to the end (or the next call of the debugger). In contrast, when we conclude that our running program can't be saved any more, the q command terminates it quickly, so that we can change it and try again. Table 7-1 lists the commands usable at the ipdb prompt.

Table 7-1. *Common Commands in ipdb*

Command	Description
l (list)	list a few lines around the one executed next
ll (long)	list a few lines more
n (next)	executes the next line
s (step)	executes the next line, if it contains a function call, jump to the first line of the function
p (print)	display contents of a variable
pp (pretty-print)	displays composite types nicely formatted
c (continue)	continues execution without the debugger
R	continue to the end of a function
q (quit)	terminates execution of the program
u, d	navigate up and down the call stack (so that you can view code there)
b (break)	list breakpoints
b <file:line>	add a breakpoint
b <function>	add a breakpoint
b <file:line>, <condition>	add a breakpoint with a condition
b <function>, <condition>	add a breakpoint with a condition
cl <number>	remove a breakpoint
?	list available commands
help <command>	shows help for a debugger command
[ENTER]	repeats last debugger command

Using Breakpoints

Breakpoints tell the debugger to stop execution at a specific line and start the debugger. They make our life more comfortable, so that we don't need to insert pdb.set_trace() in our code all the time. We can set a breakpoint at the beginning of a specific function (e.g., in the move() function) with

```
ipdb> b moves.move
```

given that the moves module is known at that moment. Alternatively, we can specify a filename and line number:

```
ipdb> b moves.py:24
```

To make use of the breakpoint, we start our program in debugging mode (as a new ipdb session). Then we press c once to reach the first breakpoint and start our analysis. If we have set multiple breakpoints, we can jump from one to the next with the c command.

Breakpoints are useful to narrow down the location of a defect. One possible search strategy is to encircle the erroneous code in a few iterations. Set a breakpoint at a moment when everything is correct, and a second at a place where things have gone wrong for sure. Set a third breakpoint halfway and check whether the fault occurred at the third breakpoint already. Depending on the result, narrow down your search in one half or the other.

Viewing and Deleting Breakpoints

You can list all breakpoints currently set by simply pressing b. The list includes a number, a location, and the number of times the breakpoint has been visited:

```
ipdb> b
Num Type         Disp Enb   Where
1   breakpoint   keep yes   at ../maze_run/debugging/maze_run.py:35
    breakpoint already hit 2 times
2   breakpoint   keep yes   at ../maze_run/debugging/moves.py:24
    breakpoint already hit 2 times
```

If you want to remove a breakpoint you can use the cl command with the same parameters you used to create a breakpoint. Most of the time breakpoints will be easier to delete using the number from Table 7-1:

```
cl 2
```

which deletes the second breakpoint from the list. Sometimes I find setting and deleting breakpoints manually in **ipdb** a bit clumsy. In PyCharm setting and deleting them requires a single click on the bar at the left side of the program code (see Figure 7-2 below).

Conditional Breakpoints

One frequent problem in debugging a complex program is that an error does not occur when the program reaches a certain line for the first time. Imagine we have 99 iterations before reaching the condition we are interested in. Manually typing c the first 99 times would let us fall asleep before finding the error. In that case, we need to stop program execution depending on the state of the program. We could add a condition to the code yourself as an if clause. For instance, we could check whether the next tile is going to be a wall:

```
if level[newy][newx] == '#':
    ipdb.set_trace()
```

However, this is not an elegant solution. As with conditional prints, this tends to mess up our code. *Conditional breakpoints* are a more elegant shortcut. We can reach the same by setting a breakpoint inside ipdb with

```
b moves:27, level[newy][newx] == '#'
```

Interestingly, it is not a problem if we mistype the conditional expression or it does not work for another reason. When Python raises an Exception from within the conditional, ipdb assumes there is a reason to look at the code closely and the breakpoint is triggered anyway.

Configuring ipdb

We can execute commands from a .pdbrc file when entering the debugger. ipdb looks for this configuration file in the directory where we started Python and in our home directory (the latter applies to all Python projects). Alternatively, we may specify a file with the option -c when running the debugger from the Python command line. A .pdbrc configuration file might look like this:

```
from pprint import pprint
ll
print(dir())
b maze_run.handle_key
```

When the debugger is entered, four things happen: First, we import the pretty-print function pprint() to examine large data structures more easily. Second, we have ipdb produce a longer excerpt of the current location in the code. Third, we display the contents of the current namespace. Fourth, we set a breakpoint that is triggered whenever the handle_key function in the maze_run module is called.

As you see, the configuration file may contain a mixture of both normal Python commands and debugger commands. The purpose of the configuration is to make our debugging easier. For instance, if you are debugging a large program, you might list your favorite breakpoints there. If you are debugging a system with critical data, you can save the data automatically before you debug. If you want to track when and where you are debugging, you can write a log message with a timestamp and so on. Commands that interfere with your program a lot or strongly depend on the kind of problem examined should not go into your .pdbrc. Taken together, a good configuration may make your crash landings even smoother.

Example ipdb Session

The main benefit of using a debugger is to **step through your code**. That is, we execute the program command by command and inspect variables on the way until we (hopefully) discover the place where a defect occurs. We can control execution of our code with the shortcuts in Table 7-1. Here, we will go through an ipdb session from the beginning to the end.

Adding a Game Control Function

After importing all necessary modules and initializing the game, we need to plug the arrow keys into our move function. In Chapter 4 we found out the key codes for the arrow keys to be used in the event loop (the integers 273-276). We can map each arrow key to one of the movement vectors in a dictionary:

```
DIRECTIONS = {
    276: LEFT,
    275: RIGHT,
    273: UP,
    274: DOWN
}
```

In the game control function, we take a key, get the move vector, perform the move in the maze, and draw everything. We start the game by passing that function as a callback into the event loop:

```
def handle_key(key):
    """Handles key events in the game"""
    move(maze, DIRECTIONS.get(key))
    img = draw_grid(maze, tile_img, tiles)
    display.blit(img, Rect((0, 0, 384, 224)), Rect((0, 0, 384, 224)))
    pygame.display.update()

event_loop(handle_key)
```

When we run the program, it looks fine at first. When we press arrow keys, the figure moves around and eats dots, and walking on the exit tile terminates the program. But if we hit a different key, the program suddenly crashes with an error message:

```
Traceback (most recent call last):
  File "maze_run.py", line 45, in <module>
    event_loop(handle_key)
  File "/home/krother/projects/maze_run/maze_run/event_loop.py", line 16, in event_loop
    handle_key(event.key)
  File "maze_run.py", line 39, in handle_key
    move(maze, direction)
  File "/home/krother/projects/maze_run/maze_run/moves.py", line 29, in move
    newx = oldx + direction[0]
TypeError: 'NoneType' object is not subscriptable
```

Stepping Through the Code

We will step through the code from the very beginning. Let's start the debugger from IPython:

```
In [2]: %run -d maze_run.py
> /home/krother/Desktop/python_maze_game/maze_run/debugging/maze_run.py(1)<module>()
1---> 1 from draw_map import draw_grid, parse_grid
      2 from event_loop import event_loop
      3 from generate_maze import create_maze
      4 from load_tiles import load_tiles
      5 from moves import move, LEFT, RIGHT, UP, DOWN
```

The debugger lets us start from the first line. We now can press n to go through the lines one by one.

```
ipdb> n
> /home/krother/Desktop/python_maze_game/maze_run/debugging/maze_run.py(2)<module>()
1      1 from draw_map import draw_grid, parse_grid
----> 2 from event_loop import event_loop
       3 from generate_maze import create_maze
       4 from load_tiles import load_tiles
       5 from moves import move, LEFT, RIGHT, UP, DOWN
```

It will quickly turn out that this is not an ideal way to proceed. First, it is boring to scroll through a long list of imports and other code not relevant to the problem. Second, we will have to get out of the event loop once we get there (you are free to try what happens). Fortunately, we already know where the error occurred, so we will start debugging on the top level of the Traceback. To get to the point in the code, we set a breakpoint in the handle_key function:

```
ipdb> b handle_key
Breakpoint 1 at /home/krother/projects/maze_run/maze_run/maze_run.py:35
```

For setting the breakpoint, we don't need to specify the module, because we are already in the scope of the game module. Now, we can continue execution:

```
ipdb> c
```

You should see that the Pygame window pops up and the debugger session is suspended. Now, if you switch the focus to the game window and press an arrow key, the debugger reaches the first breakpoint.

```
> /home/krother/projects/maze_run/maze_run/maze_run.py(37)handle_key()
1     35 def handle_key(key):
      36     """Handles key events in the game"""
----> 37     move(maze, DIRECTIONS.get(key))
      38         img = draw_grid(maze, tile_img, tiles)
      39         display.blit(img, Rect((0, 0, 384, 224)), Rect((0, 0, 384, 224)))
```

We can switch the focus back to the terminal running ipdb. Note that it matters *how* you switch the focus (if you use the mouse, Pygame won't notice, but if you use keys (e.g., Alt + Tab), they go into the Pygame event queue). We can now check the value of the function parameter key:

```
ipdb> key
275
```

This is one of the *"safe"* values that we know are working. We continue execution and return to the game window:

```
ipdb> c
```

This time, we press **the space key**. Again, the breakpoint is triggered at the same location. This time, we get a different value for key:

```
..
----> 22 move(maze, DIRECTIONS.get(key))
..
ipdb> key
32
```

We now could evaluate the first line in the handle_key function by pressing n. However, we know from the Traceback that the line calling move is the one in which the error will occur. We can now *step inside* the function with the s command:

```
ipdb> s
--Call--
> /home/krother/Desktop/python_maze_game/maze_run/debugging/moves.py(22)move()
     20
     21
---> 22 def move(level, direction):
     23     """Handles moves on the level"""
     24     oldx, oldy = get_player_pos(level)
```

Whenever entering a function during a debugging session, it is a good idea to list all its parameters. A convenient way to do that is the introspection function locals():

```
ipdb> locals()
{'level': [['#', '#', '#', '#', '#', '#', '#', '#', '#', '#', '#', '#'],
['#', '*', '.', '.', '.', '.', '.', '.', '.', '.', '.', '#'],
['#', '.', '.', '#', '.', '#', '.', '#', '.', '.', '.', '#'],
['#', '.', '.', '.', '.', '#', '.', '.', '.', '.', '.', '#'], ['#', '#', '.', '#
```

If you decide to type the names of the parameters one by one instead of using locals(), the None value of direction becomes harder to spot. We have to use the p command to actually *see* it:

```
ipdb> direction
ipdb> p direction
None
```

▓ **Hint**   If you want to analyze level in more detail, the pp command gives a much nicer output.

At this point, you may already *assume* that the None value caused the Exception. It is worth restraining ourselves from fixing the code *immediately*. First, we have identified a symptom, not the defect itself. Second, there are multiple ways to fix it. Therefore it is worth looking at the entire propagation of the defect. We will press n a few more times until the Exception is raised. Fortunately, we don't have to travel far:

```
ipdb> n
..
ipdb> n
..
ipdb> n
TypeError: 'NoneType' object is not subscriptable
> /home/krother/Desktop/python_maze_game/maze_run/debugging/moves.py(25)move()
     23     """Handles moves on the level"""
     24     oldx, oldy = get_player_pos(level)
---> 25 newx = oldx + direction[0]
     26 newy = oldy + direction[1]
     27 if level[newy][newx]
== 'x':
```

We now have the full picture: Python cannot apply the index [0] on the value None. At that point, the debugger session is of no more use to us (the values oldx and oldy are not relevant to the phenomenon). It is time to quit the session.

```
ipdb>  q
```

Fixing the Defect

Clearly, we haven't told our program what to do when an unknown key is pressed. There are different ways to mitigate the problem. First, we could add defensive code to move():

```
if direction == None:
    return
```

This makes the function more complex than necessary. The second idea is to add a default value when accessing the DIRECTIONS dictionary:

```
DIRECTIONS.get(key, (0, 0))
```

This will call move() with a value that doesn't move anything. Adding the zero vector (0, 0) as a default value is not a good idea either. In a sense, we are forcing move() to do something the function was not written for. Even though it works, it is very likely that this fix will soon grow into a more complicated defect than the one we are fixing.

The best location to fix the defect is right where it first occurs. We explicitly take care of the *missing key* situation in the game function:

```
direction = DIRECTIONS.get(key)
if direction:
    move(maze, direction)
```

Although this introduces two extra lines of code, it is easiest to read and to understand.

It Is Working!

After completing the interactive debugging session and fixing the defect, the game is working! Time to celebrate. You find the code the screenshot in Figure 7-1 was created at https://github.com/krother/maze_run. In the subdirectory buggy/ you find a version of the code containing all bugs from the last six chapters. If you wrote your own version of the game while reading this book, your own bugs will of course be sufficient.

Is the Program Without Defects Now?

There is a rule of thumb that *the number of bugs still in the program is proportional to the bugs we found already*. We know about several *design weaknesses* we discovered in Chapter 3. For instance, the program will sometimes produce a maze with inaccessible locations. There are probably others we don't know about yet. Will the program work on all computers Python runs on? How about older versions of Python/Pygame? We don't know. Thus, the answer to our question is clearly *no, there are still bugs*. But we won't worry about them—the program is *good enough* for now. Debugging is useful if we already know there is a problem. In debugging, we roll up our sleeves and get our hands dirty.

Figure 7-1. *Scene from the working game at the end of this chapter*

Other Debugging Tools

pdb, the Python Debugger

The standard Python debugger pdb has a clearly written documentation worth checking: https://docs.
python.org/3/library/pdb.html

The PyCharm IDE

The disadvantage of ipdb is that you need to know a few key commands. If you like using an IDE like
PyCharm (https://www.jetbrains.com/pycharm/), you can do exactly the same things, only that
PyCharm has buttons for everything (see Figure 7-2). You may find stepping through your program more
convenient with a graphical debugger. The PyCharm debugger provides a few useful features worth
mentioning:

- You can set and delete breakpoints with a single click next to the line number (red
  dot in Figure 7-2).

- The bottom-left tab allows you to switch to the namespaces of other frames in the
  current call stack.

- The bottom-center tab (*Variables*) in the debugger shows you the contents of the
  current namespace

- The bottom-right tab (*Watches*) lets you watch the results of expressions
  continuously as you step through your code.

ipdbplugin

ipdbplugin is a plug-in for the test framework nose. It allows you to run ipdb when running automatic tests.
In Part 3, you will see a similar option for the py.test framework. See https://pypi.python.org/pypi/
ipdbplugin.

pudb

pudb by Andreas Kloeckner is a console-based visual debugger. It creates a screen layout similar to an IDE in the console, so that you have more information than in the regular debugger. pudb is controlled by keyboard commands, which allows you to work very quickly (see `https://pypi.python.org/pypi/pudb`).

wdb

wdb is a web debugger. It can be plugged as *middleware* into a Python web server like Django or Flask, where it gives you a debugger in case a web request results in an error. wdb is capable of running the debugger on a different machine than the web server (see `https://github.com/Kozea/wdb`).

django-debug-toolbar

A plug-in for the Django web server that displays various information on a web request on a browser page (see `http://django-debug-toolbar.readthedocs.org`).

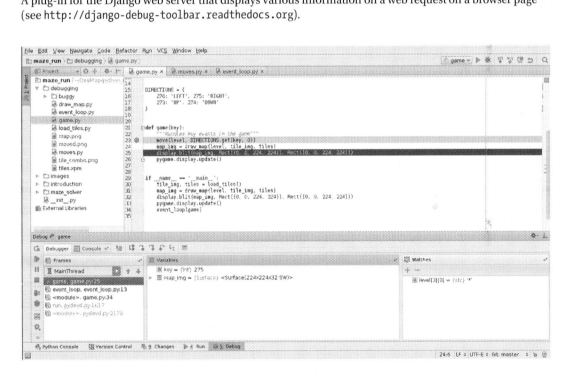

Figure 7-2. *The interactive debugger in PyCharm provides the same functionality as ipdb through a graphical interface.*

cProfile

cProfile is a standard Python module that produces detailed reports on the performance of your code. In the output of cProfile you see how many times each function was called and how much time the Python interpreter spent in each of them. If you need to optimize your code, it is a great tool to find bottlenecks in your program. See `https://docs.python.org/3/library/profile.html`.

Best Practices

- `ipdb` is an interactive debugger for Python.

- You can start `ipdb` with the interpreter or from within IPython.

- You can invoke `ipdb` at the beginning of the program, from an arbitrary line or after an Exception occurred.

- At the debugger prompt, you have a set of commands to control execution.

- You can display variables and execute normal Python commands at the debugger prompt.

- You can execute single instructions with `n` or step into functions with `s`.

- Breakpoints start the debugger at given locations without editing your code.

- Commands in the configuration file `.pdbrc` are executed when `ipdb` starts.

- There are many ways to fix a defect, some good, some bad.

- Even if everything in your program seems to work, there are probably still more defects inside.

## PART II

Automated Testing

CHAPTER 8

■ ■ ■

Writing Automated Tests

QA engineer walks into a bar. Orders a beer. Orders 0 beers. Orders 999999999 beers. Orders a lizard. Orders –1 beers. Orders a sfdeljknesv.

—Bill Sempf (*@sempf*) *on Twitter*

In the second part of the book, we will focus on a powerful programming technique: **automated testing**. Automated testing is considered an essential Best Practice by many Python programmers. Why is that? In this chapter, we are going to see a gentle introduction into what automated testing is and what it is good for. In the chapters on debugging, we checked whether our program worked by simply executing it. We compared the output to our own expectations sometimes intuitively, sometimes using a prepared table of input/output values. However, this strategy does not scale very well with the size of our program: Imagine we were adding more elements to the game (types of blocks, levels, puzzles, etc.). Every time we add something, we need to play through the game and check

- whether the new feature works.
- whether the rest of the program still works.

However good our game is, manual testing quickly becomes a daunting task. Here, automated testing comes to the rescue. Testing is a boring, repetitive task, and as such we can (and should) automate it. What is automated testing? Basically, in automated testing we write a program to test another program. In a sense, we have already done this: in the first chapters, each of our modules contained a __main__ block that we used to execute each module to see whether it is working. But automated testing has a few differences. The term **automated testing** usually means that

- The test code gives us a clear answer: The test *passes or fails*.
- We test small units of code at a time.
- We use a specialized testing framework that makes the test code *simple*.

In this book, we are going to use the test framework **py.test** to write automated tests. The automated tests work like a scaffolding that keeps our code in place as it grows. Let us consider an example: We want to add *movable crates* to our mazes. There are crates in some corridors that we can push around, but not pull them. That means that if a crate ends up in a corner, we won't ever get it out again. We may only move one crate at a time. In our example, we have to move the crate once in order to reach the exit (see Figure 8-1).

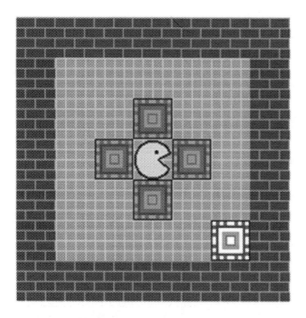

Figure 8-1. *The four blue crates around the player shall be pushed. At least one needs to be moved in order to reach the exit.*

Installing py.test

We will test the crate-moving feature using the **py.test** framework. First, we need to install **py.test:**

```
sudo pip install pytest
```

To run the tests, successfully, **py.test** needs to be able to import modules from the maze_run package. To make that possible, we need to add a file __init__.py that imports our modules:

```
from . import load_tiles
from . import moves
from . import draw_maze
```

We also need to set the PYTHONPATH variable to the directory. You can do this on a bash console with

```
export PYTHONPATH=.
```

We will have to do this every time we start a new console session. Alternatively, we can add the variable in our .bashrc file by adding the line

```
export  PYTHONPATH=$PYTHONPATH:/home/krother/projects/maze_run/maze_run
```

Of course, you need to adjust the path to your own maze_run directory.

Writing a Test Function

Next, we create the test itself in a file named test_crate.py. For now, we place that file in the same directory as the code for **MazeRun**. First, we import a few objects from earlier chapters and create a maze, using 'o' as a symbol for crates:

```
from draw_maze import parse_grid
from moves import move
from moves import LEFT, RIGHT, UP, DOWN


LEVEL = """
######
#.....#
#..o..#
#.o*o.#
#..o..#
#.....#
######"""
```

Next, we implement a small Python function named test_move_crate_right.py that checks whether our code works correctly (if you try this at home, you may choose a different name as long as the function name starts with test_). Then we move the player once:

```
def test_move_crate_right():
    maze = parse_grid(LEVEL)
    move(maze, RIGHT)
    assert maze[3][4] == '*'
```

The assert statements in the last two lines check whether the player symbol ('*') has moved one position to the right. If we run this program with the regular Python interpreter, nothing will happen, because the test_move_crate_right function isn't called anywhere. Let's see what **py.test** does with the function.

Running Tests

We execute the test by typing in the Unix terminal

```
py.test
```

and obtain the following output:

```
============================ test session starts ============================
platform linux -- Python 3.4.0, pytest-2.9.2, py-1.4.31, pluggy-0.3.1
rootdir: /home/krother/projects/maze_run/maze_run, inifile:
collected 1 items

test_crate.py .

========================= 1 passed in 0.06 seconds =========================
```

What happened? **py.test** reports that it *collected one test*. It automatically found our test function in our test module (both identified by the prefix test_). Then it executed the tests in test_crate.py. The test **passed**, meaning the condition in the assert statement evaluated to True. Our first test was successful!

Writing a Failing Test

Of course, checking whether the *player* moved is not sufficient. We need to check whether the *crate* moved as well. To check the new position of the crate, we add a second assertion to our test function:

```
assert maze[3][5] == 'o'
```

When running the py.test command again, it finds something to complain:

```
================================== FAILURES ===================================
_____test_crate_____

      def test_move_crate_right():
          maze = parse_grid(LEVEL)
          move(maze, RIGHT)
          assert maze[3][4] == '*'
>         assert  maze[3][5]  ==  'o'
E         assert '.' == 'o'
E           - .
E           + o

test_crate.py:19: AssertionError
=========================== 1 failed in 0.14 seconds ===========================
```

The test **failed**. In the output, we see the assert in line 17 is the one that failed. If the condition fails, assert raises an AssertionError, an Exception that is, honestly, not very helpful alone. However, **py.test** hijacks the Exception and tells us explicitly what the values on both sides of the comparison were. Instead of a crate ('o') we see a dot ('.'). Apparently, the crate has not moved (instead the player eats the crate). Of course, the crate did not move, because we haven't implemented the moving crate yet. If you would like to see it, you can start the game with the test level and chomp a few crates yourself.

Making the Test Pass

To move the crate and make the test pass, we need to edit the move() function in moves.py. We need to add an extra if condition for the 'o' symbol. Let's move the crate one tile to the right:

```
def move(level, direction):
    """Handles moves on the level"""
    oldx, oldy = get_player_pos(level)
    newx = oldx + direction[0]
    newy = oldy + direction[1]
    if level[newy][newx] == 'x':
        sys.exit(0)
    if level[newy][newx] == 'o':
        level[newy][newx + 1] = 'o'
    if level[newy][newx] != '#':
        level[oldy][oldx] = '␣'
        level[newy][newx] = '*'
```

When we rerun the test, it passes again.

```
=========================== 1 passed in 0.06 seconds ===========================
```

Passing Versus Failing Tests

The last example should make us concerned, or at least, think. The preceding code is only taking care of moves *to the right*. The code is, at best, incomplete. We know that the code does not work yet, but that the test passes. Concluding, we must take notice of a fundamental fact about automated testing: **testing does not prove that code is correct.**

What is testing good for, then? Let us consider the alternatives in Figure 8-2: if the code is correct, the test passes. If the code is incorrect (buggy, wrong, incomplete, badly designed, etc.), both test outcomes are possible. Thus, if we observe that our test passes, this gives us little information. We cannot decide whether the code is correct or not, because the tests might be incomplete. It works better the other way around: whenever we observe a test that fails, we **know for sure** something is wrong. We still don't know whether the code is wrong, whether the tests are incomplete, or both. But we have hard **evidence** that the situation requires further examination. In brief: **automated testing proves the presence of defects, not their absence.** Knowing that passing tests don't mean much makes automated testing a bit tricky. A Best Practice that helps us to write *meaningful* tests: you may have noticed in the preceding section that we ran the test even before writing the code for moving crates. **Writing a failing test first** helps us prove that the code we write makes a difference. If the test switches from *failed* to *passed* we know that our code is *more correct* than it was before. We will revisit this idea in Chapter 11.

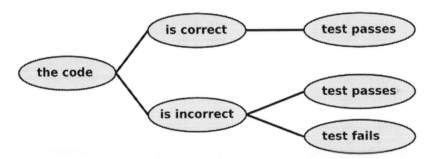

Figure 8-2. *Possible outcomes when testing code. Testing does not prove that code is correct (with incorrect code, both outcomes are possible), but failing tests prove that something is wrong.*

Writing Separate Test Functions

What can we do to push our code more firmly toward the *correct* state? The answer is astonishingly simple: Write more tests. You may notice that at the moment we have only implemented moving crates to the right. Technically, we can implement the other directions in the same way as the first. We implement each direction as a separate test function. All four function names start with test_, so that **py.test** discovers them automatically. To avoid code duplication, we place the call to move and the assertions in a **helper function** move_crate:

```python
def move_crate(direction, plr_pos, crate_pos):
    """Helper function for testing crate moves"""
    maze = parse_grid(LEVEL)
    move(maze, direction)
```

```
    assert maze[plr_pos[0]][plr_pos[1]] == '*'
    assert maze[crate_pos[0]][crate_pos[1]] == 'o'

def test_move_crate_left():
    move_crate(LEFT, (3, 2), (3, 1))

def test_move_crate_right():
    move_crate(RIGHT, (3, 4), (3, 5))

def test_move_crate_up():
    move_crate(UP, (2, 3), (1, 3))

def test_move_crate_down():
    move_crate(DOWN, (4, 3), (5, 3))
```

Using **helper functions** to keep test code short and simple is a Best Practice, because code duplication is to be avoided generally, and test code is no exception to that rule. Also, automated tests ought to be *simpler* than the code being tested (otherwise we might end up debugging two complex programs instead of one). But why do we define four one-line functions instead of grouping all four calls in a single function? Calling py.test on this code again gives us an answer:

```
3 failed, 1 passed in 0.10 seconds
```

Only test_move_crate_right passes, because when implementing the move() function, we assumed that crates will **always** move to the right, which of course is nonsense. The output given by **py.test** not only tells us that three out of four tests fail, it also tells us precisely which of them. This gives us much more information than a single bigger test function would. Clearly, it is a Best Practice to **write many small tests**. The test results give us the information to rewrite the if condition handling crates in the move() function. The updated function is

```
def move(level, direction):
    """Handles moves on the level"""
    oldx, oldy = get_player_pos(level)
    newx = oldx + direction[0]
    newy = oldy + direction[1]
    if level[newy][newx] == 'x':
        sys.exit(0)
    if level[newy][newx] == 'o':
        cratex = newx + direction[0]
        cratey = newy + direction[1]
        level[cratey][cratex] = 'o'
    if level[newy][newx] != '#':
        level[oldy][oldx] = '_'
        level[newy][newx] = '*'
```

And now all four tests pass:

```
========================== test session starts ===========================
platform linux -- Python 3.4.0, pytest-2.9.2, py-1.4.31, pluggy-0.3.1
rootdir: /home/krother/projects/maze_run/part1_debugging, inifile:
collected 4 items

test_crate.py ....

========================= 4 passed in 0.07 seconds ========================
```

▓ **Note**   Many programmers argue that one test function should contain only one assertion. This is generally a good practice, but at this point it would unnecessarily inflate our code. We will see a more elegant way to structure our tests and simplify our code in Chapter 9.

Assertions Provide Helpful Output

The assert statement will evaluate any valid boolean expression in Python. This allows us to test many different situations, a few of which are applied in the following to maze, a two-dimensional list:

```
def test_assert_examples():
    maze = parse_grid(LEVEL)
    assert len(maze) <= 7                            # comparison operator
    assert 1 < len(maze) < 10                        # range check
    assert maze[0][0] == '#' and maze[1][1] == '.'   # logical operators
    assert maze[0].count('#') == 7                   # using methods
```

As mentioned previously, **py.test** changes the output of assert from an AssertionError to a more meaningful output. A practical side of this is that we can compare lists, dictionaries, and other composite types in assert statements. As an example, we write another test using the minimalistic maze '*o#' consisting of just three tiles:

```
def test_push_crate_to_wall():
    maze = parse_grid("*o#")
    move(maze, RIGHT)
    assert maze[0] == ['*', 'o', '#']
```

The test fails when running **py.test**! Apparently, we did not take care about walls blocking the movement of crates yet. **py.test** reports the location of the mismatch between the two lists (actually, all three positions mismatch, but the first one is sufficient for the test to fail):

```
E            assert [' ', '*', 'o'] == ['*', 'o', '#']
E              At index 0 diff: ' ' != '*'
```

Similarly, we can write a test to make sure a crate blocks movement as well. This time, we compare two nested lists in the `assert` statement:

```
def test_push_crate_to_crate():
    maze = parse_grid("*oo")
    move(maze, RIGHT)
    assert maze == [['*', 'o', 'o']]
```

For a two-dimensional list, we get a precise report on the mismatching items as well:

```
E        assert [[' ', '*', 'o']] == [['*', 'o', 'o']]
E          At index 0 diff: [' ', '*', 'o'] != ['*', 'o', 'o']
```

This kind of precise output is a lifesaver when testing large lists and similar composite types. Comparing the *expected* versus the *factual* output can be done in a single assert, and we won't have to compare the lists manually in order to find the mismatch. The assert statement used by **py.test** is quite versatile. **py.test** often manages to create a meaningful output from the expression in case the test fails (with the `-v` option it gets even a bit better). Because we may use any kind of boolean expression in `assert`, we can construct most of the tests needed in practice.

Testing for Exceptions

There is one situation in which the `assert` statement does not work: if we want to test whether an Exception was raised. Let us consider an example: what should happen if we call the move() function with the direction parameter set to None? (We encountered this situation in Chapter 7.) Assume we want a TypeError to be created and want to test whether move raises the Exception. Testing that **no** Exception is generated would be easy:

```
move(maze, None)
assert True
```

But it does not work the other way around. There is no syntactically correct way to write a single `assert` statement that calls move with None **and** passes if an Exception is raised inside the function. The problem is that if we want the TypeError to *occur if everything works correctly*, the `assert` will always fail because of that Exception. We could help ourselves with a clumsy workaround:

```
try:
    move(maze, None)
except TypeError:
    assert True
else:
    assert False
```

Now the test fails if (and only if) the Exception does **not** occur. For this kind of situation, **py.test** provides a shortcut that is a recommended Best Practice. The context manager `pytest.raises` allows us to specifically test for an Exception:

```
import pytest

def test_move_to_none():
    """direction=None generates an Exception"""
```

```
maze = parse_grid(LEVEL)
with pytest.raises(TypeError):
    move(maze, None)
```

Why would we want to test against Exceptions? There are a couple of good reasons for doing so:

- First, we do not want our code to show any random behavior. If the code fails, we want to fail it in a way we have specified before. The pytest.raises function is a great way to do that.

- Second, it helps us to contain bugs—if we know what a wrong input behaves like, it will be less likely that an error propagates through our code.

- Third, the source of an error becomes easier to find.

- Fourth, it helps us to spot design flaws, things we simply did not think of before.

If the test fails, we see the message 'Failed: DID NOT RAISE'. However, it passes nicely.

Border Cases

How well do the tests we have written so far perform? Out of eight test functions, six pass and two fail. With py.test -v we obtain

```
============================ test session starts ============================
platform linux -- Python 3.4.0, pytest-2.9.2, py-1.4.31, pluggy-0.3.1
rootdir: /home/krother/projects/maze_run/part1_debugging, inifile:
collected 8 items

test_crate.py::test_move_crate_left PASSED
test_crate.py::test_move_crate_right PASSED
test_crate.py::test_move_crate_up PASSED
test_crate.py::test_move_crate_down PASSED
test_crate.py::test_assert_examples PASSED
test_crate.py::test_push_crate_to_wall FAILED
test_crate.py::test_push_crate_to_crate FAILED
test_crate.py::test_move_to_none PASSED


================================= FAILURES =================================
_____test_push_crate_to_wall_____

    def test_push_crate_to_wall():
        maze = parse_grid("*o#")
        move(maze, RIGHT)
>       assert maze[0] == ['*', 'o', '#']
E       assert [' ', '*', 'o'] == ['*', 'o', '#']
E         At index 0 diff: ' ' != '*'
E         Full  diff:
E         - [' ', '*', 'o']
E         + ['*', 'o', '#']

test_crate.py:51: AssertionError
_____test_push_crate_to_crate_____
```

```
      def test_push_crate_to_crate():
          maze = parse_grid("*oo")
          move(maze, RIGHT)
>         assert maze == [['*', 'o', 'o']]
E         assert [[' ', '*', 'o']] == [['*', 'o', 'o']]
E           At index 0 diff: [' ', '*', 'o'] != ['*', 'o', 'o']
E           Full  diff:
E           - [[' ', '*', 'o']]
E           + [['*', 'o', 'o']]

test_crate.py:57: AssertionError
=============================== 2 failed, 6 passed in 0.11 seconds =============
```

If we examine the mismatching lists in the two failing tests, we notice that the crates can be moved too easily. A crate can be pushed through everything, including walls and other crates. Pushing it further out of the playing field would crash the program. We have neglected several possible situations that can arise. These are called **border cases** or **edge cases**. Generally, border cases aim at covering *as many of the possible inputs with as little test code as possible*. Good border cases cover a diverse range of inputs. For instance, typical border cases for float numbers include typical values and extreme values like the biggest and smallest value, empty and erroneous data, or wrong data types. In our case, the border cases we have not covered explicitly include

- Pushing a crate into a wall.

- Pushing a crate into another crate.

- Pushing a crate into the exit.

To satisfy our border cases, we need to update the move() function once more:

```
def move(level, direction):
    """Handles moves on the level"""
    oldx, oldy = get_player_pos(level)
    newx = oldx + direction[0]
    newy = oldy + direction[1]
    if level[newy][newx] == 'x':
        sys.exit(0)
    if level[newy][newx] == 'o':
        cratex = newx + direction[0]
        cratey = newy + direction[1]
        if level[cratey][cratex] in '. ':
            level[cratey][cratex] = 'o'
            level[newy][newx] = ' '
        elif level[cratey][cratex] == 'x':
            raise NotImplementedError("Crate pushed to exit")
    if level[newy][newx] in '. ':
        level[oldy][oldx] = ' '
        level[newy][newx] = '*'
```

The last addition makes all our tests pass:

```
=========================== 7 passed in 0.08 seconds ===========================
```

We might test the same set of border cases for the other directions as well. But since the code we are testing is not very long or complex, we decide that our seven tests cover the possible situations *well enough* for now (also see Figure 8-3).

Figure 8-3. *"I admit the chance of finding a seven-tentacled monster below the house was low, but I found it worth testing anyway."*

Complex Border Cases

In the previous example, the border cases were relatively easy to identify. We simply considered what would happen if a certain tile got in the way of a crate. Often, border cases are not that simple to find. The reason is that the input contains many dimensions. To explore this idea, let us conduct a thought experiment: Imagine we would add powerups that make the player superstrong, so that it can move multiple crates (see Figure 8-4). Let's say each player has a **strength, represented as a floating-point number,** and a player can move up to the square root of *strength* crates at a time.

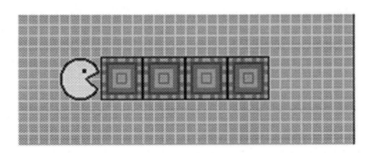

Figure 8-4. *When we add the strength of the player as an extra dimension, the border cases become a lot more complex.*

This small addition raises a bunch of questions about *how exactly* the crates are moved:

- What numerical precision is required for the strength value?
- What is the maximum number of crates that are moved in practice?
- What is the minimum number? Is it possible that the player is too weak to push anything?
- How is the rounding of the square root to be done (up, down, mathematical)?
- Can the strength ever be negative (*here be imaginary numbers*)?
- Can the strength be infinite?

If we wanted to cover all border cases for the preceding example, we would have to consider at least one representative strength value for each of these six situations. What is more, imagine we wanted to make sure the power-up feature works in all possible situations. Then we would have to combine each representative strength value with *each* of the game situations we tested previously. The result would be dozens of additional tests. With a few more dimensions like the movement directions, power-up strength, tiles that could get in the way, and so on, it becomes infeasible to exhaustively cover all situations by testing. Fortunately, a crate-pushing game is not that complex in practice, but many real-world applications are. The situations with nasty border cases range from mathematical calculations, and reading input files to all kinds of pattern matching. In more than one of my programming projects, maintaining a clean, representative collection of border cases for testing (and forcing the program to understand them) was a major portion of the work invested. A general strategy is to pick border cases that represent our inputs *well enough*. If we imagine the possible inputs of our program as a multidimensional space, by choosing border cases we try to define the outline of that space **with as few tests as possible and as many as necessary**.

Benefits of Automated Testing

With the five tests we have written so far, we have an automatic procedure in place that allows us (or other developers) to check whether the moving crates work. There are several reasons the tests could fail during future development of the program:

- We add more features to the game and accidentally break the crate feature.
- We fix a defect and accidentally break the crate feature.
- We rename the move function, so that our tests don't find it any more.
- We change the characters encoding wall and floor tiles, so that move_crate, our helper function, checks nonsense.
- We try to run the test on a computer where Pygame is not installed.

Of course, our simple tests are unable to figure out automatically *what exactly* went wrong. But the remarkable thing about automated testing is that in all these situations, **py.test** will produce failing tests, which tells us: *"Something went wrong, please investigate the problem further."* Isn't that a nice thing to have?

Without doubt, writing automated tests creates extra work up front. How does that work pay off? There are three more benefits worth mentioning. First, **automated testing saves time**. We started this chapter with the premise that manual testing does not scale. Imagine you would have to go through all border cases manually each time you change something in your code. You either would spend a lot of time testing manually or skip a few tests and spend more time working on your code. With *reproducible* automated tests, the invested effort pays off after running the tests already a few times. Second,

automated testing promotes well-structured code. It is worth pointing out that we could test the move() function entirely without initializing graphics or the event loop. The code is written in a way that is *easy to test independently*. If we were to test a single big function, high-quality tests would be complicated if not impossible to write. Third, **automated testing is rewarding**. When you execute your tests and see *failing* tests turn to *passing*, this gives the programmer a feeling of accomplishment. Often, this kind of positive feedback keeps you going, especially when biting through a difficult piece of code. At least this is what repeatedly happened to me and many other Python programmers. All three benefits are essential to the Best Practice of automated testing. To understand them in depth, we will need to revisit them when we have seen more automated testing techniques in the following chapters.

Other Test Frameworks in Python

There are a few alternatives to **py.test** worth mentioning:

unittest

unittest is the default testing framework installed with Python. Because unittest doesn't require any installation, it is good to know how it works. Practically, unittest provides a small subset of the possibilities of **py.test**, mostly grouping tests into classes.

nose

The test framework **nose** extends unittest by automatic test discovery and a couple of other convenient features. **nose** and **py.test** are distant cousins, and **py.test** is the more powerful of the two. We limit the description to a link to **nose**: http://nose.readthedocs.io.

doctest

The **doctest** framework works in a fundamentally different way. doctests are Python shell sessions written into Python documentation strings. The great thing about doctests is that they make it easy to include testable code examples in your documentation. How to include doctests in documentation is described in Chapter 17.

Writing a __main__ block

In some modules, you find test code in the __main__ block. If a program does not need the __main__ block for regular execution, we might as well write some tests for the functions in the module. For instance, we could test for the moving crate:

```
if __name__ == '__main__':
    maze = parse_grid(LEVEL)
    move(maze, direction)
    if maze[3][5] == 'o':
        print('OK')
```

This is an acceptable strategy in very small programs to test modules that are not executed directly. On one hand, we avoid a heavier infrastructure for some time. On the other hand, this kind of test quickly becomes cumbersome as the project grows. To name one thing, you cannot test *multiple* modules this way. As soon as the code grows beyond 100 lines it is worth to switch to a *"real"* test framework.

Best Practices

- **Automated tests** consist of code that checks whether a program works.
- **py.test** is a framework for writing automated tests in Python.
- To import modules under test, they need to be imported in the file _init_.py.
- **Assertions** decide whether a test passes or fails.
- **py.test** provides detailed information why an assertion fails.
- The function pytest.raises allows testing for failures explicitly.
- Writing many small **test functions** provides more information than a few big tests.
- Failing tests are the ones that provide the most useful information. Testing proves the presence, not the absence, of defects.
- Writing a failing test first and then making it pass is a more reliable approach.
- Tests should cover diverse **border cases**.
- The work to collect and maintain border cases can be considerable.
- Automated testing **saves time, promotes maintainable code,** and is **rewarding**.

CHAPTER 9

■ ■ ■

Organizing Test Data

QA Engineer walks into a bar. Quickly orders a second beer before the first is served.

—@botticus

Our tests in the previous chapter were easy to write. Each test required very little input, so that the test functions were three or four lines at max. But what if we want to write tests for more complex situations? We will need to look closer at the data related to our tests. Ideally, we want to test **diverse data** to cover as many border cases as possible (see Figure 9-1). At the same time, we cannot cover every possible input to our program by tests. How can we implement data-driven tests? In this chapter, we will encounter Best Practices for organizing our tests and the according data efficiently. We will implement tests that require prepared example data and create series of tests from data and tests that isolate intermodule dependencies inside a program. We will start by testing a few specific scenarios for moving crates in **MazeRun** we did not check yet:

- Move a crate to a corner.

- Move a crate back and forth.

- Move to the same location on different paths.

- Move several crates.

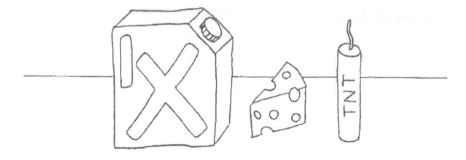

TEST DATA — Let's see which of those burn

Figure 9-1. *Test data is like collecting diverse objects and checking which of them burn*

© Kristian Rother 2017
K. Rother, *Pro Python Best Practices*, DOI 10.1007/978-1-4842-2241-6_9

Such test scenarios are more complex and could occur in a real in-game situation. Thus, they give us a chance to discover unexpected bugs that would pass simple tests unnoticed. Our scenarios have in common that they are composed of multiple steps and need some preparation.

Using Fixtures

When writing tests for multiple situations, the test data often **repeats** in a few tests. In Chapter 8 we wrote a helper function that prepared the maze and performed the assertions. Here, we will use a shortcut provided by **py.test** that allows us to reuse our test data more flexibly: **fixtures**. A fixture in **py.test** is a function that returns data for one or more tests. To create a fixture, we need to apply the @pytest.fixture decorator to the function. The fixture is called before the test automatically. Suppose we want to implement our first test scenario: *Move a crate to a corner*. We start by importing a few of our modules and use the same level as in the previous chapter (see Figure 9-2). Then we implement the fixture function:

```python
from .draw_maze import parse_grid
from .moves import move
from .moves import LEFT, RIGHT, UP, DOWN
import pytest

LEVEL = """#######
#.....#
#..o..#
#.o*o.#
#..o..#
#.....#
#######"""

@pytest.fixture
def level():
    """A level with four single crates"""
    return parse_grid(LEVEL)
```

Figure 9-2. *The level used for several scenario is provided by the level fixture*

The fixture level consists of a single line. This is not a bad thing. The process of creating our test data might grow later easily (e.g., if we decide to use classes later). Now we can use our fixture in a test function by simply adding level as an additional parameter. To move the top crate to a corner, we need to push it up, walk around it, and push it three times to the left:

```
def test_move_crate_to_corner(level):
    """Moves top crate to upper left corner"""
    for d in [UP, RIGHT, UP, LEFT, LEFT, LEFT]:
        move(level, d)
    assert level[1][1] == 'o'
```

When we call py.test with the updated move function from the previous chapter, the test passes. Note that we did not have to care about telling our test function *where* the level parameter comes from. **py.test** does that for us!

░ **Reminder**   If running the test doesn't work, try export PYTHONPATH=. before calling py.test.

Creating a fixture becomes useful only if we use it more than once. For our second scenario, we will *move a crate back and forth*. This is a simple **sanity check**. Good testing often includes a circular or repetitive operation, for instance reading a file, writing it, and reading it again just to make sure that the data doesn't change on the way. Moving the crate back and forth serves the same purpose. Even if moving a crate *once* works fine, it could be that it jams the second time. This time we will use an assert comparing two lists in our test

```
def test_move_crate_back_forth(level):
    """Sanity check: move the top crate twice"""
    for d in [LEFT, UP, RIGHT, UP, RIGHT, RIGHT, DOWN, LEFT, LEFT, LEFT]:
        move(level, d)
    assert level[2] == list('#o*    #')
```

Both tests pass. Here we may notice an important fact about fixtures: Both tests move the top crate. What is more, our first test pushed the crate *into a corner* where it ought to stay forever. Still, our second test passes. This is possible, because **the fixture is re-created before each test. py.test** takes care of resetting the crates to their starting position before each test by calling level again.

The scope Parameter

Sometimes creating fixtures takes a lot of time (e.g., reading a huge file, creating a database, starting web services, etc.). If many tests use such *expensive* fixtures, test execution will slow down. If the data does not change, we can instruct **py.test** to initialize the fixture just once for the entire test module by setting the scope parameter. We replace the fixture decorator with

```
@pytest.fixture(scope='module')
```

Note that in our example, the test executed second will fail, because the top crate in the fixture is already somewhere else. Tests interfering with each other are a lot harder to debug, which is why we will leave the scope parameter at the default value (the function level).

Test Parameterization

Another typical situation is that we want to write many *similar* tests. Suppose we want to check another test scenario: *moving to the same location on different paths.* Suppose we have the following paths leading to position (2, 2) in our level fixture:

```
PATHS = [
    (UP, LEFT),
    (LEFT, UP),
    (RIGHT, UP, LEFT, LEFT),
    (DOWN, DOWN),  # wrong on purpose
]
```

To avoid code duplication, we could test these paths using a for loop:

```
def test_paths():
    for path in PATHS:
        level = parse_grid(LEVEL)
        for direction in path:
            move(level, direction)
        assert level[2][2] == '*'
```

However, this approach has severe disadvantages:

- We cannot use our fixture level, because we need to reinitialize it inside the test multiple times.

- As soon as one path fails, the entire test fails. We obtain no information how many paths are failing.

- If one path fails, the remaining paths will not be executed. We will not learn whether they fail or not.

A better alternative is to *generate* tests from our data automatically. In **py.test** this strategy is called **test parameterization**. We write a single test function and instruct **py.test** to call that test function with different parameters. Each call will result in a single test. To use test parameterization, we apply the @pytest.mark. parametrize decorator:

```
@pytest.mark.parametrize('path', PATHS)
def test_paths(path, level):
    """Different paths lead to the same spot"""
    for direction in path:
        move(level, direction)
    assert level[2][2] == '*'
```

When we run the tests, we see four new tests. Each entry in PATHS results in a separate test function. **py.test** assigns numbers to each test, so that we can identify them more easily. In fact, the fourth test fails, because (DOWN, DOWN) is not a valid path to the top-left corner. In the output, we see that test_paths[path3] is failing (the index starts at 0 as usual):

```
test_data.py .....F

================================ FAILURES ===================================
_____test_paths[path3]_____

path = ((0, 1), (0, 1))
level = [['#', '#', '#', '#', '#', '#', ...], ['#', '.', '.', '.', '.', '.',
...], ['#', '.', '.', 'o', '.', '.', ...], ['#', '.', 'o', ' ', 'o', '.',
...], ['#', '.', '.', '*', '.', '.', ...], ['#', '.', '.', 'o', '.', '.',
...], ...]

    @pytest.mark.parametrize('path', PATHS)
    def test_paths(path, level):
        """Different paths lead to the same spot"""
        for direction in path:
            move(level, direction)
>       assert level[2][2] ==  '*'
E       assert '.' == '*'
E         - .
E         + *

test_data.py:50: AssertionError
==================== 1 failed, 5 passed in 0.09 seconds ====================
```

If we anticipate that a test fails, we can mark the test as "**expected to fail**" using the pytest.mark.xfail function when defining PATHS:

```
PATHS = [
    (UP, LEFT),
    (LEFT, UP),
    (RIGHT, UP, LEFT, LEFT),
    pytest.mark.xfail((DOWN, DOWN))
]
```

py.test will indicate this test with an 'x' in the output. A Best Practice is to treat xfail as a placeholder to mark tests that need to be fixed at a later point.

Multiple Parameters

With test parameterization, we can supply multiple parameters to a test function with a single decorator. This pattern is typically used to feed a test with *input data* and the corresponding *expected output*. We will limit ourselves to a short example here. Our input shall be a movement path, our expected output the final x/y position of the player:

```
PATH_PLAYERPOS = [
    ((LEFT,), 2, 3),
    ((LEFT, RIGHT), 3, 3),
    ((RIGHT, RIGHT), 4, 3),
]
```

```
@pytest.mark.parametrize('path, expected_x, expected_y', PATH_PLAYERPOS)
def test_move_player(level, path, expected_x, expected_y):
    """Player position changes correctly"""
    for direction in path:
        move(level, direction)
    assert level[expected_y][expected_x] == '*'
```

Inside the '@pytest.mark.parametrize' decorator, the names of the parameters are given as a string. **py.test** assigns them to the parameters of our test function automatically, which gives us three additional passing tests.

Parametrized Fixtures

Test parametrization is a good strategy to make test code *shorter* and *simpler*. **Parameterized fixtures** are an alternative to applying the @pytest.mark.parametrize decorator to a test. As an example, we could check whether the dots in the level make any difference. If we define an identical level, but without dots, we would expect the same outcome. To create the level, string replacement is sufficient:

```
LEVEL_NO_DOTS = LEVEL.replace('.', ' ')
```

Instead of duplicating all test functions written so far, we want to tell **py.test** to run everything twice: once *with* dots in the level, once *without*. Creating a parameterized fixture is similar to test parameterization. This time we need to add the test data as the params argument to the @pytest.fixture decorator, and use it inside as request.params. We do this by **replacing** the level fixture:

```
@pytest.fixture(params=[LEVEL, LEVEL_NO_DOTS])
def level(request):
    """A level with four single crates"""
    return parse_grid(request.param)
```

Every test using the level fixture is executed once with each of the two levels. As a result, we effectively test twice as many situations! By writing only four test functions we have covered a total of 16 different situations. That should make our crate feature sufficiently well-tested.

▓ **Hint**   Test fixtures and test parameterization play together very nicely in **py.test**. We can combine multiple parameterized fixtures with test parameterization in a single test functions. This way, you can easily generate hundreds of tests with little code, because **py.test** will loop through all combinations of parameters while generating tests. Keep an eye on execution time while using parameterized tests!

Mocking

In this section, we will look at a more challenging testing situation: *How can we test a part of the program connected to other components?* What if these components do things we don't want to happen in a test? Imagine we want to test a function that sends a document to the printing module. Does that mean that every time we run the test we would have to switch on the printer, insert paper, and watch the page being printed? Even worse, what if the external component is waiting for user input? Fortunately, Python offers an elegant solution for this kind scenario: **Mocking**.

Mocks are fake objects that replace real objects in our program. The Mock simulates the behavior of the replaced object, but without actually doing anything. Using Mocks, we can isolate the component we are testing from its dependencies and check whether the Mock was called. Thanks to the dynamic typing system in Python, Mocks can be inserted practically anywhere. The module `unittest.mock` gives us a comfortable interface for creating Mocks.

Suppose we want to test the graphics in **MazeRun**. Testing the graphics in detail (capturing images and analyzing their content) would cause a horrendous overhead. Most of it is not even necessary, if we assume that **Pygame** works correctly. All we need to know is whether the according calls to Pygame functions have been made. Let's go through two examples of `unittest.mock` to illustrate its usage. For simplicity, we want to test `draw`, a short function drawing a single tile:

```
from pygame import image, Rect
import pygame

pygame.init()
pygame.display.set_mode((80, 60))

def draw(surface):
    img = image.load('../images/tiles.xpm')
    surface.blit(img, Rect((0, 0, 32, 32)), Rect((0, 0, 32, 32)))
    pygame.display.update()
```

First, we will test whether the draw function is really calling `pygame.display.update` to update the screen. To do so, we replace `pygame.display.update` with a Mock. The `@mock.patch` decorator takes care of that:

```
from unittest import mock

@mock.patch('pygame.display.update')
def test_mocking(mock_update):
    display = pygame.display.get_surface()
    draw(display)
    assert mock_update.called is True
    assert mock_update.call_count == 1
```

The `@mock.patch` decorator automatically hands over the created Mock to our test function. We can assign it any name we like (here, `mock_update`). The two `assert` statements use two properties of the Mock, both verifying that our Mock function has been called.

For the second test, we want to see whether anything is drawn on the `display` object. For that, we create a Mock object from the `MagicMock` class replacing `display`:

```
def test_blit():
    mock_disp = mock.MagicMock(name='display')
    draw(mock_dist)
    assert mock_disp.blit.called is True
```

Both tests pass. How does the `MagicMock` object know that it has a `blit` method? A practical property of the `MagicMock` class is that it says *"yes"* to everything and creates new attributes for itself as they are requested. This property makes mocking a little dangerous, because we might create passing tests by accident.

```
def test_bad_mocks():

    mo = mock.MagicMock()
    assert mo.twenty_blue_dolphins()
    assert mo.foo.bar('spam')['eggs']
    assert mo.was_called()   # wrong method that passes
    assert mo.caled          # typo that passes!
```

Generally, Mocking is a Best Practice to replace external components: network operations, clocks, random numbers, input/output streams, and so on. We could mock os.environ to create fake environment variables for the duration of a test. We could mock time.sleep to cut out delays and accelerate our tests. We could mock urllib to create a web connection that always works. The module unittest.mock offers a number of interesting options worth reading about. For details, see https://docs.python.org/3/library/unittest.mock.html.

Testing Output Files

In many applications, we need to test whether output files produced by our program are correct. Tests involving files typically create at least four challenges:

- We need to read the file first (as a string or using a support library) before we can interpret its contents.

- There is usually a lot of information that we need to parse, structure, filter, and so on.

- A test reading a file can potentially fail in many ways (wrong contents, wrong path, lack of write permission). Therefore, the test results are harder to interpret.

- If our test creates a file, we need to clean it up afterwards. Otherwise, the test may pass next time, because the file is still there, even if we broke the code in the meantime.

Of these challenges, the last one is the most dangerous one, because it may cover defects in our program. We will deal with this issue first. To avoid the problem of tests leaving files around, we could try to clean up the output file ourselves with os.remove:

```
import os

def test_file_output():
    open('output.txt', 'w').write("Hello  World!")   # the code being tested
    assert os.path.exists('output.txt')
    os.remove('output.txt')
```

This works well as long as the code works correctly or terminates with an Exception. The potential defect in this test occurs with the following sequence of events:

1. The code being tested creates the file, but then crashes with an Exception. The test fails, but the output file is there.

2. Before the next test run, we try to fix the code, but accidentally it will do *nothing*.

3. In the next test run, the code does nothing, but the test still finds the file. The test passes.

A better (safer) alternative would be to delete the output file *before* the test. But then, we will litter our disk with output files. As you may already guess, there are a few nice shortcuts for this situation.

Cleaning Up After Tests

py.test offers a mechanism to clean up after tests. The functions `teardown_function` and `teardown_module` are executed after a test (or all tests in a module, respectively) completed. Corresponding functions to run *before* tests are `setup_function` and `setup_module`, respectively. To remove the output file after our test completes, we need to write

```python
import os

def teardown_function(function):
    if os.path.exists('output.txt'):
        os.remove('output.txt')

def test_file_output():
    open('output.txt', 'w').write("Hello World!")  # the code being tested
    assert os.path.exists('output.txt')
```

The key advantage of this method is that the teardown function is automatically called after each test, *even if* the test terminates with an Exception. Separating the cleanup code from our test is a Best Practice.

▒ **Hint** If you are interested in cleaning up an individual fixture, check the **py.test** documentation for **yield fixtures:** `http://doc.pytest.org/en/latest/fixture.html#fixture-finalization-executing-teardown-code`.

Using Temporary Files

Another possibility is to use **temporary files**. The `tempfile` module from the Python Standard Library allows us to create temporary file objects that are deleted automatically afterwards:

```python
import tempfile

def test_file_output():
    with tempfile.TemporaryFile('w') as f:
        f.write("Hello World!")  # the code being tested
```

In this case, our test doesn't need a teardown function. The `TemporaryFile` object requires that our code accepts file objects as input. If we need a physical file (e.g. as a filename) instead, using the `tmpdir` fixture in **py.test** is a better idea:

```python
def test_file_output_with_tempdir(tmpdir):
    tempf = tmpdir.join('output.txt')
    tempf.write("Hello  World!") # the code being tested
    content = tempf.read()
    assert content == "Hello World!"
```

A useful aspect of the tmpdir fixture is that the temporary files are **not** deleted automatically after the test finishes. On Unix, they are stored in the /tmp directory, where they are unlikely to interfere with the rest of our program. The exact path is displayed if the test fails. This makes the tmpdir a good place to store output for later diagnostics. Please consult the **py.test** documentation for details: http://docs.pytest.org/en/latest/tmpdir.html.

Comparing Output Files with Test Data

When we generate output files (results of calculations, reports, log files), there are many details to test. Instead of parsing the files and writing tests for each detail, it is often easier to create a correct sample file manually and compare the sample to the actual output. The Python Standard Library provides two modules that help us with that:

The filecmp Module

The filecmp.cmp function takes two file objects and returns True or False. Assuming we have one file 'output.txt' containing the test results and another 'expected.txt' containing a manually prepared sample, we can compare the two with

```
import filecmp

def test_compare_files:
    open('output.txt', 'w').write("Hello World!")  # the code being tested
    assert filecmp.cmp('output.txt', 'expected.txt')
```

The disadvantage of this method is that if the files are not equal, we won't see *how* they differ. For that, we need the second module.

The difflib Module

The difflib module compares two files line by line and produces output similar to the Unix diff command. The function difflib.ndiff takes two lists of strings. The output of the difflib.ndiff function is not very useful for test assertions, because **py.test** will not display the complete output if the test fails. But we can extend the previous test to print information about mismatches between the files:

```
def test_compare_files():
    open('output.txt', 'w').write("***Hello World***") # the code being tested
    lines_result = open('output.txt').readlines()
    lines_expected = open('expected.txt').readlines()
    print('\n'.join(difflib.ndiff(lines_result, lines_expected)))
    assert filecmp.cmp('output.txt', 'expected.txt')
```

py.test only displays the standard output (and the diff), if the test fails. This is why the example contains a few extra asterisks. We obtain the mismatches down to single characters:

```
------------------------- Captured  stdout  call -------------------------
- ***Hello World***
? ---            ^^^

+  Hello  World!
?               ^
```

Best Practices for Tests Involving Large Files

When testing large data files, finding differences is not the only problem. Also, designing the tests in the first place is challenging. What should we test? How many tests do we need? With a large output file it is obvious that we cannot test everything. In the following list, you find a few typical tests that cover many situations:

1. Test whether the file is there in the first place.

2. Test whether the file is not empty.

3. Read the file and check whether it has the right number of entries.

4. Match the file to a sample file.

5. Check a few exemplary details, not all of them.

6. Test the output data *before* writing it to a file. Often the writing itself is trivial or can be delegated to a support library like `csv` or `json`.

Generating Random Test Data

Many tests require sample data records containing names, e-mail addresses, or simply text. Inventing a few virtual persons ourselves is fun, but inventing a whole phone book is not. The **faker** package helps us to generate random data for many common and less common fields. We can install **faker** with

```
pip install faker
```

The package provides us with a Faker object, whose methods generate data randomly:

```
In [1]: import faker
In [2]: f = faker.Faker()

In [3]: f.date()
Out[3]: '1979-12-17'

In [4]: f.name()
Out[4]: u'Sonji Moore'

In [5]: f.sentence()
Out[5]: u'Unde ea quidem asperiores voluptate eos adipisci sed.'
```

The generated data covers many border cases. For instance, `f.name()` frequently spits out PhDs, royalty, and other prefixes and suffixes that give developers headaches if considered too late. There are plenty of methods for generating random test data in **faker**. It is worth taking a look at the output of `dir(f)`.

Where to Store Test Data?

So far, we stored most of our test data *inside* the Python files with the test functions. This is an accepted Best Practice that is found even in very large test sets (e.g., in tests for the Python standard library). However, there are some alternatives that are worth mentioning. Here, we will look at them briefly.

Test Data Modules

Group test data (e.g., all fixtures) in a separate module. This approach has the advantage that multiple test modules have access to the same data.

Test Data Directories

If your tests require files (input with good/bad/exotic examples, sample output) it is worth grouping them in a separate directory. This collection may develop a life of its own after some time. If you store nasty examples you or your users found, the test data becomes a valuable part of the collective memory of a project.

Test Databases

When your program uses a database, you may need a dedicated test database. Two approaches are found frequently in practice. First, you could **create the database in the tests**. Each time you start the tests, a fixture creates a new database, fills it with data, and destroys the database afterward. The disadvantage of this approach is that creating a database from scratch is usually slow. Even if the delay is only a few seconds, this will drag down your development speed. Second, you could **maintain a dedicated test database**. You permanently keep a database around for testing. This approach tends to be faster, and it gives you a place to store your test examples. The disadvantage of this method is that it is more difficult to maintain *data consistency*: There is always a risk that your code accidentally changes the data and ruins the test database. There are strategies to mitigate the risk (e.g., read-only access or using transactions), but in general you need to keep an eye on how you administrate the database.

There is no perfect solution, and maintaining a very large set of test data is an interesting project in its own right.

Best Practices

- **Fixtures** are functions that prepare data for test functions.

- **Parametrized tests** create multiple tests from a list of data entries.

- **Mocking** uses fake objects generated with the unittest.mock module.

- Replacing external objects by **Mocks**, the dependencies of the tested code become simpler.

- **Cleanup functions** in **py.test** are called after a test finishes.

- **Temporary files** created by tmpfile and the tmpdir fixture are a good place for output files generated by tests.

- The **filecmp and difflib modules** help comparing files.

- The **faker** library creates random data for testing.

- With **multidimensional input** it may be impossible to cover all border cases exhaustively. A rough guideline is to write as many tests as necessary and as few as possible.

CHAPTER 10

■ ■ ■

Writing a Test Suite

If you don't care about quality, you can't meet any other requirement.

—Gerald M. Weinberg

Up to now, we have been creating a set of test functions for our game. We can run all tests from the Linux command line simply by typing 'py.test' or 'py.test filename.py'. If we are testing a larger program, the number of tests will easily grow into hundreds. With parameterized tests, even thousands of tests are common. How can we organize such a large number of tests and still use them efficiently?

To organize our tests better, we will create a **test suite** in this chapter. A test suite is a complete, structured set of tests accompanying a given program. To write a test suite for MazeRun, we will use the tests we have already written. We will structure our tests into **modules, classes,** and **packages**. We will **refactor** our test code to be more concise. We will also execute the tests in different ways, so that we do not need to run the entire test suite every time. Finally, we will calculate **test coverage** in order to measure how much of our code has been tested. A good test suite is a powerful diagnostic tool that recognizes a variety of issues in your program. A test suite can test whether elementary functions work (Unit Testing), whether components of a software system work together (Integration Testing), or whether the functionality demanded by a user is there (Acceptance Testing)—more on these three in the next chapter. We wrote our first tests by placing each test in a separate function. We stored test functions in separate modules deliberately. After the last two chapters the output of **py.test** looks like this:

```
============================== test session starts ==============================
platform linux -- Python 3.4.0, pytest-2.9.2, py-1.4.31, pluggy-0.3.1
rootdir: /home/krother/projects/maze_run/tests, inifile:
plugins: cov-2.3.0
collected 33 items

test_crate.py ........
test_data.py .......x...x......
test_files.py ....
test_mock.py ...
===================== 31 passed, 2 xfailed in 0.30 seconds =====================
```

As the number of test functions grows, we need to pay more attention to the overall structure. To improve the structure we will clean up or **refactor** our test suite. Similar to normal code, we will group our functions into reasonable higher-order structures. The first thing we will do is to improve the structure of our test modules. Then we will group our tests into classes.

© Kristian Rother 2017
K. Rother, *Pro Python Best Practices*, DOI 10.1007/978-1-4842-2241-6_10

Test Modules

With many tests, **test modules** offer a straightforward way of structuring our test suite. We can split our tests into multiple modules. Technically, this is easy to do: we simply copy the according tests into a new Python file. If these modules carry test in their names like those preceding, the autodiscovery in **py.test** will collect all test modules accordingly. Normally, we do not have to import our test modules explicitly. There are, however, a few Best Practices to keep in mind when organizing test modules:

- First, **the names of test modules should be the same like the tested modules**. By convention, if we are testing the maze_run/moves.py module, the according test module should be test_moves.py. This makes finding the test code for a given piece of code and vice versa a lot easier.

- Second, **helper functions and test data should be kept in separate modules.** Having an extra nontest module (e.g., util.py or fixtures.py) in our test directory, where test modules can import them, helps to avoid redundancy in the test suite.

- Third, all test modules should be in the same place.

There are a couple of improvements that we can make in the structure of our modules. Reorganizing our test modules involves mainly grouping similar tests together and giving a descriptive name to each module. First, we move our fixtures into a separate module, fixtures.py, from which other tests can import them. The fixture module contains our parametrized fixture level:

```python
import pytest
from maze_run.draw_maze import parse_grid


LEVEL = """#######
#.....#
#..o..#
#.o*o.#
#..o..#
#.....#
#######"""

LEVEL_NO_DOTS = LEVEL.replace('.', ' ')

@pytest.fixture(params=[LEVEL, LEVEL_NO_DOTS])
def level(request):
    """A level with four single crates"""
    return parse_grid(request.param)
```

Next, we figure out that the tests for moving the player figure and crates from Chapters 8 and 9 cover very similar functionality. We merge them into one module, test_moves.py. We leave the tests for the graphics (with mocking) and file output where they are, only rename the files to test_graphics.py and test_file_output.py, respectively. As a result, we have three modules and one helper module.

░ **Best Practice**   Before we proceed after reorganizing code, it is worth checking whether all tests still pass.

Test Classes

With **py.test**, there is not much to do to create a test class. A simple recipe to create a test class is as follows:

1. Collect a few test functions that belong together.

2. Indent the functions by one level.

3. Write a `class` statement on top.

4. Give the class a name starting with `Test`, so that **py.test** knows there are tests inside.

5. Add a docstring describing what the test class is good for.

6. Add the `self` parameter to each of the functions.

Let's clean up the tests for moving players and crates in the module `test_moves.py`. When merging our previous code, the module contains the following functions:

```
move_crate(direction, plr_pos, crate_pos)
test_move_crate_left()
test_move_crate_right()
test_move_crate_up()
test_move_crate_down()
test_assert_examples()
test_push_crate_to_wall()
test_push_crate_to_crate()
test_move_to_none()
test_move_crate_to_corner(level)
test_move_crate_back_forth(level)
test_paths(path, level)
test_move_player(level, path, expected_x, expected_y)
```

Although you may notice that the code itself could be improved, we will group the tests into classes first. Looking at the code, one might identify two potential classes. The first, `TestCrateMoves`, is for everything related to crates, and the second, `TestPlayerMoves`, is for the remaining tests. The function `test_assert_examples` is not related to any of the functionality in the module. We decide to **delete** it, because it does not serve any purpose in **MazeRun**. The resulting structure of the module with `self` added to each method is as follows:

```
def move_crate(direction, plr_pos, crate_pos):

class TestCrateMoves:
    def test_move_crate_left(self)
    def test_move_crate_right(self)
    def test_move_crate_up(self)
    def test_move_crate_down(self)
    def test_push_crate_to_wall(self)
    def test_push_crate_to_crate(self)
    def test_move_crate_to_corner(self, level) def test_move_crate_back_forth(self, level)

class TestCrateMoves:
    def test_move_to_none(self)
    def test_paths(self, path, level)
    def test_move_player(self, level, path, expected_x, expected_y)
```

A test class behaves like a normal Python class. We don't need to write a constructor (_init_) or instantiate the class: **py.test** will take care of that for us. With [NEWLINE]`from fixtures import level,` `LEVEL[NEWLINE]` makes the tests pass.

▨ **Hint**   If you are familiar with `unittest`, the test framework of the standard Python library, you might expect us to create a subclass of `unittest.TestCase`. You still can do that when using **py.test**, and all assertion methods from `unittest` work in the same way. Here we are going to implement all tests using **py.test** assertions instead (which is incompatible with `unittest`-style classes). The resulting code is a little shorter and easier to read.

Refactoring Test Functions

Now we turn to improving the code itself. We will take the opportunity to perform a few small refactorings. The first construction site we will take care of are the four tests test_move_crate_left, test_move_crate_right, and so on. They all use the LEVEL data instead of the level fixture. In fact, we can apply test parameterization described in Chapter 9. As a bonus, we get rid of the helper function move_crate as well. We will not change the implementation of the other four tests. The code is the same as in Chapter 8. The refactored test class would look like this:

```python
from maze_run.draw_maze import parse_grid
from maze_run.moves import move
from maze_run.moves import LEFT, RIGHT, UP, DOWN
from fixtures import level
import pytest

CRATE_MOVES = [
    (LEFT,  (3, 2), (3, 1)),
    (RIGHT, (3, 4), (3, 5)),
    (UP,    (2, 3), (1, 3)),
    (DOWN,  (4, 3), (5, 3)),
]

class TestCrateMoves:

    @pytest.mark.parametrize('direction, plr_pos, crate_pos', CRATE_MOVES)
    def test_move_crate(self, level, direction, plr_pos, crate_pos):
        """After move player and crate moved by one square"""
        print(direction, plr_pos, crate_pos)
        move(level, direction)
        assert level[plr_pos[0]][plr_pos[1]] == '*'
        assert level[crate_pos[0]][crate_pos[1]] == 'o'

    def test_push_crate_to_wall(self):
        ...

    def test_push_crate_to_crate(self):
```

```
    ...

def test_move_crate_to_corner(self, level):
    ...

def test_move_crate_back_forth(self, level):
    ...
```

In the `TestPlayerMoves` class, we will merge the test functions `test_paths` and `test_move_player`. Both use test parameterization and the code is mostly redundant. The refactored function uses a single list of parameters, which makes our test class considerably shorter:

```
PATHS = [
    ((UP, LEFT), 2, 2),
    ((LEFT, UP), 2, 2),
    ((RIGHT, UP, LEFT, LEFT), 2, 2),
    pytest.mark.xfail(((DOWN, DOWN), 0, 0)),
    ((LEFT,), 2, 3),
    ((LEFT, RIGHT), 3, 3),
    ((RIGHT, RIGHT), 4, 3),
]

class TestPlayerMoves:

    def test_move_to_none(self, level):
        """direction=None generates an Exception"""
        with pytest.raises(TypeError):
            move(level, None)

    @pytest.mark.parametrize('path, expected_x, expected_y', PATHS)
    def test_move_player(self, level, path, expected_x, expected_y):
        """Player position changes correctly"""
        for direction in path:
            move(level, direction)
        assert level[expected_y][expected_x] == '*'
```

After this refactoring, we once more verify that all tests pass. They do:

```
test_file_output.py ....
test_graphics.py ...
test_moves.py ...................x.......x...

====================== 35 passed, 2 xfailed in 0.44 seconds ======================
```

What have we gained—apart from four additional tests? Now, the module `test_moves` contains just 7 methods instead of 13. Consequent usage of fixtures and parameterization results in a test suite that is **shorter and simpler**, which will facilitate future maintenance or fixing defects if one of the tests fails. With a little care spent on grouping tests into classes and modules, it becomes very easy to find the according tests by looking at the file names. In Figure 10-1 you find an overview of the test modules and classes we have created.

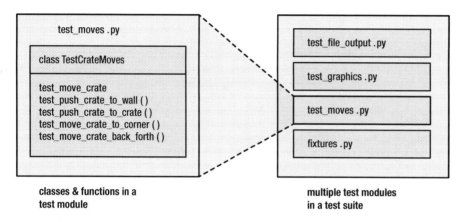

Figure 10-1. *Example test suite. Test functions (left) are nested in a test class, which in turn is nested in a test module. A test suite usually contains many test modules.*

Fixtures in Test Classes

You might ask yourself why we moved the `level` fixture to a separate module (the `fixtures` module contains only one fixture, and we only use it in `test_moves`). On the other hand, this structure leaves room for growth: if we invent more fixtures or use them elsewhere, an adequate structure is already in place. But let us examine one possible alternative briefly anyway: placing the fixture in a class.

```
class TestCrateMoves:

    @pytest.fixture(params=[LEVEL, LEVEL_NO_DOTS])
    def level(self, request):
        """A level with four single crates"""
        return parse_grid(request.param)

    ...
```

Apart from the extra `self`, there is almost no syntactical difference to the fixture we defined previously. Parameterization works in the same way, too. Of course a fixture inside a class is available only inside that class. This is why we will stick with the `fixtures` module (`level` is used by both classes). As a last detail, you need to be aware that we can set the `scope` parameter to the `@pytest.fixture` decorator:

```
@pytest.fixture(scope="class", params=[LEVEL, LEVEL_NO_DOTS])
```

In that case, the fixture will be created *once* for the class, respectively. The motivation to setting the scope to `class` (or `module`) is that building the fixture once will save time and thus speed up our tests. The drawback is that our tests could potentially interfere. We already saw an example for interference via fixtures in Chapter 9. To conclude, this option needs to be used carefully.

How Do Tests Find the Tested Code?

When we wrote our first tests in Chapter 8, we simply placed the `test_crate.py` module in the same directory as the module we tested. With one or two test modules it does not hurt to keep the tests in the folder with our code. As our program grows, this gets cumbersome quickly. Therefore, we will place our test modules and classes in a separate `tests/` folder in the main project directory (also see Chapter 13). This will help us to keep our program code and the tests apart cleanly. Now we need to make sure that our tested code can be properly imported. Because of the package import mechanism in Python, there are a few Best Practices to make both the tests **and** the program executable. I recommend the following procedure:

1. Create a `test/` folder in the main project directory, parallel to the `maze_run` folder containing the Python modules we want to test.

2. Make sure there is an `__init__.py` file in the `maze_run` folder (it may be empty).

3. Change the imports in your program modules to **absolute** imports (e.g., `from draw_maze import parse_grid` becomes `from maze_run.draw_maze import parse_grid`). Do this in **all modules** of the program.

4. Make sure there is no file `maze_run.py` inside the `maze_run` folder. Rename it to `__main__.py`.

5. Set the PYTHONPATH variable to your main project folder.

If the Python modules for the game are in the `/home/krother/projects/maze_run/maze_run` directory, we would add the following line to the `.bashrc` file in our home directory:

```
export PYHTONPATH=$PYTHONPATH:/home/krother/projects/maze_run
```

As soon as we **open a new terminal**, the PYTHONPATH becomes updated. Afterward, we can write in our test modules (or anywhere else):

```
from maze_run.moves import move
```

Alternatively, we can tell `pip` to install the package in editable mode. If we have a `setup.py` file, we can go to the `/home/krother/projects/maze_run` directory and type

```
pip install -e .
```

Which will add the path to `maze_run` to the import path (`sys.path`). The second method requires the project to have a `setup.py` file. Both approaches for importing code under test are accepted Best Practices, although the second one integrates more seamlessly with **virtualenv** discussed in detail in Chapter 13.

As a result, the imports inside our program and in our tests work in the same way. Now we can execute the game from the main project folder with

```
python maze_run/
```

and our tests with

```
cd tests/
py.test
```

Please note that no __init__.py file is required in the test/ folder or its subpackages. Once again, the test autodiscovery takes care of everything. Not having __init__.py files also avoids installing the tests when running python setup.py install (which is pointless most of the time).

░ **Hint**   If you have not worked with package imports at this scale before, getting the paths and directories working can be frustrating. A dirty workaround to get the tests running on the code from previous chapters is to add a deeper folder level to the PYTHONPATH variable: for example, /home/krother/projects/maze_run/maze_run.

Multiple Test Packages

When the number of tests grows further, we can group our test modules into multiple **test packages**. Which packages should you use? Like for modules, there is a simple Best Practice similar to the one for test modules: **create your test packages using the same structure as the packages of the project under test.** The only difference is that the name needs to have test as a prefix or suffix, so that **py.test** finds the tests within automatically. As a result, we get two parallel directory trees: one contains the packages and modules of our program, and the other, usually found in a directory named tests/, contains the entire test suite and possibly further test packages and test modules. Suppose we want to test two Python packages: maze_run containing the game and maze_run.graphics containing all code for drawing things on the screen. In our project, we will have a test/ directory for maze_run and a test/test_graphics for the subpackage (see Figure 10-2). By following this naming convention, it becomes easy to find the tests for a particular part of the program.

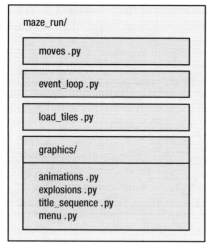

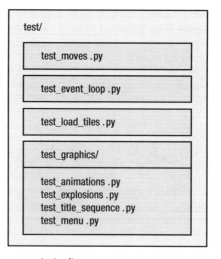

code being tested   test suite

Figure 10-2. *Structure of test modules and packages. The code units under test (left) correspond with the names of the according tests (right).*

Test Autodiscovery

At this point it is worth spending a few thoughts on how exactly **py.test** identifies tests. The **test autodiscovery** built into **py.test** first checks all subdirectories of the current directory and compares their names to a pattern. Every directory that

- starts with test_ or
- ends with _test

is examined further, including subdirectories. In each directory, all Python files that

- start with test_ and ends with .py or
- end with _test.py

are collected and imported as **test modules**. Importing modules as **test modules** differs from normal imports in a subtle way, because these are the ones where **py.test** changes the assert statement to cause tests to pass or fail. In all other modules (in particular, all imported nontest modules), the assert statement works normally.

Test autodiscovery does not stop on the module level. Inside each module, test classes and test functions are discovered using a very similar pattern:

- test classes start with Test
- test functions inside classes start with test
- test functions outside classes start with test

Everything else will be ignored by test autodiscovery, allowing us to define any helper functions/classes/modules we like, as long as they don't look like tests.

Executing a Test Suite

Now we are ready to run our test suite. So far, we simply typed py.test and let the test framework do all the work. Here, we will explore a few alternatives. The regular py.test command lists the test modules, marking passed tests with a dot '.', failures with a 'F', expected failures with an 'x', and errors with an 'E':

```
test_file_output.py ....
test_graphics.py ...
test_moves.py ...................x........x...
```

We can get a more concise output with py.test -q or even py.test -q --tb=no. When running a longer test suite, it is easier to get an overview of what is going on. Usually, the result is one of three situations:

```
...........................x........x...
```

All tests pass. If we see only dots, this is the most boring case, and our test suite does not give us any additional information. Upon seeing this, we can continue writing more code (or better, more tests) right away.

```
.......EEEE..EEEEEExEEE
```

A majority of tests fails with an error. These errors are usually easy to find. When we see this kind of output, the reason is either that we broke something fundamental in our code (in this case the `level` fixture is broken). Another reason might be a configuration problem (e.g., a misplaced configuration file). Note that an `ImportError` is caught by **py.test** before any tests are executed.

```
..............FFFF.......x..F...x..F
```

Some tests pass and some fail. This is the most interesting situation. A few failing tests may mean that there is a border case we forgot to fix or we even did not know about. In any case, we have obtained new information to evaluate. Now it is worth investigating the output produced by **py.test** in detail and find out what caused the tests to fail. In this case, changing a single character in the `maze_run.moves.move` function caused the defect. I encourage you to add tiny defects yourself and see how the outcome of changes.

```
py.test -q --tb=no
```

Partial Execution

What can we do if a few of our tests are failing? Because our tests work independently, we can take a *divide-and-conquer* approach: we examine the failing tests one after the other and fix them individually. Fortunately, in **py.test** there are lots of options to execute parts of our test suite.

Executing Test Modules and Packages

To run a single module, we give its name as a parameter to **py.test:**

```
py.test test_moves.py
```

By providing the name of a test package, we can run all test modules within a directory:

```
py.test tests/
```

Executing Test Classes

To select a single test class from a module, add its name using the pattern `module::class` like the following:

```
py.test test_moves.py::TestCrateMoves
```

Executing Single Tests

We can narrow down the executed tests further by specifying the name of the executed test using the pattern `module::class::test`

```
py.test test_moves.py::TestCrateMoves::test_move_crate
```

Selecting Tests by Keywords

A shorter way to select similar names is to specify keywords that occur in the test name with the -k option. For instance, to run all tests containing *'push'*, we can write

```
py.test -k push
```

To see which tests we picked exactly, we add the -v and --tb=no options:

```
py.test -k push -v --tb=no
```

which gives us

```
test_moves.py::TestCrateMoves::test_push_crate_to_wall PASSED
test_moves.py::TestCrateMoves::test_push_crate_to_crate PASSED
```

Examining Failures

To examine failing or erroneous tests, we can use our whole repertoire of debugging techniques. A handy shortcut is the --pdb option, which catapults us directly into the debugger as soon as an assertion fails. However, it is not advisable to use this option by default, because we will end up in the debugger once for *each* failing test. A better practice is to get an overview of the entire test suite first, and then run a smaller subset with the --pdb option. For example:

```
py.test -k push --pdb
```

Rerunning Tests

After fixing code, we need to know whether the fix made the failing tests pass. We also need to know whether the previously passing tests *still* are passing (or whether we messed up everything). Once we have fixed any defects in the code, we will have to rerun the rest of the test class/module/suite again. Several options of **py. test** help us with such test runs:

- The -x option stops test execution on the first failing test. This is helpful if we already *know* that many tests will fail in a similar way and want to start a more detailed diagnosis for one of them.

- When we already have fixed something and want to see the effects on the whole test suite, the --lf option reruns only the tests that failed in the previous run.

- The --ff (failed-first) option executes the failing tests first. If we see that no improvement took place, we can abort the test run by pressing Ctrl+C.

There are plenty of other options **py.test** understands. A summary of some frequently used options is given in Table 10-1.

Table 10-1. *Frequently Used Options in py.test*

Option	Description
-q	concise output
-s	disable output capturing
-x	stop on first fail
-k [keyword]	keyword occurs as a substring in name of test or class
-v	list all tests explicitly
-pdb	start the debugger on failing tests
-x	stop test execution on first failing test
-lf	rerun failing tests from previous run
-ff	execute tests that failed first, then all others
-tb=line	shorten traceback to one line
-tb=no	switch traceback off

Calculating Test Coverage

When running a test suite, we have seen how many tests were executed and how many of them pass or fail. We did not yet learn *how much of the code* was executed by our tests. This is where **test coverage** comes in. In Python, the pytest-cov package allows us to check which sections of the code were tested. We first use pip to install pytest-cov the **py.test** plugin for coverage analysis:

```
pip install pytest-cov
```

Now we can run our tests with the --cov option:

```
py.test --cov
```

We can calculate coverage explicitly for a specific module or package by giving it as a parameter to **pytest-cov**:

```
py.test --cov=../maze_run/
```

Note that the preceding command will run the entire test suite, not just test_crate.py. Of course, the regular options of **py.test** can be combined with the coverage module. In the background, the results of the coverage analysis are stored in a hidden file .coverage, whose contents are not meant to be read by people. For convenience, we obtain a report containing all Python files that have been executed. The abridged report for the maze_run directory looks as follows (full paths abbreviated):

```
----------- coverage: platform linux, python 3.4.0-final-0 -----------
Name                               Stmts   Miss  Cover
--------------------------------------------------
../maze_run/__init__.py                3      0   100%
../maze_run/draw_maze.py              23      5    78%
../maze_run/event_loop.py             13      9    31%
../maze_run/generate_maze.py          37      8    78%
../maze_run/load_tiles.py             18      6    67%
../maze_run/maze_run.py               27      1    96%
../maze_run/moves.py                  40     10    75%
../maze_run/util.py                    8      2    75%
--------------------------------------------------
TOTAL                                169     41    76%
```

In this table, Stmts is the number of Python statements (not counting empty lines), Miss is the number of lines not executed by any test, and Cover the percentage of lines executed. The 76% total coverage already gives us some useful information: we now have hard evidence that our test suite executes more than half of the code. That means there might be lots of spots where even nonsense code like a = 1/0 would pass our test suite unnoticed. There is obviously still work to do!

We can identify the problematic areas by creating an HTML report:

```
coverage html
firefox htmlcov/index.html
```

The newly created htmlcov/ directory contains a HTML page for each module. On the HTML pages, the executed and missed sections are highlighted (see Figure 10-3). It turns out that most of the code sections not covered by our test suite are the event loop and the __main__ blocks of each module. Although our tests aimed mainly at moving crates, it turns out that they executed almost the entire program!

```
22
23  def move(level, direction):
24      """Handles moves on the level"""
25      oldx, oldy = get_player_pos(level)
26      newx = oldx + direction[0]
27      newy = oldy + direction[1]
28      if level[newy][newx] == 'x':
29          sys.exit(0)
30      if level[newy][newx] == 'o':
31          cratex = newx + direction[0]
32          cratey = newy + direction[1]
33          if level[cratey][cratex] in '. ':
34              level[cratey][cratex] = 'o'
35              level[newy][newx] = ' '
36      if level[newy][newx] in '. ':
37          level[oldy][oldx] = ' '
38          level[newy][newx] = '*'
39
40
41  if __name__ == '__main__':
42      tile_img, tiles = load_tiles()
43      maze = create_maze(12, 7)
44      maze = parse_grid(maze)
45      maze[1][1] = '*'
46      for i in range(100):
47          direction = random.choice([LEFT, RIGHT, UP, DOWN])
48          move(maze, direction)
49      img = draw_grid(maze, tile_img, tiles)
50      image.save(img, 'moved.png')
```

index   *coverage.py v4.1, created at 2017-01-10 01:13*

Figure 10-3. *HTML output of the* coverage *tool. The executed code parts are marked by the green bar to the left. The sections shaded in red were not executed. In this case, the module* moves.py *has been covered mostly by the tests, but we did test whether the exit ('x') works and the __main__ block was never called.*

How to interpret the **test coverage** of a program? What does 100% test coverage mean? In the first place, it just means that every instruction was executed at least once. 100% test coverage does not mean that all instructions in the program *work*, let alone that the program as a whole is *correct*. Why is that? There is a simple explanation: there are too many possible **execution paths**. Imagine our program contains a single decision (e.g., an if statement). Then, there are two separate paths through the program. Each path could contain a defect and therefore needs to be tested separately. If our program contains a series of eight decisions, there are already 256 possible paths. As the complexity of our program grows, the number of execution paths grows toward infinity. Unless the program is very simple, it is likely that our tests will fail to cover all paths through the program. Let us consider a small, slightly contrived example. Suppose we have the (*wrong!*) code for calculating a logical XOR:

```
def xor(a, b):
    if a is False and :
        if b is True:
            return True
    if b is False:
        return True
```

and a test function:

```
def test_xor():
    assert xor(True, False)
    assert xor(False, True)
```

This test will result in a coverage of 100% of the code within the xor function. However, even a superficial explanation will find out that half of the possible inputs produce a wrong result (our tests fail to cover the relevant border cases (True, True) and (False, False). And test coverage does not give us the slightest hint that the function is broken. This limitation is one of the reasons why measuring **test coverage** is a bit dangerous. Having 100% test coverage is very delusive. It suggests we have tested everything, when in fact we have only made sure every line is covered *by at least one path*. By the way, a correct way of calculating the logical XOR in Python would be

```
def xor(a, b):
    return bool(a) != bool(b)
```

In practice, measuring test coverage is still useful. Of course, the higher test coverage we have, the better. However, we don't need to aim straight for 100% coverage. If a program changes frequently that even might impede development. Often, we can reach 50% test coverage with comparatively few tests and a small but helpful test suite. A test coverage of 75% starts feeling solid, 90% is rigorous, and 100% is for projects that do not evolve very quickly but require a high integrity (e.g., a language processor like Python itself). The main benefit of analyzing test coverage is that it allows us to identify problematic areas and assess risks better.

A Test Suite Needs Maintenance

A test suite is a part of a software, much like the code that does the work. Keeping the test code clean is therefore as important as keeping the code of the program itself clean. This means splitting large functions or files into smaller ones, avoiding code duplication, and keeping an eye on coding style. Documenting *why* certain tests were written is an important Best Practice that makes cleaning up tests easier. A test suite evolves like any program: it grows, it changes, and it needs to be restructured (refactored) from time to time, too.

Fortunately, test code is generally easier to maintain than regular code. Test functions tend to be short already. As a rule of thumb, try to keep test code *very simple*. Avoid multiple assertions in the same test: many small tests are better than a few big ones. Also avoid multiple loops or if conditions; in most cases, these can be moved to a helper function or a parametrized test. Remember that if a test fails during debugging, the error could be in the test or in the code. We don't want to debug two programs at the same time (the program and the test); therefore maintaining a test suite that is very easy to understand makes development more reliable.

Best Practices

- A **test suite** is a structured collection of tests for a given program.

- Test functions can be grouped into **test modules, test classes,** and **test packages**.

- Test modules and packages should carry the same names as the code units they test.

- A test suite should be located in a separate folder tests/.

- Test **autodiscovery** in **py.test** finds tests by matching their names.

- The most interesting test results are when only a small fraction of tests fail.

- **py.test** offers many options to execute a test suite partially.

- **Test coverage** is the percentage of code lines executed during tests.

- **Test coverage** can be calculated with the `pytest-cov` package.

- A test coverage of 100% does not mean that we have tested every possibility.

- Automated tests are program code that needs to be cleaned up and restructured.

CHAPTER 11

Testing Best Practices

"Code without tests is broken by design."

—Jacob Kaplan-Moss, Django core developer

Over the last few chapters, we have seen that automated testing is a powerful technique to examine whether a Python program works. The **py.test** framework is a versatile tool to write tests for small units of code, use test datasets, and manage Test Suites with many assertions and test functions. Obviously, testing is a very useful technique in the toolkit of every advanced Python programmer. However, we haven't looked at the big picture so far: **Where in the development process does automated testing have its place?**

The statement *"Code without tests is broken by design."* by Jacob Kaplan-Moss, core developer of the Django web server, is a bold claim. It says we cannot write **correct** code without automated testing. Can we reverse the claim and say that *"code with tests is correct"*? In this chapter, we are going to examine both claims. We will look at software testing as a part of the development process and turn our attention to questions like the following:

- What different types of tests are there?

- When is it best to start testing during development?

- What are the benefits of automated tests?

- In what situations are tests difficult to write?

- What are the limitations of testing in general?

- Are there any alternatives?

- What distinguishes good from bad tests?

I hope that the Best Practices of testing covered in this chapter will help you to write automated tests that optimally support your programming, so that you can produce working software faster and maintain it efficiently.

Types of Automated Tests

First of all, there are a few recurring kinds of tests. They differ more in the purpose they are written for and the scope in which they are used than in the usage of **py.test** to implement them. This section introduces vocabulary used by many professional developers when they talk about automated testing. Table 11-1 gives an overview of different types of tests.

Table 11-1. *Types of Automated Tests*

Test	Description
Unit Test	tests small, isolated units of code.
Integration Test	tests the collaboration of two or more larger components.
Acceptance Test	tests features from a user's perspective.
Regression Test	rerunning tests to make sure previously built features are still working.
Performance Test	tests execution speed, memory usage or other performance metrics.
Load Test	tests performance under high workload, especially for web servers.
Stress Test	tests functionality under adverse conditions (failure of components, attacks, etc.)

Unit Tests

Tests for a single function, class, or module are called **Unit Tests**. Unit Tests prove that a single piece of code fulfills its basic requirements. Unit Tests may perform very detailed checks and include a fair amount of nitpicking. When writing Unit Tests, we usually want to cover many border cases, such as empty input, long input, weird input, and so on. A Best Practice for writing Unit Tests is the **FIRST** acronym introduced by Tim Ottinger and Jeff Langr. Unit Tests should be

- **F**ast—execute in a few seconds or less

- **I**solated—test only one piece of code at a time

- **R**epeatable—can be rerun with the same outcome

- **S**elf-verifying—the Test Suite does not need additional information to evaluate the test

- **T**imely—tests are written before the code (more on this in section "The Test-First Approach")

Other common Best Practices found in Unit Tests are using only one `assert` per test (although this is rather a rule of thumb) and using *mock objects* to replace complex components by simpler placeholders, so that the test depends only on the code unit being tested.

Integration Tests

Testing components in isolation is not enough. Tests for the collaboration between components are required as well; they are called **Integration Tests**. Typically, this means testing collaboration between bigger components like a database, a web server, or an external application rather than testing two classes in two adjacent Python modules. Integration Testing also might include testing the software on different versions of libraries or Python versions. In Python, a couple of tools for Integration Testing exist, for example, **Tox** (`https://tox.readthedocs.io/`), which supports running a Test Suite on a series of Python versions. When writing Integration Tests, the actual program components need to be used (no mock objects or other placeholders). An Integration Test attempts to reproduce the environment in which a software is used as accurately as possible.

Acceptance Tests

The third type of tests focuses on the user's point of view. An **Acceptance Test** checks whether the features of a program work "*as advertised.*" A typical Acceptance Test runs a program as a whole and checks a few features of the output. They simulate what a real user would be doing (e.g., executing the program from the command line or sending HTTP requests via a browser). A Best Practice for Acceptance Tests is that we don't need to test every thinkable situation. This is what Unit Tests are for. We rather make sure that our application processes input and deliver the desired output under the assumption that all individual components are correct.

How to implement Acceptance Tests in practice strongly depends on the kind of user interface of our program. If we are developing a program library, Acceptance Tests will look like the tests written with **py.test** we have seen before, only they will test the part of the interface we want to expose to users. With a command-line application we could execute the program with os.system and redirect the output. A primitive test for a command-line application could look like this:

```
def test_commandline_app():
    """Make sure a maze with at least one wall is produced"""
    cmd = "python create_maze.py > output.txt"
    maze = open('output.txt').read()
    assert '#' in maze
```

Writing Acceptance Tests for graphical interfaces is more challenging. There exist dedicated tools for Acceptance Testing of web interfaces (e.g., **Selenium, Cucumber,** and **Codecept.js**), but sometimes, reasonable testing can be done with regular tests in a web framework (using **py.test**). In no instance do automated Acceptance Tests replace a manual check of whether a program does its job. In any case, communication between programmers and users is needed to find out whether *what the software does* is relevant in the first place (e.g., it makes their life easier, improves their business, is fun to play).

Regression Tests

An important application of testing is called **Regression Tests**. Regression Tests simply mean rerunning tests after changes to the program. This could include rerunning Unit Tests, Integration Tests, Acceptance Tests, or all of the above. Regression Tests emphasize that it is a Best Practice to rerun tests in a couple of standard situations:

- after adding a new feature

- after fixing a defect

- after reorganizing your code (refactoring)

- before committing code to a repository (see Chapter 12)

- after checking out code from a repository

Regression Tests make sure that everything we created so far still works after we have edited the code. If we have a fast test set, it is a very powerful technique to rerun tests during programming every couple of minutes. Regression Testing makes sure that we don't inadvertently break a feature while focusing our attention on some other part of the program. The command-line options of **py.test** make our life easier during Regression Testing (e.g., rerunning only failed tests speeds up our work considerably). Whether you decide to rerun failing tests, Unit Tests, Integration Tests, or all tests you can get your hands on during a Regression Test depends on how big the change to the code was, and how close you are to releasing a program.

Performance Tests

All tests presented so far test the *functionality* of a program: *Does the program work or does it not?* But some other metrics might be worth testing as well: Is the program fast enough? Does it react to user input in an appropriate time? Is the program memory-efficient or does it consume excessive system resources? All of these can be found under the term **Performance Tests**. In Python, there are some great tools for manual Performance Testing. For instance, we can check the performance of our functions using the %timeit magic method in IPython:

```
In [1]: from generate_maze import create_maze
In [2]: create_maze(10, 10)
In [3]: %timeit create_maze(10, 10)
1000 loops, best of 3: 589 s per loop
```

The %timeit function is smart in figuring out how often it needs to run a piece of code to determine a reliable average execution time. A slower function generally needs less runs than a fast one. If we, in contrast try range, a million runs are necessary. In addition, IPython warns us that the results fluctuate a lot:

```
In [4]: %timeit range(100)
The slowest run took 9.16 times longer than the fastest.
This could mean that an intermediate result is being cached.
1000000 loops, best of 3: 392 ns per loop
```

Using timeit is to be preferred over measuring the execution time with an external program. In particular, **do not** try to measure the performance of individual Python functions with the Unix command-line tool time. This way, you will measure a lot of overhead as well (e.g., starting the Python interpreter), and the result will be imprecise. By importing the timeit standard module, we can measure the execution time of any Python command inside a regular Python program. By comparing the number returned by the timeit.timeit function against an expected maximum time, we can write simple Performance Tests:

```
def test_fast_maze_generation():
    """Maze generation is fast"""
    seconds = timeit.timeit("create_maze(10, 10)", number=1000)
    assert seconds <= 1.0
```

Performance Optimization

How can we use of the information on timing to improve performance? The cProfile module allows us to examine the performance of a program in more detail. For instance, if we use the create maze() function to create a very big maze, the function becomes slow. With cProfile.run() we obtain a report on where exactly the program spends its time:

```
cProfile.run("create_maze(200, 200)")
        395494 function calls in 19.689 seconds

Ordered by: standard name

ncalls tottime percall cumtime percall filename:lineno(function)
     1    0.003    0.003  19.689  19.689 <string>:1(<module>)
     1    0.000    0.000   0.009   0.009 generate_maze.py:22(get_all_dot_pos)
     1    0.009    0.009   0.009   0.009 generate_maze.py:24(<listcomp>)
```

```
39204    0.078    0.000    0.078    0.000 generate_maze.py:27(get_neighbors)
    1    0.262    0.262   19.670   19.670 generate_maze.py:35(generate_dot_pos)
39204    0.126    0.000    0.126    0.000 generate_maze.py:42(<listcomp>)
    1    0.000    0.000   19.686   19.686 generate_maze.py:49(create_maze)
    1    0.017    0.017    0.017    0.017 generate_maze.py:9(create_grid_string)
...
39204   18.914    0.000   18.914    0.000 {method 'remove' of 'list' objects
```

The ncalls column tells us how many times the function was called. tottime is the total time Python spent inside this function, followed by the time per call (percall). cumtime is the *cumulative time*, the time Python spends inside this function and others called from it, again followed by the time per function. In the output, we see that the function get_neighbors was called 39,204 times. We could try to make get_neighbors faster, but it would not speed up our program (the total time spent there is only 78 milliseconds). The real bottleneck is list.remove, which accounts for almost the entire execution time. At this point it is worthwhile to look at the code (the complete maze generator is presented in Chapter 3):

```python
def generate_dot_positions(xsize, ysize):
    """Creates positions of dots for a random maze"""
    positions = get_all_dot_positions(xsize, ysize)
    dots = set()
    while positions != []:
        x, y = random.choice(positions)
        neighbors = get_neighbors(x, y)
        free = [nb in dots for nb in neighbors]
        if free.count(True) < 5:
            dots.add((x, y))
        positions.remove((x, y))
    return dots
```

Inspecting the code we see that each position is used exactly once. The reason for using the slow list.remove method is that the positions are processed in random order. To make the code run faster, we instead shuffle the list *once* and then process each element of the list in a for loop. Here is the updated implementation after deleting two lines and adding the two highlighted ones:

```python
def generate_dot_positions(xsize, ysize):
    """Creates positions of dots for a random maze"""
    positions = get_all_dot_positions(xsize, ysize)
    dots = set()
    random.shuffle(positions)
    for x, y in positions:
        neighbors = get_neighbors(x, y)
        free = [nb in dots for nb in neighbors]
        if free.count(True) < 5:
            dots.add((x, y))
    return dots
```

But is this implementation really faster? Running %timeit or cProfile again, gives us an answer:

```
In [13]: %timeit create_maze(200,200)
1 loop, best of 3: 279 ms per loop
```

By changing a few lines of code, we have accelerated the function by almost **two orders of magnitude!** Using `cProfile` was crucial to **measure** performance and locate the bottleneck. When optimizing code, **Unit Tests** are a valuable tool for **Regression Testing** to verify that our program not only fast but also *correct*. Performance Testing may include many other situations as well. For example:

- **Load Tests**: how does the program (e.g., a web service) handle a lot of simultaneous traffic?

- **Stress Tests**: how does the program handle malicious conditions (rapidly changing conditions, failure of components, or even external attacks attempting to crash the program)?

- **Robustness**: is the execution time stable or does it fluctuate a lot?

Because Performance Tests tend to be more time-consuming than Unit Tests, it is a Best Practice to keep them separate from other tests. In general, writing Performance Tests is more challenging. Fortunately, many programs don't need them at all.

The Test-First Approach

In Chapter 8 we wrote a test although we hadn't implemented the code satisfying the test yet. Writing tests before writing the program is a key Best Practice of testing. *Why is writing tests first a good idea?* Let us consider the opposite approach first, which is the one most of us would think of intuitively. We first write a program. Then we debug the program and fix all defects. Only after that, we write tests, and we are done. However, this approach creates a couple of severe problems:

- The tests give us little additional information, because the program works already: they all pass by default.

- Writing tests is boring if they don't have any immediate impact. It is easy to write low-quality tests if having them is not essential.

- If during testing we find things that could be done better, we need to repeat the entire process (write code, fix bugs, test, repeat).

- We don't know when we have written enough tests.

- We don't know when we are done fixing bugs.

- We don't know when we are done writing the program.

Especially the last point should raise considerable doubt about the approach unless we have detailed and accurate knowledge what "*done*" means. It turns out that very often, our knowledge is not sufficiently accurate when we start programming, because the goals of a programming project evolve with the code itself. For a long time, software was first developed and then tested (using both manual and automated tests). With the beginning of the Agile movement in the early 2000s, it became increasingly popular to write tests before implementing the code that satisfies the test. In brief, the test-first approach follows this procedure (also see Figure 11-1):

1. Write a test function.

2. Run the test and make sure it fails.

3. Write code.

4. Run the test and make sure it passes.

5. Clean up the code and run regression tests.

6. Repeat the procedure until you are done.

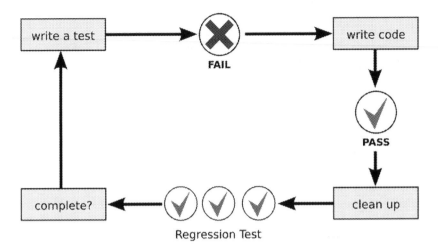

Figure 11-1. *The test-first approach. We write a failing test first, and then the code to make it pass. After that, Regression Tests check whether everything else is still working. The process is repeated until the program is complete.*

The test-first approach has a couple of advantages: First, **seeing the test fail proves its correctness**. When we write a test, we don't know whether it is correct by default. The test is program code, and thus might contain defects. A test for which the according code does not exist yet can be expected to fail. If the test passes anyway, we would know the test contains a defect or tests something that is already there. That way, we make sure that the test provides us with extra information. Seeing a test fail first is essential for developing useful tests.

Second, writing tests first promotes writing code that is easy to use. When writing the test, we need to think about *how* the code is going to be used. This exposes design weaknesses earlier. For example, if we find out that even writing the test is complicated, the interface may have to be redesigned.

Third, writing tests first is motivating for programmers. If we see our tests switch from FAIL to PASS, this is much more rewarding than the thought "*Oh my, do I need to write tests for all that code?*"

The test-first approach is today known a Best Practice that promotes higher quality of the software. It can be applied in a variety of situations. Three of them are presented in the following.

Writing Tests Against a Specification

If we have a written specification—a document describing everything a program should do—we can write a lot of tests before writing the code. We can even write a full Test Suite. Afterward we start implementing the code and see more and more of the tests pass. The main advantages of this approach are that writing tests first helps you to develop a good interface for the code, and that seeing more and more tests pass is highly motivating for developers. If we are working in an area with established domain knowledge (i.e., we understand the problem the software will solve in high detail), writing tests against a specification is feasible. In many other situations (computer games, startups, and research projects), either we have no written specification to start with, or the specification is very likely to change. In that case writing tests against the complete spec would be a waste of time. A more pragmatic approach is to pick one component from the specification, write tests for that component, and then implement it, pick the next, and so on. This way we limit the amount of wasted effort.

Writing Tests Against Defects

As we saw throughout the first chapters, finding and fixing defects can be stressful, tiring, and annoying. It is even worse to fix the same defect twice. The test-first approach protects us against that. The workflow of testing against defects is a slight adaptation of the test-first procedure:

1. Identify a defect or program failure.

2. Write a test against the defect or the resulting failure.

3. Make sure the test fails.

4. Fix the defect.

5. Run the test again and make sure it passes.

We can use the same procedure whenever we find a defect in our program. The failing test serves as a *proof* that the program contains a particular defect. As we investigate how the defect propagates through the program, we may add more specific tests (that also fail) to catch the defect earlier. Once we fix the defect, all of the newly written tests should pass. This way we make sure that the same defect will not occur again. Writing tests against bugs is a very helpful strategy to make software more robust. It is also the least dogmatic way to use the test-first approach. You will find a majority of programmers to agree that this is a Best Practice. A slight drawback of using writing many automated tests against bugs is that the resulting Test Suite will be unsystematic. Then, refactoring the tests from time to time is a good idea.

Test-Driven Development

Test-Driven Development (TDD) is the most rigorous interpretation of the test-first idea. TDD applies the test-first approach to the entire development process. Before writing any code, we write a test. Then we write sufficient code to make the test pass, write the next test, and so on. We structure the program as we alternate between writing tests and writing code. The idea behind TDD is that it helps to structure the program, because to write a test, we first need to fully understand what the program should do. Applied rigorously, TDD leads to very short development cycles (in the range of minutes). The main difference between TDD and other test-first approaches described earlier in the chapter is that in TDD, the person writing the test and the person writing the code must be identical. In the approaches described previously, testers and developers could be separate persons or even teams. Opinions on whether using TDD is a good idea differ. On one hand it prevents *coding too much*. When all tests pass, we are done. It also promotes thinking before writing code. Both are accepted virtues in programming. On the other hand, TDD is not easy to do and requires both experience and discipline. A bigger drawback is that it is difficult to keep an eye on the overall architecture of the software while working from one test to the next. One criticism of TDD is that, it promotes design that is hard to maintain. A balanced discussion on TDD was given in the EuroPython 2014 keynote by Emily Bache (`https://archive.org/details/EuroPython_2014_5ZLqAvRe`). In any case, trying TDD is a good learning experience and I highly recommend you try it out.

Advantages of Automated Testing

We have seen that automated testing can be applied to small and large units of code, from single functions to entire software packages. We have seen a few examples, in which tests are more difficult but possible to write. Finally, we have seen that writing tests before the code is an accepted Best Practice. On the other hand we have also seen that testing does not prove a program correct. It only proves the presence of defects, not their absence. The rationale that tests only prove **incorrectness** is given in Figure 11-2.

		tests	
		correct	incorrect
code	correct	**PASS**	**FAIL**
	incorrect	**FAIL**	**PASS** or **FAIL**

Figure 11-2. *Possible outcomes if code and tests are correct or wrong*

Are there any other benefits or limitations of automated tests that we have missed so far?

Testing Saves Time

First of all, using tests is much faster than manual checking of program features. But what about the time invested in writing automated tests? Ideally, the time invested in writing tests pays off quickly. Whenever we change a program, there is a risk to accidentally break something that was working before. Having a test eliminates the time to discover and fix these defects manually. This is true regardless whether we are adding new features, fixing defects, or reorganizing (refactoring) our code. The main benefit of automated tests is that we will never have to worry about the same issue twice. Thus, the effort invested should pay off after a few rounds of development.

Some programmers skip automated tests, arguing they do not have the time for that. For a small program (100 lines or less) there is little doubt about that. Running the code and manually checking it will be faster most of the time. Above 100 lines, automated tests start becoming more useful. Depending on the project (and the damage done if there is a bug) both programs with and without tests work. Above 1000 lines, not writing automated tests becomes very risky. Generally, the program size a single experienced programmer can handle without automatic tests is bigger than a team with mixed skill levels. Over time, tests accelerate development, because the existing features can be tested quickly and in an automated way. The bigger your program grows and the longer you maintain it, the bigger the benefit of automated testing.

Testing Adds Precision

In a dynamically typed language like Python, testing is necessary. Python catches very few errors before running the program, whereas statically typed languages point out many defects during compilation. In Python, we need tests to reach a comparable level of precision. We can use tests to define precisely what a function, class, or module is expected to do. By writing a test we clearly state that we are *expecting* a given behavior and that an observed behavior is not a coincidence.

Testing Makes Collaboration Easier

Testing facilitates collaboration among developers in many ways. Tests make it easy to check quickly whether the code received from other programmers is working. This is a necessary step before starting to modify someone else's code. With tests we can carry out such checks without consulting the other programmer. This is especially valuable when engaging in an Open Source project, onboarding into an existing team, or taking over a project whose original developers are not available any more. On the opposite site, writing tests protects your back when your latest change to the code do not work on someone else's computer. Asking *"did the tests pass?"* pulls the discussion in a constructive, fact-based direction instead of assigning blame on mere assumptions.

Limitations of Automated Testing

Testing Requires Testable Code

To write good tests, the structure of the code itself needs to be testable. Imagine we would write the entire game (setting up the level, drawing graphics, the event loop handling moves, etc.) in a single monolithic function. This would lead to a couple of serious impediments:

- It would be very complicated to get our test data into the program (e.g., to replace the random map by our own test scenario).

- The graphics would be displayed all the time, slowing down tests.

- It would be difficult to hijack the keyboard in order to get commands into the event loop and to leave the program afterward.

Having a single big program would inflate our test code considerably and slow down the tests. In practice, splitting the code into small functions and classes that are easy to test is already half of the work. The relationship between well-structured code and useful tests is mutual. Good tests make it easier to structure your program, whereas well-structured code is easy to test.

Testing Does Not Work Well for Projects Evolving Quickly

If a programming project is changing very rapidly, testing may not be worthwhile. For instance, if you do exploratory data analysis (e.g., collecting data from files and databases and generating tons of diagrams), writing automated tests usually is a wasted effort. Also, when implementing a prototype, development speed is often more useful than correctness. In both cases, writing tests would unnecessarily slow down development. However, some change in programs is normal. If everything in a program changes all the time, this can indicate that the program is not well-structured. In that case, testing can help to stabilize the parts that will not change: that the program finishes without an error, that it produces an output file, that the output file is not empty, and so on. Even if such tests may seem trivial, they will cover a lot of code.

Testing Does Not Prove Correctness

It is not possible to test everything. Automated tests are necessarily incomplete. Even with very detailed border cases, there is a lot of uncertainty remaining. As said in Chapter 10, a test coverage of 100% does not mean we have tested everything. Problems like *path complexity*—multiple execution paths through the program—create more possible ways a program could execute than we can test. Even in a program with a small number of branching instructions, the number of possible paths exceeds the number of situations we can test in practice. Even if we *would* cover all possible paths, we usually cannot cover every possible input. Finally, there is always a chance that our tests do not precisely describe all possible ways we intend the program to be used. There are many studies confirming that it is rather normal that a program contains unknown defects. Unfortunately, Python programs with automated tests are no exception. Concluding, **automated testing does not prove correctness.**

Programs That Are Difficult to Test

Random Numbers

By definition, random numbers are unpredictable. Whenever random numbers are involved, tests need to cover all possible outcomes. A Best Practice to test programs using random numbers is to control the seed value using `random.seed()`, so that we *know* what sequence of random numbers will be created, and your test results will be at least consistent. Here, it is important to set the seed value for each test module independently to avoid our tests interfering with each other.

■ **Hint** I read that the implementation of the Python `random` module is consistent on all platforms. With the same seed value you should obtain the same result everywhere. I also checked and found random numbers generated by Python 2.7 and 3.5 consistent, but I would be cautious when testing random numbers anyway.

Graphical User Interfaces

If your program has a textual interface, it is quite easy to write tests for it. Basically we can catch the standard output (via `sys.stdin` or redirect the output on Unix) and replace user input by our test data. With graphical interfaces, things get cumbersome quickly. The basic problem is that it is hard to instruct an automatic test to check whether what we see on the screen makes any sense to a human being (as an extreme example, white font on a light gray background may be correct to an automated test, but completely useless for human users). Also, it is possible to simulate a series of mouse clicks to specific positions in a user interface. However, the positions of GUI elements are frequently subject to changes, resulting in frequent changes to tests.

Generally, writing tests for dynamic web pages is a bit easier, because the separation of HTML, CSS, and Python helps to focus tests on the functionality. Test strategies for both the HTML and the back-end part include diverse technologies such as the **Django test framework** (very similar to the tests seen in this book) and **Selenium** (test scripts that remote-control a web browser). For Django developers, *Test-Driven Development with Python* by Harry J. W. Percival (O'Reilly Media, 2014) is a great expert-level book on the subject.

A Best Practice when dealing with graphical user interfaces is to separate the visual components cleanly from the rest, as follows: First, write a well-tested library or command-line tool that does the work. Test it using the techniques presented over the last few chapters. Second, write the graphical part on top of it. Depending on your abilities, write rudimentary tests or resort to manual testing of the graphical part. You will need to do some manual testing of a graphical interface anyway.

Complex or Large Output

If the output of your program is very complex or simply large, good tests can be challenging to write. Such situations could include generation of images, audio, video, or large text files. The main problem is that comparing the output of your program to a sample file does not work well. Imagine you introduce a small change in your program that results in a few extra spaces in a file that is several MB large. Reinspecting the test data quickly becomes costly.

Two strategies come to the rescue in this kind of situation: First, for many file formats **support libraries** written in Python already exist. For instance, if you use the `PILLOW` library to generate images, you can use the same library to verify the output of your program. If you have a library for reading and writing the target format (and assuming that it works correctly), you won't have to check every detail of the output. Checking some main characteristics (e.g., the number of images, their size, and a few other key properties) is often sufficient. If such a support library does not exist, writing one might be a good investment.

Second, you can write detailed tests for a very small sample dataset. If your regular dataset is larger, testing a small file alone is insufficient. A Best Practice would be to additionally test a larger file, but limit the testing to a few key metrics: Is the output nonempty? Does the file have the right size and the right number of entries? Does the image have the right number of pixels? What is the minimum/maximum amplitude of the audio signal? What is the average color of the video? Such metrics cover 80% of the situations and make even testing large output manageable.

Concurrency

Testing things that happen in parallel is my personal nightmare. It does not matter whether you are testing concurrent processes, threads, greenlets, or any other kind of parallel processing; concurrency is very difficult to test. The reason for that is in the nature of concurrency itself: Imagine we have a player and a ghost moving through the maze (like we designed in Chapter 15). If we implement this feature as a single thread, we have full control over the sequence of events. We can write normal tests that examine what is in the Pygame event queue. If we create one thread for the player and one thread for the ghost, we give up that control. Now, if we write a test that aims at checking both threads, the test very easily interferes with these threads. For instance, the test could slightly delay some of the events. As a result, the bug could disappear as an effect of the testing. If you are familiar with *Heisenberg's uncertainty principle*, you may recognize a similarity. Consequently, bugs that disappear when they are tested are called **Heisenbugs**. In brief, in a concurrent environment tests and the system under test interfere with each other, making things a lot harder to test.

My recommendation if you must use concurrency is to read deeper into the subject. Pick one library (**asyncio, gevent,** or **Twisted**) and understand it thoroughly. Look for specific recommendations on testing in the documentation. Probably you will have to log a lot of information. If concurrent programming is bound to become your daily business, programming languages with strong concurrency support like **Go** and **Scala** are worth a look as well.

Situations Where Automated Tests Fail

Computer scientists have found a couple of very nasty situations where testing makes little or no sense. Think about the following:

- Can you test whether a program finishes (e.g., whether there is an endless loop)?

- Can you test how a program behaves when it runs out of memory?

- How many different environments (operating systems, Python versions, library versions, and combinations thereof) can you practically test your program on?

- Can you test infrastructure (network connections, web services, helper scripts)? In what situations is that useful?

Alternatives to Automated Testing

In a company manufacturing safety-critical software I heard the following statement: "*We usually do not rely on unsafe techniques like automated testing.*" Given that automated tests only prove the presence of bugs, we need to acknowledge the fact that automated testing per se does not make a program safe, secure, or correct. But what are the alternatives? Here, we briefly look at a few alternatives to **verify correctness** that are found in the toolbox of a software engineer.

Prototyping

In the classic software engineering book *The Mythical Man-Month* (Addison-Wesley, 1995), Fred Brooks states that one needs to *prepare to throw away your first implementation*. This experience directly points to the technique of **prototyping**. In prototyping, a first version of the program is written as a proof-of-concept with the explicit condition that it will not be used afterward. A working prototype exposes problems that were unknown before. By creating a concrete implementation, many conceptual or architectural issues nobody had thought of can be identified. To create a prototype rapidly, testing is not essential. After the prototype, a second, more thoroughly designed program that avoids the flaws of the prototype is written. There, automated testing has its place again. Prototyping is a very useful technique for us, because Python is a great language for writing prototypes. Writing a prototype is fast, and often writing a new program from scratch is much faster than trying to correct the flaws introduced in the first attempt.

Code Reviews

Code reviews have already been introduced in Chapter 4 as a method to identify defects. Code reviews have many kinds of benefits beyond debugging: Reviews help to improve software quality in general. Reviews help developers to work together (if the review is supportive and does not end up in finger-pointing). Reviews promote learning and retention of knowledge in a team. Personally, I think reviews are fun. If you would like someone to look at your code, feel free to send me it to me and I'll have a look.

Checklists

Checklists are a useful tool to maintain software quality as well. A checklist is simply a series of steps, questions, or reminders that are checked one by one. For a couple of years I have been using a checklist to pack my suitcase for business trips. One of the things on my list is a toothbrush. Of course, I would remember to pack my toothbrush, wouldn't I? But if I get up at 4 a.m. or if I have to pack up and leave in a hurry, I wouldn't be so sure. When things get hot, I don't want to leave it to chance whether I have my toothbrush with me. The checklist makes sure of that.

In a software project, the items on a checklist could be the following:

- Typical bugs you want to exclude, for example, "*Have all variables been initialized?*"

- Steps during the release of a software, for example, "*Create a zipfile. Upload it to the project page.*"

- Explicit manual tests, for example, "*Can the zipfile be downloaded and unzipped?*"

By checking things explicitly, checklists take the human factor out of the equation. There is a good and a bad side to this. The bad side is that using a checklist is repetitive and after some time becomes boring. This is why checklists tend to work better with two people (e.g., during a review). The good side is that checklists *simplify* very complex situations. They therefore work under stress conditions: there is a reason that checklists are used heavily by people doing medical surgery or operating planes and helicopters. *The Checklist Manifesto* by Atul Gawande (Metropolitan Books, 2010) is a book that provides more background knowledge on creating and using checklists.

Processes Promoting Correctness

Writing correct software has a lot to do with the underlying development process. For instance, a process where safety is a priority needs to identify safety risks at the very beginning and address these risks explicitly. This involves nonprogramming activities like risk assessment and contingency planning. On an organizational level, quality standards like **ISO9001, CMMI,** and **ITIL** are common. They aim to control, document, and improve quality in a development process. However, these are methods for big teams and organizations. Knowledge of quality standards is not very useful for the average Python project, unless your organization uses them. A more useful approach is to adopt a few basic **Kaizen** practices like the **5-Why** technique and **Kanban**. Both focus on improvement and help to discover the predominant values in an organization. Organizational values (e.g. quality, customer service, personal integrity) have a huge impact on code quality, often in nonobvious ways. This is why I think that basic knowledge about processes, leadership, and team dynamics is indispensable for an experienced programmer interested in quality.

Conclusions

All approaches to manufacture correct software come at a price. Verifying code or working with a process that promotes correctness takes much longer than writing *untested* Python programs. In a scientific Python programming project, I calculated that each team member wrote on average about 20 lines of Python code per day (lots of time was also spent on testing, debugging, rewriting code, reading and writing scientific articles, attending conferences, teaching, administrative duties, etc.). That number corresponds well with literature. For software development in safety-critical environments, that number might even drop to 10 lines of code per day and programmer. Thus, writing fully verified software is very expensive. In rapid prototyping or a startup environment a single developer might easily produce more than 100 lines of code. Of course the outcome of rapid development will be more difficult to maintain. But to be *functionally correct*, a program only needs to answer a business hypothesis within a couple of month, whereas in a safety-critical system the software needs to run reliably for a long time, usually years up to decades.

When thinking about correctness, the **Swiss Cheese Model** is helpful: Imagine that every measure we take to improve correctness is a slice of cheese. Each slice has holes, because each measure has its limitations. But if we stack many slices like prototyping, code reviews and—of course—automated testing on top of each other, the number of holes through which a defect could penetrate the entire stack will hopefully be very small. It is good to know alternatives to testing exist, if only to deprive us of the delusion that automated testing is the one and only Best Practice to write correct code. Python is a language that allows fast development and quickly evolving projects. Automated tests are a technique that makes a software project more robust without sacrificing speed of development. Python and automated testing fit together well.

Best Practices

- **Unit Tests** are tests for small units of code. A Best Practice is to write **Unit Tests** that are *Fast, Isolated, Reproducible, Self-validating, and Timely.*

- **Integration Tests** test whether two or more components collaborate correctly.

- **Acceptance Tests** test user-level features.

- **Regression Testing** refers to rerunning tests after refactoring code, fixing defects, or making other changes.

- The timeit and cProfile modules analyze the execution time of Python statements and allow writing **Performance Tests**.

- Writing failing tests before writing code that makes them pass proves that a test is working correctly.

- Writing tests before code is useful to implement new features or fix bugs.

- **TDD** is a rigorous interpretation of the test-first approach, promoting very short cycles of writing tests and code.

- **Automated Testing** is certainly not the only way to create working software. There are plenty of other techniques to **verify and validate** programs, such as **manual testing, code reviews,** and **checklists**.

## PART III

Maintenance

CHAPTER 12

Version Control

Judging by the pollution content of the atmosphere, I believe we have arrived at the latter half of the twentieth century.

—Spock, *Star Trek IV: The Voyage Home*

Once I was contributing to a research project involving a database, a public web server, and lots of Python code. One day the hard disk of the server crashed, wiping out everything. We tried to restore the service from files that were scattered on different peoples' computers—and failed. The project never came to life again. We would have needed a *time machine* to restore the previous state of the project. Ironically, when I was working on another web-database project one year later, history repeated itself. The disk on the server crashed *again*. This time, we *did have* a time machine. We could take all code and data like it had been *before the crash*. Although we had to configure a few things manually, the site was soon running again. Now you may wonder how we could recover the old code. Or, more precisely: *"How did you build yourself that time machine?"* Our time machine is called **Version Control** (see Figure 12-1). In this chapter we will see what Version Control is and how to use it.

© Kristian Rother 2017

K. Rother, *Pro Python Best Practices*, DOI 10.1007/978-1-4842-2241-6_12

Figure 12-1. *Version Control is a bit like time traveling in your source code—temporal paradoxa included. To see a world without program bugs, you would have to travel back into the 19th century before Ada Lovelace wrote the very first computer program.*

Over the previous chapters, our program has changed considerably. We have applied various debugging and coding strategies and edited our code accordingly. While trying out different approaches, we might have copied Python files to preserve both the old and the new version. After some time, we would see files accumulating (e.g., for the module drawing the playing field as a grid of tiles):

```
draw_grid.py
draw_grid2.py
draw_grid2_new_version.py
draw_grid3.py
draw_map.py
draw_map_buggy.py
draw_map_with_introspection.py
```

It seems our program has proliferated and developed a life on its own. After a few days of not working with the code it will be very difficult to use these files correctly. Questions similar to the following arise: Is the most recently modified file really the one you should use? What was the difference between draw_map and draw_grid again? Is it safe to delete all the others, or do they still contain important code fragments? If our code contains files distributed over multiple directories, the situation gets even worse. In brief, the result is that our program is in danger of becoming a total mess.

Version Control is the way out of this problem. Version Control means tracking all changes in your program code and related files, so that over time you are building a log of how your code developed. Version Control enables us to revert to any previous point in time later. Because of that, Version Control is considered the most basic, essential Best Practice for maintaining any project over longer time. Even for small, one-person projects it pays off quickly.

In this chapter, we will use the Version Control system **git**, to track changes in the **MazeRun** code, and place it in a public source code repository.

Getting Started with git

git was written by Linus Torvalds, the inventor of Linux. It is today the most commonly used and most advanced Version Control system. Almost needless to say, it is available for free. Things you can do with **git** include the following:

1. Create a repository

2. Add files to a repository

3. Examine the history of your project

4. Jump to an earlier state and back

5. Publish the code on a public repository

6. Manage multiple code branches in parallel

On Ubuntu Linux, you can install **git** with

```
sudo apt-get install git
```

Creating a Repository

Projects in **git** are organized in **repositories**. Generally speaking, a repository is a group of files that are versioned together. What does that mean? Let us consider a concrete example. Imagine you have all files for the **MazeRun** game in a directory called maze_run (including Python code, images, and maybe a few data files). We want to use **git** to track changes in these files. First, we create a new repository from the command line with the git init command:

```
cd maze_run/
git init
```

You should see a message like this:

```
Initialized empty Git repository in /home/krother/projects/maze_run/
```

At first, nothing seems to have changed. But if you look more closely (with ls -la), you notice a hidden folder called .git. This is where **git** is storing changes applied to your files over time. Now our project can start developing its own *history*.

Adding Files to a Repository

When we initialize a repository, does **git** start tracking the existing files automatically? We can check what **git** knows about the current directory at any time by typing

```
git status
```

We obtain a message like this:

```
Untracked files:
    (use "git add <file>..." to include in what will be committed)

        draw_maze.py
        event_loop.py
        generate_maze.py
        load_tiles.py
        maze_run.py
        moves.py
        util.py
        images/

nothing added to commit but untracked files present (use "git add" to track)
```

What **git** is telling us is that it sees files it has never seen before, and thus are not in the repository yet. We can add these files and entire directories to the repository with the git add command:

```
git add *.py
git add images/*
```

By using git status again, you can check which files **git** took note of. Adding works for any type of file (source code, text files, images, Word documents). However, **git** works most efficiently for *changes in text files.*

To tell **git** that we are done adding files, we can use the **commit** command and attach a message:

```
git commit -m "added first working version of MazeRun"
```

After which git status reports:

```
nothing to commit, working directory clean
```

The **commit** command copies the contents of our files to **git**'s internal files in the .git directory. We now have completely recorded the changes. Whatever we change in our Python code later, we can restore the previous state as long as we don't mess with the .git directory (which usually is not a good idea unless you really know what you are doing).

Tracking Changes in Files

The main use of Version Control is to keep track of changes in our files. Imagine we want to edit the description of the *random maze generator* introduced in Chapter 3. Like before, we open the file (generate_maze.py) in our favorite text editor, and make changes. For instance, we could replace the spartan comment

```
# Code for chapter 03 - Semantic Errors
```

with a more illustrative docstring that explains what the module does and what its limitations are:

```
"""
Random Maze Generator

Creates X*Y grids consisting of walls (#) and floor tiles (.),

forming a network of connected corridors.

Warning: Sometimes, the algorithm will create enclosed spaces,
but it is good enough to experiment with debugging techniques.

This module was introduced in chapter 03 - Semantic Errors
"""
```

When we save the file, the changes are not automatically added to the **git** repository. We can check with git status again which files have changed:

```
> git status
On branch master
Changes not staged for commit:
  (use "git add <file>..." to update what will be committed)

    modified: generate_maze.py

nothing added to commit but untracked files present (use "git add" to track)
```

You can also check see what exactly has changed with git diff. The output contains the prefix + for each line we added and the prefix - for each line we deleted:

```
> git diff
index c0d5a33..2ea0321 100644
--- a/part1_debugging/generate_maze.py
+++ b/part1_debugging/generate_maze.py
@@ -1,5 +1,13 @@
+"""
+Random Maze Generator
```

```
-# Code for chapter 03 - Semantic Errors
+Creates X*Y grids consisting of walls (#) and floor tiles (.),
+so that the floor tiles are connected.
+
+Warning: Sometimes, the algorithm will create enclosed spaces.
+
+This module was introduced in chapter 03 - Semantic Errors
+"""
```

```
 import random
```

To write these changes into the repository, we need to add the files and commit the changes again:

```
git add generate_maze.py
git commit -m "improved module docstring for maze generator"
```

As a shortcut, you can do both adding and committing changes in one step, as long as the file generate_maze.py has been added to the repository earlier so that **git** knows about it:

```
git commit -a -m "improved module docstring for maze generator"
```

The git commit -a -m command will add *all* files from your repository that were changed recently. This is useful, because it saves you the effort of adding each file one by one. In bigger projects, it is sometimes desirable to create multiple *commits* from a round of edits (e.g., if you're writing a book, the commits could be labeled *"added figure to chapter 12," "fixed code example in chapter 15,"* etc.). **git** gives you very fine-grained control over what goes into an individual commit. As a Best Practice I recommend adding the files manually anyway instead of using git commit -a -m, simply to be conscious about what you are adding.

▓ **Commit Daily**   It is a good habit to commit all your changes at least at the end of a working day. If you are collaborating with other people or developing intensively, commits may happen much more frequently. In peak times, I am using git commit every few minutes.

Moving and Deleting Files

Apart from changing the content of files, we may want to move a file to a different place or throw it away altogether. The normal Unix commands mv and rm still work, but **git** will become confused because a file it expected is not there anymore. Instead, we need to tell **git** explicitly that we want to move or delete a file.

The git mv command is an equivalent of mv for moving files. It works in exactly the same way as mv, only that a note is added to our repository that the file used to be somewhere else. A full command could look like this:

```
git mv foo.py examples/foo.py
```

Similarly, git rm deletes a file, but still remembers the previous contents in the repository:

```
git rm bar.py
```

It is possible to override changes using the -f flag, but I do not recommend using -f as a Best Practice. With git status we can check that **git** took note of the moved and deleted files. After moving and deleting files, the changes need to be committed to the repository with git commit like we did previously when editing files.

Discarding Changes

While editing code, it sometimes turns out that an idea does not work. Or it turns out that we have entangled ourselves so badly in our own edits that it is better to throw away all changes and start over. Or we simply delete our code accidentally. In a text editor, it is very easy to destroy hours and days of work by pressing Ctrl+A, Backspace, Ctrl+S. In these situations we can use the repository to undo our changes and fall back to a known state. Imagine we have messed up the file generate_maze.py (this is safe to try at home given that you have committed the most recent changes to a repository).

We can restore the file with the git checkout command:

```
git checkout generate_maze.py
```

This re-creates the file as it was at the last commit. We can revert all files in the current directory with one command as well:

```
git checkout .
```

With frequent commits, git checkout works like a project-wide **undo** function.

Navigating the History of Our Code

When tracking changes in our code for a while, we do a lot of **commits**. Our repository is accumulating its own *history*. Ideally, this history is silently stored in the .git directory and we will never need to look at it again. However, one day we may notice that we messed up something that worked before. In such cases, we can use **git** as our time machine to go back and see how the code looked before (see Figure 12-1).

The first thing we need to figure out is which date to enter into the time machine. The command git log gives us a list of all commits we have done previously:

```
> git log
commit a11d542accc755a47533783b462c69992e218e73

Author: krother <krother@academis.eu>
Date:   Fri Jul 1 11:45:40 2016 +0200

    improved module docstring for maze generator

commit b865b483a7e042e02724464cc6bd944b23e2324e
Author: krother <krother@academis.eu>
Date:   Fri May 27 21:18:51 2016 +0200

    cleaned up scripts for part 1
...
```

Each commit contains a *hash code*, the author, a timestamp, and the message we wrote (at this point it pays off to write descriptive commit messages). We can restrict the output for the log messages concerning a single file as well:

```
> git log util.py
commit b9699d1e57292d33aa908a790013c93e15f24962
Author: krother <krother@academis.eu>
Date:   Sat May 21 06:29:25 2016 +0200

    reorganizd part1
```

To get an overview over a longer stretch of history, it is useful to condense each commit to one line with the --pretty=oneline option:

```
git log --pretty=oneline generate_maze.py
a11d542accc755a47533783b462c69992e218e73 improved module docstring
b865b483a7e042e02724464cc6bd944b23e2324e cleaned up scripts for part 1
6c3f01bb1efbe1dfdf6479a60c96897505c1d7a4 cleaned up code for chapter 03
b9699d1e57292d33aa908a790013c93e15f24962 reorganized part1
```

▓ **Why do we need hash codes instead of simply numbering commits from 1 to X?** The time-traveling analogy provides us with a good explanation: Imagine we traveled back in time to give an earlier self the results of an exam. We would create an alternate history with two versions of the present (one with a failed exam and one with a perfect one). Apart from the scientific problems created, it will be difficult to unambiguously refer to one of the two alternate realities by a date alone.

With a time-traveling machine like **git**, we have the possibility to alter the history of our code. What is more, you (or a team of people) can create *multiple* histories in parallel. In a nutshell, a linear history does not go together well with time travel. The way **git** avoids paradoxa resulting from that is to treat each commit as a unique event that is independent of a timeline—and in computer science, *hash codes* are the tool of choice to identify such data items. I haven't seen hash codes applied to time travel in real life, but the idea doesn't sound too bad.

Checking out Older Commits

Having identified a commit of interest, we can jump back in the history of our project. Let us assume we would like to check how the code looked like after the commit labeled *"reorganized part1"*. We need the git checkout command and the according hash code b9699d1e572.. copied from the output of git log. We travel back in time with

```
git checkout b865b483a7e042e02724464cc6bd944b23e2324e
```

git gives us a warning message (*"detached HEAD"*) that basically means that time traveling is potentially dangerous, and git will discard any changes unless we explicitly state otherwise. When we take the opportunity to simply look around in the past and open generate_maze.py in an editor, we notice that our recent docstring has disappeared. The header of the module once again reads

```
# Code for chapter 03 - Semantic Errors
```

git has changed all files in the repository to resemble the state in which they were at that point in the commit history.

Traveling Back to the Most Recent Commit

With git log we see only the commits older than the point we jumped to. That is, our newer commit is invisible (and we cannot see its hash code). Are we trapped forever in the past? Fortunately, our time machine has a "go back" button. When we have seen enough of the past, we can return to the present with

```
git checkout master
```

And once again, our docstring appears in generate_maze.py on the disk (depending how well your editor handles files being edited by other programs, you may get more or less surprised reactions from your text editor).

Publishing Code on GitHub

Even if you are not developing code with **git**, it is practically impossible not to come across **GitHub** at some point. **GitHub** is a website hosting millions of repositories containing everything from *Hello World* programs to entire operating systems. **GitHub** serves as a marketplace for developers to share code and work on collaborative projects (see Figure 12-2). Using **GitHub** has many advantages:

- You can access your program code from multiple computers without SSH.

- Publishing code on GitHub works as a backup system.

- You can browse source code of published repositories in a web browser.

- Other programmers can copy a project, improve it, and kindly ask you to reincorporate their changes.

- The README file is automatically rendered and displayed on the project page.

- Each project has an issue tracker that works as a lightweight project management tool.

- You can plug additional services into a Github repository. For instance, tests can be executed or documentation can be published automatically.

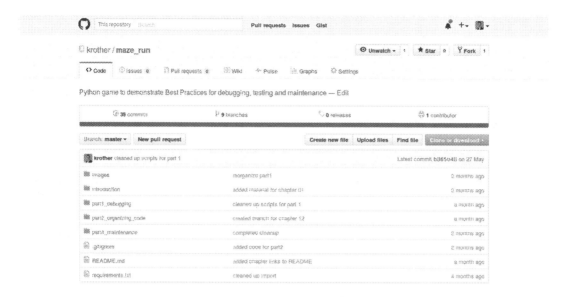

Figure 12-2. *GitHub is a platform to share source code and to collaborate with other developers. The screenshot shows an earlier version of the MazeRun repository.*

At the time of writing, GitHub is the de facto central platform for open source development on this planet. Nevertheless, you can use it for private repositories as well (with a paid plan). Many programmers I have met see someone's presence on **GitHub** as a kind of business card. A GitHub profile does not provide a very accurate estimate of programming skills (e.g., because most commercial projects are not publicly visible), but being familiar with the platform can be considered a Best Practice for most programming languages. Fortunately, all you need to remember for using GitHub are three commands: `git push`, `git pull`, and `git clone`.

Starting a Project on GitHub

Starting your own project on GitHub is easy. You go to `http://github.com`, create yourself an account, and find the button *"**create a new repository**"*. After that, you mostly follow the instructions on the screen like entering a project name and description. The most relevant decision is whether you *copy the new repository from GitHub to your computer or from your computer to GitHub*. GitHub will display the commands for both options, so that you can copy-paste them into a Unix terminal. You only need to do this once, so we won't discuss the exact commands in detail.

Which option is better? That depends on what you already have: If you haven't created a repository with `git init` on your computer yet, copying the repository from GitHub to your computer with `git clone` is simpler. If you already have used **git** locally, even for one or two commits, it is better to copy the existing repository to GitHub with the commands given on the page. Currently, the commands proposed by GitHub for that situation, for instance for the MazeRun repository, are as follows:

```
git remote add origin https://github.com/krother/maze_run.git
git push -u origin master
```

Using GitHub as a Single Contributor

Once we have set up our project on GitHub and gone through the first configuration steps, things get easier. How can we publish our code? Let us consider we are the only person working on a project. We write code locally and commit the changes to the local repository with `git commit`. In regular intervals (e.g., daily), we would like to submit our changes to GitHub, so that other people can read it, and our code is safe in case the computer's drive crashes. After committing, all we need to type is

```
git push
```

git will ask us for our user name and password, and we are done. If anything goes wrong the first time, the two most common reasons are ither that the git repository was not set up correctly (in this case, you can safely delete the repository on GitHub, create a new one, and try again) and that your Internet connection works through a proxy server that doesn't allow the connection by default (some companies and public locations do that). In that case, please consult your network administrator.

This kind of workflow is not only useful for one-person programming projects. It also works well if we publish tutorials or training material via GitHub (e.g., using `http://gitbook.com`) or manage our own website via GitHub Pages (`http://pages.github.com`).

Working on Projects Started by Other People

Originally, **git** was created for teams of developers working together. The idea is that two or more developers can work on the same code in parallel. They exchange changes in the code, so that the common code base grows much faster than if they had to wait for the other person to finish. Starting to work on an existing project through GitHub is easy. Basically anyone can use `git clone` to get a copy of a repository. For instance, we could start developing a local variation of the MazeRun game:

```
git clone https://github.com/krother/maze_run.git
```

The `git clone` command creates a local copy of the GitHub project. It also copies the `.git` directory, so that the entire history of the project is copied as well. At a later point, we can check with `git pull` whether there are any changes in the repository on GitHub:

```
git pull
```

To use `git pull`, we need to commit our own changes first.

Projects with Multiple Contributors

By default, only the owner of a repository may change its contents. But if we wanted to collaborate on a project with someone, we can add multiple contributors in the *Settings* for that Github project. By adding a contributor, we allow that person to add code to the project, change its settings, or even **delete the project** altogether. These privileges should only be given to people you know and trust.

With multiple contributors, a typical workflow is as follows:

1. Update our local copy with `git clone` or `git pull`.

2. Edit the code.

3. Commit the changes with `git commit`.

4. Run `git pull` once again to check for changes.

5. Right afterward, publish everything with `git push`.

Merging Changes by Two People

When two or more people edit the same code, there is a big problem around the corner. Imagine that you and someone else *edited code at the same time*. Both of you commit the code (step 3 from the preceding list). What happens in steps 4 and 5? If both people worked on different files, **git** will **merge** both edits automatically. While merging, the newest files from each commit will be used. If the same file was edited by two people, the merge is more complicated. Usually, **git** will ask you to merge the files manually. You get a file in which the conflicting changes are marked. You then have the chance to resolve the conflict and contribute the code with `git add` and `git commit`.

Pull Requests

There are many advanced options that facilitate collaboration with other developers: for instance, you can create your own copy of a published project (called a **Fork**). You can change your Fork without modifying the original project. However if you think that your changes are worth being incorporated back into the original project, this is done with a **Pull Request**. Say you create your own **Fork** of **MazeRun** on GitHub and have added sound effects to the game in your copy of the project. What happens if we decide that this would be a good addition to my code as well:

- You create a Pull Request of your commit to my repository on GitHub.

- I receive the Pull Request and review what changes are coming.

- I accept the changes.

- The code is merged (assuming there are no merge conflicts).

A good Pull Request requires some kind of communication between the people involved, otherwise the developer receiving a Pull Request will be confused easily. A Pull Request is similar to a merge, only it happens entirely on GitHub. Pull Requests are a common way to make small as well as big improvements to open source software.

Development with Branches

A key feature of **git** is that we can work on multiple things in parallel. To stretch the time machine equivalent a bit further, imagine we have multiple alternate realities (the 2009 Star Trek movie contains a superb example of the practical problems this creates). With **git**, these alternate realities or **branches** fortunately are not that difficult to manage.

By default, there is a single branch, called `master`. Let's assume we want to work on a new experimental feature for the game (e.g., *sound effects*). We can create a dedicated branch for that with the command and give it the name `sound_effects`:

```
git branch sound_effects
```

Now we have two code branches, `master` and `sound_effects`, and both are still identical. We can see all branches with

```
git branch
```

We see a list of branches, with the currently active branch marked by an asterisk (*):

```
* master
  sound_effects
```

To work on the new branch, we need to switch to it:

```
git checkout sound_effects
```

You can verify with `git branch` that we are really in the new branch now. We can now edit code, add files, and commit normally. Here, we simply create a placeholder:

```
echo "print('BEEP')" >> sound.py
git add sound.py
git commit -m "created file for sound effects"
```

The new file is added to the repository for the new branch. Let's switch back to the `master` branch:

```
git checkout master
```

We notice that the newly created file `sound.py` has disappeared! We now have two alternate realities in our code.

Merging Branches

At some point we may decide that the sound effects are mature enough to be included in the main line of the program. We can apply the changes from one branch into another one. Assume that we still are in the `master` branch. We can use `git merge` to incorporate the changes from the `sound_effects` branch into `master`:

```
git merge sound_effects
```

Note that the `master` branch could have developed further in the meantime. In that case, **git** will merge the changes and ask us to merge manually in case they overlap. That way, we can make sure that the code is always consistent.

There are several practices for development with branches in **git**. The most important Best Practice is to keep stable code in the `master` branch and newly implemented features somewhere else (e.g., a `development` branch). As soon as a feature is stable enough, it gets merged into `master`. For the code repository of this book (`http://github.com/krother/maze_run`), I created separate branches for many of the chapters. This way I could keep the context of the code cleanly separated. I merged different branches into each other regularly. The branches and their relationships got quite impressive (see Figure 12-3). Understanding what branches are and how to use them requires a bit of thoughtwork. I recommend not using branches in your very first **git** project. They are however an essential technique in professional development.

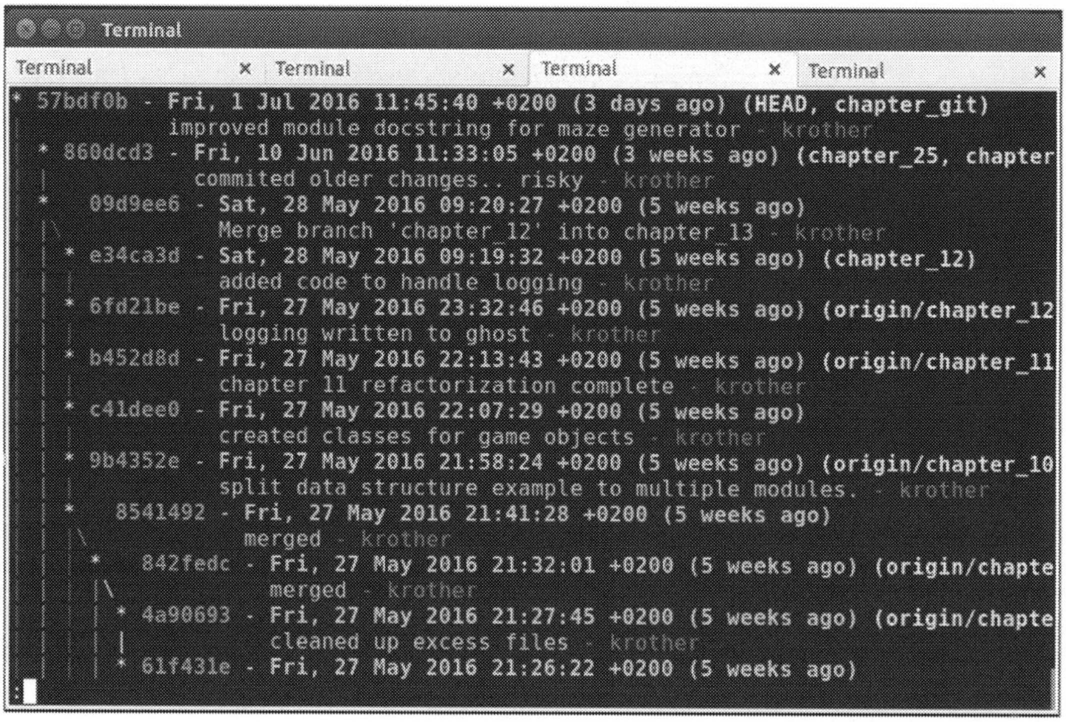

```
● ● ●   Terminal

Terminal          ×  Terminal           ×  Terminal           ×  Terminal          ×
* 57bdf0b - Fri, 1 Jul 2016 11:45:40 +0200 (3 days ago) (HEAD, chapter_git)
           improved module docstring for maze generator - krother
  * 860dcd3 - Fri, 10 Jun 2016 11:33:05 +0200 (3 weeks ago) (chapter_25, chapter
           commited older changes.. risky - krother
  *   09d9ee6 - Sat, 28 May 2016 09:20:27 +0200 (5 weeks ago)
  |\          Merge branch 'chapter_12' into chapter_13 - krother
  | * e34ca3d - Sat, 28 May 2016 09:19:32 +0200 (5 weeks ago) (chapter_12)
  | |         added code to handle logging - krother
  | * 6fd21be - Fri, 27 May 2016 23:32:46 +0200 (5 weeks ago) (origin/chapter_12
  | |         logging written to ghost - krother
  | * b452d8d - Fri, 27 May 2016 22:13:43 +0200 (5 weeks ago) (origin/chapter_11
  | |         chapter 11 refactorization complete - krother
  | * c41dee0 - Fri, 27 May 2016 22:07:29 +0200 (5 weeks ago)
  | |         created classes for game objects - krother
  | * 9b4352e - Fri, 27 May 2016 21:58:24 +0200 (5 weeks ago) (origin/chapter_10
  | |         split data structure example to multiple modules. - krother
  | *   8541492 - Fri, 27 May 2016 21:41:28 +0200 (5 weeks ago)
  | |\          merged - krother
  | | *   842fedc - Fri, 27 May 2016 21:32:01 +0200 (5 weeks ago) (origin/chapte
  | | |\          merged - krother
  | | | * 4a90693 - Fri, 27 May 2016 21:27:45 +0200 (5 weeks ago) (origin/chapte
  | | | |         cleaned up excess files - krother
  | | | * 61f431e - Fri, 27 May 2016 21:26:22 +0200 (5 weeks ago)
: ▮
```

Figure 12-3. *Graphical log of a git repository with multiple branches*

Configuring git

Generally, working with **git** integrates well with most day-to-day programming activities once you become familiar with the basic commands (i.e., add, commit, status, push, and pull). There are a couple of configuration options that make using **git** even more pleasant.

Ignoring Files

When importing Python modules, Python 3 creates *bytecode* in the __pycache__ directory to speed up execution. In **MazeRun**, the __pycache__ directory contains files like generate_maze.cpython-34.pyc as soon as we run the program once. Python automatically updates the cached files, so we can ignore them safely. However, git status will constantly pester us to add the __pycache__ directory to our repository:

```
> git status
Untracked files:
    (use "git add <file>..." to include in what will be committed)

    ___pycache___/
```

There are good reasons **not** to add the __pycache__ directory to our repository. First, Python manages them automatically, so they are useless for other people. Second, they would change each time we run the code, creating a lot of unnecessary messages. We would prefer if **git** would not remind us all the time about such files every time we type git status. We achieve both by creating the file .gitignore in our main project directory. The .gitignore file contains names and patterns that **git** will not bother us with. This file could contain the following line:

```
__pycache__/*
```

Now, git status will not mention the cache directory any more. What is more, when we try to add it by git add or git add *, it is rejected. Apart from bytecode files, most projects contain other files that do not need to be tracked by Version Control. These include, for instance

- local configuration settings (e.g., containing our home directory)
- log files
- databases
- temporary files
- passwords

The first three inflate a repository unnecessarily and produce a lot of *background* noise when using git status and git diff. The last is a serious security risk (**simply never add passwords to a repository**). A Best Practice is to add these types of files to .gitignore as patterns. A typical .gitignore file could contain the following items:

```
__pycache__/*
*.conf
*.log
*.db
*.tmp
password.txt
```

The **pyscaffold** tool introduced in Chapter 13 creates a more detailed .gitignore file for us automatically. When multiple people are working on a program together, it sometimes occurs that they are changing one line of code back and forth. This could be a directory name or an import statement that is different on their respective machines. When we observe this pattern, it is a hint that some configuration needs to be managed outside the repository (e.g., in an environment variable or the .bashrc file). Whenever you see people changing code back and forth it is a good time to **stop coding and start talking**.

Global Settings

A second place where **git** stores configuration options is the .gitconfig file in our home directory. Here, we can define our user name and useful shortcuts. The file can be edited using the git config command or in a text editor. For simplicity I will stick to the latter. My own .gitconfig file looks like this:

```
[user]
    email = krother@academis.eu
    name = krother
[alias]
    ci = commit
    st = status
    l = log --pretty=oneline
```

The [user] section simply contains my user name on **github**, so that I don't have to enter it each time I connect to a public repository. The [alias] section defines shortcuts: git ci works like git commit, git st works like git status, and git l summarizes the log in one-line mode.

Usage Examples

If you have not worked with Version Control before, you may find using **git** highly rewarding. When I started using a Version Control system, after a short time I wondered how I could ever have written any program without it. Yet, you can use **git** in many different ways, depending on the size of the project and the number of contributors.

Twenty Characters: A Small Project with Low Traffic

In a small project, you can treat Version Control as your private time machine. **git** maintains a clean history for code, data, documentation, or anything else. For instance, I write and maintain lots of course materials with git. There is nothing bad in maintaining many small repositories on GitHub. I have started 25 repositories on GitHub and 5 more on *Bitbucket*. One of my smallest repositories contains just three commits, two Python scripts, and a few image files (http://github.com/krother/twenty_characters). It serves the purpose to preserve a project in case I erase my backup drive accidentally. I also have contributed to repositories started by other people. In some cases, my contribution was as little as one line. There is really no minimum size.

Python: A Huge Project with Daily Commits

On the other end of the scale, a shared repository can get quite big. For instance, the repository of CPython, the standard Python interpreter (mirrored on http://github.com/python/cpython), contains more than 93,000 commits by 131 contributors. Guido van Rossum himself holds 10,800 commits, added more than a million lines of code, and removed 700,000 lines (see Figure 12-4). The history dates back to 1991. Changes are committed many times daily.

Figure 12-4. *Contributions to the Python interpreter by a few core developers over time. The red/green numbers indicate the lines contributed/deleted. Taken from* `http://github.com/python/cpython`.

grep: A Long-Term Project

Other repositories have less traffic. For instance, the repository of `grep`, a Unix command-line tool to search text in files, has been around for a longer time. The *GNU grep* repository was populated with 35,000 lines of code in 1999, but the history can be traced back to the first release by Mike Haerkal in 1988, which is a rewrite of the original grep by Ken Thompson from 1973. Although `grep` is generally considered a very stable tool, a team of developers change a few lines once or twice a week. Without Version Control, it is quite improbable that this program could have been maintained over more than four decades!

As the example shows, there appears to be no maximum size, either. We usually find one repository per project. I strongly discourage putting more than one project in the same repository. Repositories are not costly, after all.

git is a very powerful tool. So far, we have only scratched the surface. In Table 12-1 the most common commands are given. To learn more, I strongly recommend ***Pro Git*** by Scott Chacon and Ben Straub (Apress, 2009), a whole book dedicated to the possibilities and workflows that **git** offers.

Table 12-1. *git Commands*

Adding Files to a Repository

`git init`	creates a new git repository in the current directory
`git add <files>`	tracks changes in the given files
`git commit -m "message"`	writes tracked changes in the repository
`git commit –amend`	changes commit message or add files to last commit

Navigating Revisions

`git status`	displays added, modified, and untracked files
`git checkout .`	discards local changes
`git diff <file>`	displays changes since the last commit
`git rm <files>`	removes a file from the next commit
`git log`	lists commit messages
`git log <file>`	lists commit messages for the given file

Configuring git

`git config`	changes a configuration variable

Using a remote repository

`git clone`	creates a local copy of a local repository
`git pull`	updates the local copy
`git push`	submits changes to a remote repository (e.g., GitHub)

Advanced options

`git branch`	displays branches
`git branch <branch>`	creates a new branch
`git checkout <branch>`	switches local copy to given branch
`git merge`	merges two branches
`git blame <file>`	shows who edited which line
`git cherry pick <file> hash`	copies a file from an older commit
`git rebase`	rearranges two branches into a linear history
`git bisect`	guides you through a binary search in the commit history

Other Version Control Systems

There are some alternative Version Control systems worth mentioning:

Mercurial

A beginner-friendly distributed Version Control system. It has slightly fewer features than git, but the regular workflows are easier to use than with git. The website `http://hginit.com` is a good place to start.

Subversion (SVN)

A nondistributed Version Control system that was there long before git and Mercurial. There is little reason to use it in a new project today. The most convincing argument for using SVN that I heard was by a company manufacturing safety-critical software. They want to be 100% sure that they are using a stable technology that has not changed in the past ten years and is unlikely to change in the future. See `http://subversion.apache.org/`.

Concurrent Versions Software (CVS)

This is an even older Version Control system that has earned itself a worthy spot in a museum.

Bitbucket

A code repository like **Github** that allows for a limited number of public and private repositories free of charge. Bitbucket is compatible with **git** and **Mercurial**. See `https://bitbucket.org/`.

Sourceforge

A code repository dedicated to open source projects. For more than a decade (before GitHub became widely popular), Sourceforge was the main marketplace for open source software. See `https://sourceforge.net/`.

Best Practices

- **git** is a Version Control system that keeps track of changes in code.

- **git** records subsequent versions of the code as it develops over time.

- The repository is a history of changes stored in the `.git` directory.

- To track changes in a file, you need to `git add` the files and `git commit` the changes.

- `git log` displays the commit history. Each commit is identified by a **hash code**.

- Via `git checkout` you can return to an earlier commit, and return to the present.

- The history of a project is not necessarily linear. Multiple parallel **branches** can exist.

- GitHub is a platform for publishing and exchanging code. It also serves as a simple backup mechanism.

- When two contributors edit different files at the same time, **git** merges the changes automatically.

- When two contributors edit the same code, you need to **merge** the changes manually.

- The `.gitignore` file contains file name patterns that will not be tracked.

- There is no minimum and no maximum size for using a repository reasonably. All Python projects benefit from using a Version Control system.

CHAPTER 13

▨ ▨ ▨

Setting Up a Python Project

For proper home improvement, you need three things: First, a cleaned-up construction site. Second, the right tools. Third, beer in the fridge.

—My dad

When we started writing a small program from scratch, we did not worry much about organizing files. We simply collected everything in the same place, and that was fine. The MazeRun game started with a few Python files and a few images. But as the project grew, other files started accumulating. We already have seen various input and output files, tests, test data, configuration files, documentation, and of course more Python modules. How to organize these files properly? And how can we keep dependencies on external Python modules in check? Realizing that *only a part of the software consists of code*, what are Best Practices for organizing files and structuring a Python project in general?

A solid project structure helps us to

- find files quickly.

- apply standard tools (e.g., for testing and packaging) without much configuration.

- get other programmers involved without explaining too much.

- switch between multiple projects easily.

- prevent projects from interfering with each other.

In this chapter we will carry out the excavation work that makes further growth of our project possible (see Figure 13-1). First, we will establish a structure for our files and directories using the **pyscaffold** tool. Think of this structure as a large ditch with supported walls where everything will fit in. Second, as a foundation for our project, we will use the **virtualenv** tool to manage the installed Python modules.

▨ **But what if I have already set up my project?**   In contrast to a building, we can adopt an existing program to the structure proposed here. Even if we already have a git repository, files can be rearranged to fit a given structure quickly via `git mv`. As a result, not only our program code but all other parts supporting the code will have their place.

© Kristian Rother 2017

K. Rother, *Pro Python Best Practices*, DOI 10.1007/978-1-4842-2241-6_13

"When I said I wanted a bigger cave,
I surely didn't expect this"

Figure 13-1. *If programs were buildings, setting up a project would look like an excavation. The project contains a few things that are not a part of the program* ***directly****: a versioning system, a test environment, documentation, and so on.*

Creating a Project Structure with pyscaffold

Fortunately for us, there is a ***de facto*** standard for the file and directory structure of Python projects. This structure is found in big and small projects alike. Sticking to it counts as a Best Practice, because this structure is well-known among Python programmers and cooperates well with other Python tools; that is, it facilitates running automated tests and creating releases of your software. The **pyscaffold** tool creates a standard structure for Python projects according this standard. It creates important directories and files in a new project folder. Of course, we could set up most of it with a few Linux commands as well. The advantages of using **pyscaffold are** that we ensure consistency over multiple projects, and that it creates a cleanly written setup.py script that makes our software a lot easier to test, build, and distribute over its entire life cycle.

░ **When is pyscaffold not applicable?**   Not all Python projects use the directory structure created by pyscaffold. Most notably, the big Python web frameworks like **Django, web2py,** and **Zope / Plone** have their own scripts for creating directories and configuration files for a new project. The book *Two Scoops of Django* by Daniel Greenfield and Audrey Roy (Two Scoops Press, 2015) is an excellent source for organizing Django projects (or Django in general).

Installing pyscaffold

pyscaffold can be installed painlessly via pip:

```
sudo pip install pyscaffold
```

Apart from the Python package, pyscaffold also requires an installation of **git.** See Chapter 12 for details. To create a new project with **pyscaffold**, we start in the folder used for Python development (e.g., `projects/`) and run the `putup` script that comes with pyscaffold:

```
cd projects/
putup maze_run
```

Here `maze_run` is the name of the Python project **and** the Python package we want to create. We observe that pyscaffold created a `maze_run` directory with four more subdirectories and ten files, although some of them are hidden. Typing `ls -la` results in

```
.git/
docs/
maze_run/
tests/
.coveragerc
.gitattributes
.gitignore
AUTHORS.rst
LICENSE.txt
MANIFEST.in
README.rst

requirements.txt
setup.py
versioneer.py
```

In the following, we will look at the created directories and files (and some others) in more detail.

Typical Directories in a Python Project

Generally, in a good directory structure there is one obvious place for every file. In the typical project structure, **pyscaffold** creates four directories and a few additional files.

Directories Created by pyscaffold

Pyscaffold creates four directories that contain most things you will need in a typical Python project. We will look at them one by one:

The Main Python Package Directory

This is the directory where the Python code of our program has its home. In our example, it is the `maze_run` directory. The directory is an importable Python package; it already contains an `__init__.py` file. It also contains the file `_version.py` that automatically determines version numbers from `git`. We don't need to edit the version.py file at all. This directory is also the place where we can add our own Python modules and subpackages.

The tests/ Directory

This is where automated tests are stored. Apart from an __init__.py file, the directory should be empty. If we have already installed py.test, we can run the test suite with

```
python setup.py test
```

or

```
py.test
```

The docs/ Directory

This is a separate folder to keep documentation. Initial files for the documentation tool **Sphinx** are already there. If we have installed Sphinx (and the **make** tool), we can create and view our documentation with

```
cd docs
make html
firefox _build/html/index.html
```

You find a detailed introduction to Sphinx in Chapter 17.

The .git/ Directory

We see that pyscaffold has automatically created a new git repository and added all files as an initial commit. The hidden folder .git contains the internals of that git repository. If you already have an existing git repository, simply move all directories and files (except the .git folder) to your existing repository and run git add there. There is no *"hidden magic"* done by pyscaffold in the background.

Directories Not Created by pyscaffold

There are some other directories frequently found in Python projects, but not created by **pyscaffold**. Some will be created by scripts; others we need to create ourselves:

The bin/ Directory

By convention, the bin/ directory contains programs (both Python and non-Python) meant for execution from the command line. When installing a Python package with

```
python setup.py install
```

the programs in the bin/ directory will be installed for all users. On Linux, these will be typically installed in the /usr/bin/ directory. Installing scripts this way is a convenient method to make our Python tools available system-wide.

The Directories build/, dist/, and sdist/

As soon as you start creating releases of your program, the directories build/, dist/, and/or sdist/ will appear.

The .hg/ Directory

If you see a `.hg` directory in a project you know that the version control system **Mercurial** has been used in this project. Both `.git` and `.hg` may occur in the same directory (in this case you need to be a bit careful, because using two version control systems in parallel is not the best idea).

Data Directories

We also might want to have separate directories for input and output data in our project. It is generally wise to keep data separate from our program code. Whether we want to have data directories in our project folder or in a completely different place depends on whether we want to add data to the same `git` repository. If not, it is better to choose a separate location and use an environment variable to specify its location.

Files

Files Created by pyscaffold

README.rst

The `README` file is by far the most important file in any project. Because it is visible in the file system and on a public `git` repository, it is the first thing most developers read if they want to install the program or simply want to know what the project is about. This file should contain a brief summary of what the program does, how to install and use it, and where to find more information.

Having a README file in the **ReStructuredText** format (`.rst`) allows us to use markup language that is used by the public repositories **github** and **bitbucket** to format our description nicely. Alternatively, you can use the Markdown format (with the suffix `.md`). Both are rendered very similarly on the according GitHub page.

setup.py

The `setup.py` file is the central piece of a Python project. It contains instructions to build our program, create releases, and run tests. We can configure `setup.py` to release your program to the **Python Package Index** (pypi.python.org) or to create executables on Windows with **py2exe**. With the `setup.py` file created by pyscaffold, many of these things work out of the box. The most common use is to build your program. For instance, the following command collects everything needed to run the `maze_run` Python package in the `build/` directory:

```
python setup.py build
```

We can also install the package alongside other Python modules installed on our system:

```
python setup.py install
```

AUTHORS.rst

This file contains a simple list of developers and their contact data.

LICENSE.rst

The LICENSE.rst file is a document covering the legal aspects. By default, you as an author are the copyright holder for your software, whether this file is there or not. But if you intend to grant other people the right to use, modify, or republish your software or to make money with it, many subtle legal aspects come into play. Unless your peers are lawyers, they will prefer spending their time using the software or improving it instead of finding legal loopholes between customized licenses. Therefore it is a Best Practice to use one of the standard software licenses (MIT License, LGPL, GPL, Apache License, depending on what kind of use you want to allow) and paste the default text into this file. An overview of Open Source Licenses and their meaning in human language is available at http://choosealicense.com/.

MANIFEST.in

The MANIFEST.in file contains a list of file names and file name patterns. This list is being used to identify files that are to be included in builds and source code releases. For instance, we will find Python files from the maze_run package here, but not the tests. We can create a .tar.gz archive for distributing all files specified in the MANIFEST.in file with a single call to setup.py:

```
python setup.py sdist
```

versioneer.py

This script facilitates updating version numbers with git. It normally takes very good care of itself, so we don't have to modify it at all.

requirements.txt

This file is used by pip to keep track of required Python modules and their versions. We will take care of installing them in the section on virtualenv.

.coveragerc

A configuration file for calculating coverage by automated tests using coverage.py. We are not going to touch it in this book.

.gitattributes and .gitignore

The default configuration files for git. See Chapter 12 for details.

Files Not Created by pyscaffold

Some other files not created by pyscaffold are worth mentioning, because they are frequently found in Python projects. See Table 13-1 for an overview.

Table 13-1. *Additional Files Frequently Found in Python Projects Not Created by pyscaffold*

File Name	Description
CONTRIBUTING.md	Instructions for people who want to submit bug reports, bug fixes, or other kinds of improvements.
Makefile	If a program contains components written in C, the Makefile is the script equivalent to setup.py.
fabfile.py	A script that facilitates communication between a local and remote server installations via the **fabric** tool.
manage.py	When you see this script, you know that you are in a **Django** project.
Dockerfile	The virtualization technology **Docker** has gained a lot of popularity. The Dockerfile contains instructions to create a Docker image that encapsulates a service or other component.
tox.ini	Configuration file for the build tool **tox**.
.travis.yml	Configuration file for the ***Continuous Integration*** tool **Travis**.

Setting the Version Number of Our Program

The mechanisms established by pyscaffold facilitate managing version numbers of our project. To set a version number, use the git tag command. By convention, a version number always starts with a small 'v':

```
git tag v0.3
```

Thanks to the infrastructure created by **pyscaffold**, our Python package will find this tag automatically:

```
>>> import maze_run
>>> maze_run.__version__
'0.3'
```

Managing a Python Project Environment with virtualenv

With directories and files for our project set up, we are ready to deal with a second, fundamental aspect of our project: ***Python itself***. When managing a Python installation, we quickly run into a number of practical questions:

- Which Python version are we going to use?

- Can we test the game with Python 3.3 and Python 3.6 alike?

- Can we install additional modules without superuser privileges?

- How can we prevent Python libraries we need for different projects from interfering?

- How can we set the PYTHONPATH variable and other environment variables conveniently?

When developing a software, all of these situations are common. Sometimes, we need a Python library with a specific version in one particular project, but not in another. Sometimes, we want to develop our program further while a stable version is installed on the same machine. And in all cases, we want to prevent different projects from interfering with each other. In all these cases, **virtualenv** comes to the rescue.

Virtualenv manages multiple projects, each having a separate set of installed Python libraries. It allows us to switch quickly between projects, and our entire Python environment changes with it. At the same time it is a lightweight approach that does not produce a lot of administrative overhead. In practice, virtualenv is like a moat around our project and its Python installation. It makes sure that errors in the Python installation or configuration of libraries in our project do not spoil our entire system and vice versa (see Figure 13-2).

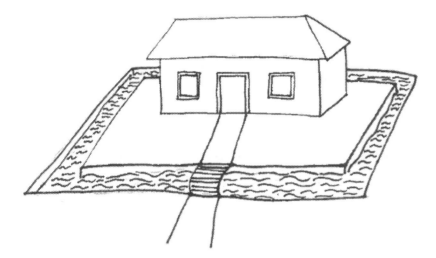

Figure 13-2. *Virtualenv is like building a moat around the house. It prevents a fire from spreading—in both directions. Likewise, a virtual environment prevents that Python projects interfere with each other.*

Installing virtualenv

For working conveniently with virtual environments, two Python packages are required. Both can be installed with `pip`. The first one is the `virtualenv` package itself:

```
sudo pip install virtualenv
```

The second, `virtualenvwrapper`, is a collection of tools that make creating virtual environments and switching between them easier:

```
sudo pip install virtualenvwrapper
```

We also need to add a few lines to the `~/.bashrc` file to let virtualenv know where to find its configuration:

```
export WORKON_HOME=$HOME/.virtualenvs
export PROJECT_HOME=$HOME/projects
source /usr/local/bin/virtualenvwrapper.sh
```

Finally, we need an extra line to make Python3 the default interpreter for projects managed by virtualenv:

```
export VIRTUALENV_PYTHON=/usr/bin/python3
```

Connecting a Project to virtualenv

We now can tell virtualenv to take over responsibility for the project folder we created with pyscaffold. First, we start a new virtualenv project with the following command:

```
mkvirtualenv maze_run
```

Using virtualenv on a pyscaffold project is not a prerequisite; virtualenv works with any kind of directory, even an empty one. We can specify a Python version explicitly:

```
mkvirtualenv maze_run -p /usr/bin/python3
```

We get the following message:

```
Running virtualenv with interpreter /usr/bin/python3
Using base prefix '/usr'
New python executable in maze_run/bin/python3
Also creating executable in maze_run/bin/python
Installing setuptools, pip.done.
```

What has happened behind the scenes? First, virtualenv creates a new subdirectory in its own folder `~/.virtualenvs/maze_run`. There, libraries and configuration scripts will be stored. In the subfolder `~/.virtualenvs/maze_run/bin/` you will find copies of Python and `pip`. These will be used instead of `/usr/bin/python3` or wherever your Python interpreter is. In practice, you now have an independent Python installation. A good thing is that we have little reason to dig around in the `~/.virtualenvs` folder; most of the time, it manages itself pretty well. In a second step, we need to connect the virtual Python environment to our project folder:

```
cd maze_run/
setvirtualenvproject ~/.virtualenvs/maze_run/ .
```

And with that, we are done! The virtual environment is ready to be used. In Figure 13-3, you find an overview what the project directory and the hidden virtualenv directory contain.

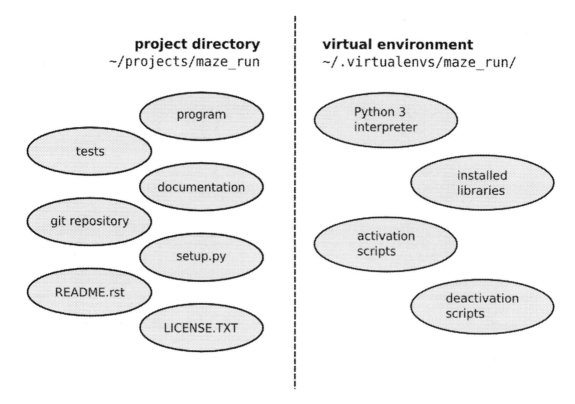

Figure 13-3. *Contents of a project directory and the according virtual environment directory. Most of the time, it is sufficient to edit only the files/directories on the left side.*

Working with a virtualenv Project

The main benefit of virtual Python environments is that we can switch between them freely. A couple of straightforward commands turn a virtual environment on or off. To start working on the maze_run project, type

```
workon maze_run
```

We see the project name (maze_run) appearing at our prompt. For example:

```
(maze_run)~/projects/maze_run:master$
```

Now, whenever we run Python, the Python installation for the virtual environment will be used. We can check it with

```
>>> import sys
>>> sys.executable
'/home/krother/.virtualenvs/maze_run/bin/python'
```

We have successfully detached our working environment from the rest of the system. Even if we replace or delete our main Python installation, the virtual environment will continue to work.

Installing Packages in virtualenv

When using the Python interpreter inside a virtual environment, you may notice that all the Python libraries you installed on your system previously have disappeared. virtualenv changes the search path for modules, so that the standard installation directory is not included any more. This might feel a little cumbersome at first, but it is exactly the point of using virtualenv. We don't need to care whether libraries installed system-wide have the right version or are broken or buggy. They are literally out of the game. Instead, our project now has its ***own*** libraries. If we need a library for our project, we have to install it from scratch using pip or python setup.py install ***within*** the virtual environment:

```
pip install pytest
```

This will install the py.test testing framework like in Chapter 8, this time in the ˜/.virtualenvs/maze run/ directory.

▓ **No administrator privileges are required to install packages**   This is a nice side effect of using virtualenv that is not only convenient but also avoids compromising system security by installing potentially harmful packages as root.

If our program requires installation of specific versions of libraries, we can write them into the requirements.txt file. For instance, we obtain the version of py.test with pip freeze and can place the result in requirements.txt. The file would then contain one library:

```
pytest==2.9.2
```

The following command installs all dependencies of a project:

```
pip -r requirements.txt
```

▓ **Doesn't installing libraries twice generate extra overhead?**   In brief, yes. If we create ten virtual environments that each require the same ten libraries, each library will be installed ten times on our system. Of course, this will use ten times more disk space. Fortunately, most Python libraries are not that big. virtualenv basically trades disk space for the freedom in modifying each installation separately.

Leaving a virtualenv Session

When we are finished working inside the virtual environment and want to switch it off, we can type

```
deactivate
```

The virtual environment is specific for a single terminal session. Thus, we can work on many projects simultaneously, as long as they are open in separate terminals.

Other shell commands for managing virtual environments include

```
lsvirtualenv
rmvirtualenv
cpvirtualenv
```

▓ **How to create many virtual environments for testing?**   If you want to test your software with many combinations of Python interpreter and library versions, you can automate the process with **Tox**. Tox automatically creates virtual environments from a list of versions and runs tests for each combination you specify. See `https://testrun.org/tox/latest/`

Configuring virtualenv Startup and Deactivation

Setting up a project environment often requires more things than creating a few directories and installing Python libraries. These could include

- setting the PYTHONPATH variable

- setting paths to C libraries

- setting environment variables with login names and passwords

- setting other environment variables

- starting database servers

- starting other services and daemons

- starting virtual machines

Also, these things need to be cleaned up when we are done working. Fortunately, `virtualenv` offers a natural place for the setup and cleanup of project-specific configurations. In the ˜/.virtualenvs/maze run/bin/ directory, there are four command-line scripts for that purpose: Each time you activate the virtual environment, preactivate and postactivate will be run. And each time you deactivate the environment, predeactivate and postdeactivate are executed. You find the precise order of events in Figure 13-4.

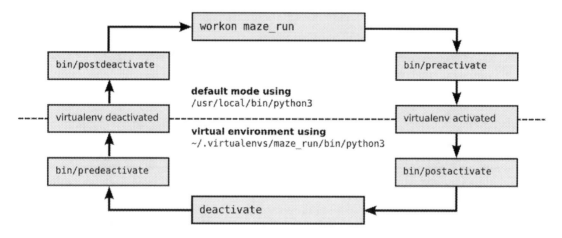

Figure 13-4. *Activation/deactivation sequence in virtualenv*

We cannot go through each of these tasks in detail here. Instead, we will look at one or two examples. Integrating others is not that difficult as long as they can be expressed as a command-line script.

Setting the PYTHONPATH Variable

By far the most common thing to place in a startup script for **virtualenv** is setting the PYTHONPATH variable. By doing so, we want to make the maze_run package available for importing in our entire project. We cannot do this system-wide (e.g., in the .bashrc file), because then our environments would start interfering with each other again. To set the variable, we need to ***export*** it in the postactivate script. The according line in the script looks like this:

```
export PYTHONPATH=/home/krother/projects/maze_run/
```

Python 3 takes good care about paths to installed libraries, so you do not need to include anything else in the PYTHONPATH most of the time.

When exporting the PYTHONPATH variable, you may also have seen the following expression:

```
export PYTHONPATH=$PYTHONPATH:/home/krother/projects/maze_run/
```

It copies the contents of the PYTHONPATH variable and appends our project directory. However, there is a nasty problem when combining this command with virtualenv! If we now would activate and deactivate our virtual environment a few times, PYTHONPATH becomes longer and longer. This will produce unwanted side effects quickly!

Installing Pygame with virtualenv

Most of the time, installing Python libraries inside virtual environments with pip works well. One notable exception is **Pygame**. To install it, we need to perform a couple of manual steps. First, several C libraries are required on the system level (mainly the SDL media library and the Version Control System **Mercurial**). On Ubuntu Linux, they can be installed with

```
sudo apt-get install mercurial python3-dev python3-numpy libav-tools \
    libsdl-image1.2-dev libsdl-mixer1.2-dev libsdl-ttf2.0-dev libsmpeg-dev \
    libsdl1.2-dev libportmidi-dev libswscale-dev libavformat-dev libavcodec-dev
```

Second, we retrieve the source code for the **Pygame** package from its repository and compile the packages:

```
hg clone https://bitbucket.org/pygame/pygame
cd pygame
python3 setup.py build
```

Now we can switch to our virtual environment and install **Pygame** there:

```
workon maze_run
cd pygame/
python3 setup.py install --prefix="$HOME/.virtualenvs/maze_run"
```

As you can see, the isolation of our project is not perfect. Because we have to install system-wide libraries, they still could possibly interfere with other projects. Also, **virtualenv** does not take care of safety or security aspects. If we accidentally write a script that deletes all files from all other projects (or a malicious attacker does so deliberately), **virtualenv** does nothing to prevent that. The isolation created by **virtualenv** makes development more convenient, nothing else. If we wanted to isolate our project more strongly, we could use a ***heavier*** virtualization technology (e.g., **Vagrant, VirtualBox, Docker,** or even deploy our program to a cloud-based service like **AWS)**. But getting any of these to work properly is a different story.

Best Practices

- Code is only one part of a Python software project.

- The **pyscaffold** tool creates a standard project structure including directories and files.

- The standard directories are for program code, tests, and documentation.

- The `setup.py` script is an entry point for testing, building, and installing your program.

- Version numbers of your software can be set with the `git tag` command.

- The **virtualenv** tool allows you to manage multiple Python environments.

- Each virtual environment manages its own set of installed libraries.

- Installing libraries in **virtualenv** does not require superuser privileges.

- Upon activating or deactivating a project, custom shell scripts can be executed.

- Virtual environments do not provide any safety or security precautions.

CHAPTER 14

Cleaning Up Code

"First make it work, then make it right, and, finally, make it fast."

—Stephen C. Johnson and Brian W. Kernighan in"The C Language and Models for Systems Programming," *Byte* magazine (August 1983)

When we learn to program in a new language, we write very small programs at first. In Python, small programs are tiny; tasks like searching a text file, shrinking a digital image, or creating a diagram can be completed with ten lines of code or less. At the beginning of a programmer's learning path, each of these lines is hard work: learning simple things such as appending a value to a list or cutting a string in two seems to take forever. Each line contains at least one bug. Consequently, we make progress in microscopic steps. But after some time our knowledge of the language becomes more firm. What seemed unachievable a few hours, days, or weeks ago, suddenly is *easy*. So we start writing more ambitious programs. We start writing code that does not fit on a single screen page any more. Quickly, our programs grow beyond 100 lines. This is an interesting size for a program, and we have reached it with the MazeRun game. We started developing the MazeRun game from scratch in the first part of the book. We incrementally added new features one by one. In this chapter, we will add one more feature. How does our programming style need to adapt to a growing program? Can we continue to add small features one by one forever? Or do we have to take care of aspects we did not consider before?

Organized and Unorganized Code

As an example, we will ***load tile data from a text file***. In Chapter 2, we implemented the tiles as a list of tuples. Placing this information in a file would make it easier to extend the in-game graphics and to test our program. We can easily store the tiles and their indices in a text file `tiles.txt`:

```
REMARK x and y positions of tiles in the .xpm file
#    0   0
     0   1
o    1   0
x    1   1
.    2   0
*    3   0
g    5   0
```

To use this information, we need to **read the text file, parse its contents, and collect the bounding rectangles of all tiles as a dictionary containing Pygame.Rect objects**. We also need to ignore the line starting with REMARK. Both reading and parsing can be done with a small Python program. The first working version of the code written by a less experienced Python programmer might look like this:

```python
tilefile = open('tiles.txt')
TILE_POSITIONS = {}
for text_str in tilefile.readlines():
    print([text_str])
    x = text_str[2]
    # print(data)
    # if 'REMARK' in data == True: # didn't work
    data = text_str
    if text_str.find('REMARK') == 0:
        text_str = text_str.strip()
        #print(line[7:]) # doesnt need to be printed
        continue
    else:
        import pygame
        y = int(text_str[4])
        r = pygame.rect.Rect(int(x)*32, int(y)*32, int(32), int(32))
        key = data.split()[0]
        TILE_POSITIONS[key] = r
        # print(TILE_POSITIONS[-1])
    continue
print(TILE_POSITIONS)
```

This program works correctly, but it looks very messy. The code is hard to understand, mostly because we have to read and understand all the lines to figure out what the program does. For sure, the program contains unnecessary lines, although we may not easily see which. For skilled Python programmers, on the other hand, parsing a text file won't be a real challenge. They might give in to the temptation to solve the task with as few lines as possible:

```python
from pygame import Rect


mkrect = lambda x: (x[0], Rect(int(x[1])*32, int(x[2])*32, 32, 32))
tile_positions = dict(map(mkrect, [l.split('\t') for l in open('tiles.txt')\
    if l[0]!='R']))

print(tile_positions)
```

This program works correctly as well. Although shorter, it not easy to comprehend either. We could argue which of the two programs is the uglier one: one might prefer the second for brevity or the first because it uses less complicated language features, making it (theoretically) more accessible for a novice programmer. I will leave that decision up to you, because there is a lot to improve in both programs! In this chapter, we will **clean up** these programs for reading tile coordinates from a text file.

Software Entropy: Causes of Unorganized Code

When a program grows, it becomes **unorganized** more easily. Keeping our programs clean becomes more important. But why do programs become unorganized in the first place? Why do we need to organize more and do more cleanup work when a program grows? As we saw in the preceding section, there are multiple possibilities to solve the same programming problem. Obviously, the number of possible implementations grows with increasing size. Suppose we divide a four-line program into functions. For simplicity, let us assume we can move the boundaries between functions freely. We could create four functions with one line each, or we could have one four-line function, two two-line functions, and three other combinations (see Figure 14-1). Now consider dividing an eight-line program into functions. With the code being twice as long, we could create eight one-line functions. We could create one eight-line function. We could create between one and four two-line functions. We could create any combination of sizes in between. The number of possibilities grows much faster than the number of lines. If we take into account not only functions but all kinds of program constructs (lists vs. dictionaries, for loops vs. list comprehensions, classes, modules, etc.), the number of possible implementations for the same problem becomes practically infinite.

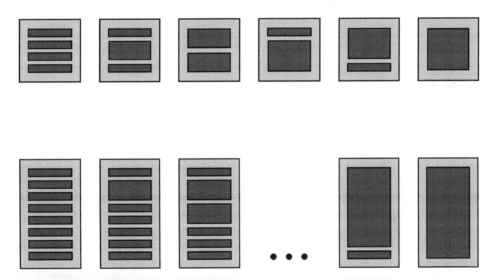

Figure 14-1. *Possibilities to structure a program into functions. Top row: a four-line program; all six possibilities are shown (four one-line functions, two two-line functions, etc.). Bottom row: an eight-line program; only five out of many possibilities are shown. With more rows, the number of possible structures grows exponentially.*

Which of these possible implementations is the best? That depends on what our program does, the kind of input used, what libraries we are using, and the expectations of the users. We will call this briefly the **context** of your program. Now there is a nasty fact: **When a program grows, the context will change**. When we add new functionality, new types of input, new libraries, the context shifts gradually. When the context changes, code that seemed the best solution before becomes an inferior one. Changing context is one main reason why finding the *ideal* implementation is hard.

A second cause of unorganized code is that programs are written by humans. For instance, it is easier to write code that works than code that works **and** is neatly written. Programs are usually written in multiple sessions. It occurs that we start adding something to the program one day, but forget to finish it the next. Last but not least, time pressure causes code to be written quickly instead of cleanly. Keeping code clean requires high self-discipline by the programmer and is a constant battle against laziness, forgetfulness, haste, and other manifestations of human imperfection.

For both reasons, ***changing context*** and ***human imperfection***, it is an intrinsic property of all programs that they become ***unorganized*** over time. This phenomenon of code unorganizing itself has been termed **Software Entropy**, borrowing the concept from the ***Second Law of Thermodynamics***. In less glamorous terms the law says: ***Disorder grows by itself***. Whatever the reasons are, it is us who have to clean up. We need to know how to recognize, clean up, or prevent unorganized code.

How to Recognize Unorganized Code?

There are many ways in which code can be unorganized. Some of them have been given fancy names like **code smells** or **unpythonic code**. These terms are good to start a conversation about coding practices with other Python programmers. However, when we are looking for clear rules these keywords are of little use. There is no definition what ***pythonic*** code is and what not. Here, we will instead examine four aspects of code that needs cleanup: **readability, structural weaknesses, redundancy, and design weaknesses.**

Readability

In a bigger program, we spend more time reading than writing code. Therefore it is crucial that the code is understandable. We can ask ourselves a very simple question: **Do we understand the code when we read it?** Code written by both beginners and advanced programmers can be more or less readable. Clearly, littering code with `print` statements and commented lines like in the first example makes it less readable. In the second example, playing ***code golf*** (solving the problem with as few keystrokes as possible) doesn't help either. Readability starts with small things. Compare the line

```
if text_str.find('REMARK') == 0:
```

with the semantically identical line

```
if line.startswith('REMARK'):
```

The second expression is closer to English, more ***explicit***, and thus more readable. Readability manifests itself in many aspects of the code: choosing descriptive variable names, code formatting, reasonable choice of data structures (imagine writing a program using only tuples), code modularization, and use of comments. Of course, experience matters when reading code. Knowing advanced language features and some libraries is part of the game. But many times it is necessary to look at a section of code and quickly figure out **what** it does and **why** it exists instead of manually tracing the code line by line. If you find it difficult to answer these questions without executing the code in your mind, readability needs to be improved.

Structural Weaknesses

There are two very common kinds of structural weaknesses: The first is lack of structure. A typical sign that structure is lacking are big blobs of code not containing any structure: functions with 100 lines and more, programs without any functions, and so on. In Python, it is ok to write programs without any functions. For instance, I frequently write short data analysis scripts without even thinking about functions. But above 100 lines, they become throwaway code very quickly. Above 100 lines, structuring is necessary, and the bigger the program, the more important it becomes.

The second structural weakness are pseudostructures, code that looks structured but in fact is another form of monolithic blob. A straightforward example are multiple `for` loops, `if` conditions, and other code blocks like in the following example:

```
for line in tilefile:
    if not line.startswith('REMARK'):
        try:
            columns = line.split('\t')
            if len(columns) == 3:
                x = int(columns[1])
                y = int(columns[2])
                if 0 < x 100:
                    if 0 < y < 100:
                        r = Rect(...)
                        ...
```

As a rule of thumb, when you reach the fourth level of indentation in any Python program (everything before column 16 being whitespace), something is weird. Usually the code can be improved by restructuring it. Especially, if there are multiple nested `for` loops, performance may quickly suffer.

A less obvious example of pseudostructures is code split into multiple functions, but with responsibilities that are not clearly defined. Consider the following example:

```
def get_number():
    a = input("enter first number")
    return a

def calculate(a):
    b = input("enter second number")
    result = float(a) + (b)
    print("the result of the addition is:", end="")
    return result

def output(r):
    print("{}".format(r))

num = get_number()
result = calculate(num)
output(result)
```

In this example, input and output are partially performed by the `calculate` function. The boundaries between functions are hard to understand, and the code becomes harder to manage. This kind of structural weakness becomes very common when the code becomes longer. There are many other kinds of structural weaknesses.

Redundancy

Redundancy violates the ***Don't Repeat Yourself*** principle (DRY) of programming. Commonly, redundancy emerges from copy-pasting code fragments. The most obvious form of redundancy are duplicate lines. For instance, in the first code example of this chapter, the `continue` statement occurs twice:

```
...
if text_str.find('REMARK') == 0:
    ...
    continue
...
continue
```

In this case, the first `continue` is redundant, because the second one will be executed. The second `continue` is redundant as well, because the loop terminates anyway. Redundant lines like these increase the size of the program and compromise readability. In this case, we can simply remove them. Another kind of redundancy is when blocks of code repeat with small variations. Sometimes, repetitive blocks emerge, because the programmer uses `Ctrl-C` + `Ctrl-V` as a programming tool; sometimes they evolve by themselves. In both cases, duplicate code blocks can be removed by moving the redundant lines into a separate function or class. Such reorganizations, called **refactoring**, can become complex operations in a bigger program. A more subtle form of redundancy is redundancy in data structures. Given that redundancy occurs on many levels and is sometimes hard to see, it is not surprising that redundancy is among the top reasons for defects in larger programs.

Design Weaknesses

Program design is a more difficult aspect. Good program design leads to ***robust*** programs that are tolerant toward unusual inputs and have a well-defined range of accepted values and clear error messages when the input is wrong. In general, robust design prevents defects from creeping in. In the MazeRun game, there is at least one design weakness: the random maze generator sometimes creates inaccessible spots in the maze. This is not a problem at the moment, but it might become one in the future.

A second aspect of good design is ***extensibility***: How easy or hard is it to add something new to the program without breaking existing functionality. The fewer places need to be changed in order to implement a simple feature, the more extensible the design is. Good design ***anticipates*** what kind of changes will occur in the future. When you would like to evaluate a design, ask yourself: **How comfortable would you feel about changing the code?** If there are regions you would prefer not to touch, the design might need improvement.

Taken together, code that is hard to read, unstructured, redundant or contains design flaws may be considered ***unorganized*** (see **Figure** 14-2). Often, several of these symptoms occur together. You can find all four symptoms in the two code fragments for loading the tile coordinates. Now imagine similar symptoms in a 1000-line program that stretches over many screen pages—again, the problem grows with increasing size. But it does not help us to complain about badly organized code; we need to think about how to improve it. Therefore, we will look at a few Best Practices of cleaning up Python programs next.

Figure 14-2. *"I don't get it. The kitchen got dirty all by itself." Software becomes messy over time.*

Cleaning Up Python Instructions

I hope that the preceding examples have convinced you that cleaning up code is a necessity. The principle of Software Entropy tells us that code becomes unorganized by itself, but it does not clean up itself (also see Figure 14-2). Cleaning up code is an everyday programming task. Cleaning up code involves a number of very simple tasks. Most of them require little knowledge of Python, so that we can start right away to improve our initial implementation. To clean up code, it helps to have a ***working*** version of the code to start with. Ideally, there are automated tests that tell us if we broke anything. Let's brush, wipe, and polish until our code shines!

Place import Statements Together

To understand a program, it is necessary to know which other modules it requires to work (its ***dependencies***). In Python, dependencies are mainly reflected by import statements. The first functional unit of a Python program should therefore be a separate block with all import statements. We simply collect all import statements from our program and move them to the beginning of the file. This way, it is easy to see which components the code requires at one glance. It is worth importing only the Python objects that are really used. In our case, there is a single import statement, and we only use pygame.Rect. Our import block becomes:

```
from pygame import Rect
```

We separate the imports from any code that follows by an empty line.

Place Constants Together

After the import section is a good place for all **constants**. A constant is a variable whose value does not change during program execution. Typical constants are input and output file names, path variables, column labels, or scaling factors used in calculations. We will simply collect all these constants in a separate section after the import block. In Python, there are no technical means to make a variable *constant*; their values can always be overwritten. To make it easier to distinguish constants from variables that change their value, Python constants are by convention written in UPPER_CASE letters. We have two constants in the tile coordinate loader. First, there is the size of tiles in pixels we need for calculating rectangles. We will place it in a constant SIZE. Second, there is the file name "tiles.txt". This file name assumes the file is in the current directory. To make the program usable from different locations, we need to provide the full path. We could write

```
TILE_POSITION_FILE = '/home/krother/projects/maze_run/tiles.txt'
```

However, this will only work on my own computer, which makes the code very inflexible. A better alternative for file names is to use the expression os.path.dirname(__file__) to determine the location of the current Python module. We can then add our filename to the path with os.path.join. The complete import and constant sections of the program are now:

```
import os
from pygame import Rect

CONFIG_PATH = os.path.split(__file__)[0]
TILE_POSITION_FILE = os.path.join(CONFIG_PATH, 'tiles.txt')
SIZE = 32
```

Again, we separate the constants from other code blocks by one or two empty lines. In the initial messy code, the variable **TILE_POSITIONS** looks like a constant but is modified by the program. We change it to lower case for later use:

```
tile_positions = {}
```

As a program evolves, many constants will change. In a program below 1000 lines, such changes are often easy to accommodate by editing the code. But if the values of constants change every second time you run the program, it is time to move them to an input file, to create a command-line option using the **argparse** module or read a configuration file using the **configparser** module.

Remove Unnecessary Lines

In programming, lines we think are important at first, later may turn out to be not important at all. A frequent intuitive reaction is to think *"**maybe I will need them later**"* and leave the unnecessary code in. However, a program is not a warehouse! Unnecessary code needs to be culled rigorously. If you have illustrative code examples that you don't want to lose, copy them to a separate file and create a separate git commit for it. In our example, we have many examples of unnecessary lines: print statements, commented lines, and the redundant continue statements mentioned previously. We can simply delete them (seven lines in total). The program becomes much more readable immediately! Now it becomes easier to notice that there is an redundant variable assignment:

```
data = text_str
```

The variables data and text_str are identical. We can get rid of the extra assignment. We might also recognize that the following if condition is a blind alley:

```
if text_str.find('REMARK') == 0:
    text_str = text_str.strip()
```

The modified variable text_str is not used afterward. We can therefore get rid of this code block and replace the following else by the opposite of the if statement. As a result, our procedure becomes a lot clearer than it was before:

```
tile_positions = {}
for text_str in open(TILE_POSITION_FILE).readlines():
    x = text_str[2]
    if text_str.find('REMARK') != 0:
        y = int(text_str[4])
        r = Rect(int(x)*32, int(y)*32, int(32), int(32))
        key = text_str.split()[0]
        tile_positions[key] = r
print(tile_positions)
```

After removing lines, it is a very good moment to verify that the program is still working. We have already cleaned up many issues in our code, but we are not done yet.

Choose Meaningful Variable Names

Well-chosen variable names have a ***huge*** impact on readability. As a general rule, names containing English words are better than acronyms. English words that describe ***meaning*** are better than words describing a ***variable type***. Very short variable names are often fine if the variables themselves are short-lived (e.g., x and y in our example). We can improve the readability by replacing r with rect, key with name, and text_str with row. Table 14-1 contains a few examples of good and bad variable names.

Table 14-1. *Examples of Bad and Good Variable Names*

Bad	Good	Explanation
xs	xsize	xs is too short
str_list	column_labels	str_list describes a type
dat	book	dat is not meaningful
xy	position	xy is not meaningful
plrpos	player position	explicit words
line_from_text_file	line	too much reference
l	?	The worst variable name of all time! Depending on the font, it could be easily mistaken for a 1.

It is worth rechecking variable names from time to time. Their meaning changes while you develop the code—an incomprehensible variable name is bad, but a misleading one is even worse. With cleaned-up variable names, defects usually become easier to find.

Idiomatic Python Code

There are a few minor improvements to be made. We can use **Python idioms**, short, precise expressions that are applicable in many situations. Here, I would like to give just two short examples. First, we can make the conditional expression more readable, as mentioned previously:

```
if not row.startswith('REMARK'):
```

Second, we can use the `csv` module to pick the columns of the file apart. This is less error-prone than parsing the file yourself. Also, using the `with` statement is a generally recommended way to open files (because they are closed automatically afterward):

```
with open(filename) as f:
    for row in csv.reader(f, delimiter='\t'):
```

Finding the right idioms is difficult, and opinions on which idiom is the best differ. It requires a combination of knowledge and experience. There is neither a complete catalog of Python idioms nor a set if clear rules when to use them. The closest thing is the book *Fluent Python* by Luciano Ramalho (O'Reilly, 2015).

Refactoring

Until now, our cleanup was mostly focused on individual lines. In the next section, we will examine the structure of the program as a whole. Improving the program structure is referred to as **refactoring**. Refactoring is an important Best Practice to maintain larger programs. Entire books are devoted to refactoring techniques, and we can only get a glimpse of the topic here. If you would like to get an idea what kind of refactorings exist, the website `https://sourcemaking.com/refactoring` is a good starting point.

▓ **Hint**   When refactoring code on a larger scale, having a good Test Suite is essential. The goal of refactoring is **always** to have the program do the same thing as before. It is quite easy (and tempting) to take a program apart, reassemble it, and miss a detail that causes the program to work differently afterward.

After the basic cleanup, we will focus on improving the structure of our code further. Generally, structuring means creating clearly separated functions, classes, modules, and other units of code.

Extract Functions

Probably the most important refactoring is to divide code into well-chosen functions. There are different reasons to write functions in Python. Here we do it mainly to divide a longer piece of code into smaller chunks. To extract a function from existing code, we need to write a function definition and define input parameters and a return statement for the output. We indent the code in between and add a call to the function, and a docstring. For instance, we can extract a function for creating Rect objects from our code:

```
def get_rectangle(row):
    """Returns a pygame.Rect for a given tile"""
    x = int(row[1])
    y = int(row[2])
    return Rect(x*SIZE, y*SIZE, SIZE, SIZE)
```

Creating a separate function for just three lines might seem overkill at first. You may object that the code inside get_rectangle is too simple. But this is exactly the point! **We want simple code.** First, simple code stays clean for a longer time when Software Entropy sets in; for instance, if our function needs to cover one or two special cases (and grows), the code still will be readable. Second, simple code is understandable by other people (colleagues, interns, supervisors, or our successor). Third, simple code is more reliable under pressure: when programmers are plagued by deadlines, nervous managers, and after-dark debugging sessions, simple code is their best friend. We call the get_rectangle function from a second function load_tile_positions that contains most of the remaining code:

```python
def load_tile_positions(filename):
    """Returns a dictionary of positions {name: (x, y), ..} parsed from the file"""
    tile_positions = {}
    with open(filename) as f:
        for row in csv.reader(f, delimiter='\t'):
            name = row[0]
            if not name.startswith('REMARK'):
                rect = get_rectangle(row)
                tile_positions[name] = rect
    return tile_positions
```

When you want to split your own program into functions, you first need to identify a coherent piece of code and then move it into a function. There are some typical functions that frequently occur in Python programs:

- **reading input** like data files or web pages

- **parsing data** (i.e., preparing data for an analysis)

- **generating output** such as writing a data file, printing results, or visualizing data

- **calculations** of any kind

- **helper functions**, code extracted from a bigger function to make it smaller

A reasonable function size when restructuring a program is 5–20 lines. If the function will be called from multiple places, it may even be shorter. Like modules, functions deserve a triple-quoted docstring right after the function definition. The documentation string should describe what the function is doing in human language (avoid Python terminology if possible).

Create a Simple Command-Line Interface

After dividing our code into functions, it is time to create a top-level interface for the program. This interface avoids code being executed accidentally (e.g., by an import). To create the interface, we group all remaining function calls at the end of the program and wrap them in a separate code block. By convention, it starts with a weird if statement:

```python
if __name__ == '__main__':
    tile_positions = load_tile_positions(TILE_POSITION_FILE)
    print(tile_positions)
```

The if expression is a Python idiom that appears strange at first (especially if you have seen other programming languages). Expressed in human language it means: "***Execute the following block of code if this file is started as the main Python program. If this file is imported as a module, do nothing.***" The __main__ block helps us to avoid accidental execution of the code. We now can import the module from somewhere else:

```
from load_tiles import load_tile_positions
tiles = load_tile_positions(my_filename)
```

In this case nothing is printed because the __main__ block is not executed when importing. The second use of the __main__ block is that we can run load_tiles.py as a Python program:

```
python3 load_tiles.py
```

Now we see the output produced by the print statement and can check whether it matches our expectations. Having a __main__ block in our program serves as a general entry point. If our module is not meant to be executed directly, we can use the __main__ block for simple test code (the code for the first part of this book contains a few examples). If we are writing a program that is to be used as a command-line tool, using the argparse module instead of sys.argv is a Best Practice. In a Python project, the bin/ directory is a good place for the command-line front end.

Structuring Programs into Modules

We have created separate modules throughout the first chapters already. In this chapter, we have worked on a single module. Therefore, we will simply list a few Best Practices to keep in mind when developing your own modules:

- Modules shouldn't become too big. Modules of 100-400 lines are of a good size; modules up to 1000 lines are tolerable, but I recommend splitting them up as soon as possible.

- Each module should have a clearly defined purpose. For instance, loading data, writing data, and doing a calculation are all separate purposes that justify having their own modules. Also, if your constant section becomes large, it may be worth placing it in a separate module.

- Creating a module is as simple as moving a piece of code to a new file and adding import statements in the original file.

- Avoid circular imports at all costs. Whenever you come across a relation like *A needs B, but B needs A,* it is worth thinking about a better structure. It is always possible to avoid circular imports. You can avoid the problem by keeping A and B together, but probably this will cause problems later.

- When importing your own modules, write explicit imports (avoid import *).

- Add a triple-quoted docstring on top of each module.

Decomposing a program into separate modules is one of the easiest ways to structure programs.

The Cleaned Code

When we are done with these cleanup steps, it is time to verify that the program still works. The completely cleaned and refactored program to read tiles is

```python
"""
Load tile coordinates from a text file
"""
import csv
import os
from pygame import Rect

CONFIG_PATH = os.path.dirname(__file__)
TILE_POSITION_FILE = os.path.join(CONFIG_PATH, 'tiles.txt')
SIZE = 32

def get_rectangle(row):
    """Returns a pygame.Rect for a given tile"""
    x = int(row[1])
    y = int(row[2])
    rect = Rect(x*SIZE, y*SIZE, SIZE, SIZE)
    return rect

def load_tile_positions(filename):
    """Returns a dictionary of positions {name: (x, y), } from a text file"""
    tile_positions = {}
    with open(filename) as f:
        for row in csv.reader(f, delimiter='\t'):
            name = row[0]
            if not name.startswith('REMARK'):
                rect = get_rectangle(row)
                tile_positions[name] = rect
    return tile_positions

if __name__ == '__main__':
    tile_positions = load_tile_positions(TILE_POSITION_FILE)
    print(tile_positions)
```

We realize that the program has not become shorter than our very first implementation. It even is a bit longer. But our implementation has several advantages worth pointing out:

- It is easy to see what the program does.

- Many parts of the code are easier to read than before.

- The module can be imported and put to customized use (e.g., loading a different file or multiple ones).

- We can use both functions independently. This is very valuable for writing automated tests (in Part 3 of this book).

- When debugging the program, it is sufficient to read a maximum of 10 lines at a time.

- The program has a built-in self-test in form of the __main__ block.

207

Taken together, the program is a lot cleaner and more readable. Defects will have a much harder time hiding in this program. Also, this code will be considered well-written or *pythonic* by most experienced programmers.

PEP8 and pylint

Python has a standard coding style guide, known as **PEP8** (https://www.python.org/dev/peps/pep-0008). The PEP8 standards give clear guidelines on variable names, imports, docstrings, length of functions, indentation, and so on. Adhering to PEP8 is a Best Practice, because it makes our code readable for others. It also helps us to write in a consistent style. Fortunately, we don't need to learn the complete PEP8 guideline by heart. The **pylint** tool helps us to check whether our code conforms to the PEP8 standard. As an example, we will examine our code *before* and *after* our cleanup session with **pylint**. First, we need to install the tool with

```
pip install pylint
```

We can then analyze any Python file with

```
pylint load_tiles.py
```

The program produces several pages of console output. For us, two sections are interesting: *warning messages* and the *code score*.

Warning Messages

At the top of the **pylint** output, we find a section with warning messages that refer to PEP8 violations. Each warning contains the line number the warning refers to. For the code attributed to an inexperienced Python developer, we get

```
C: 1, 0: Missing module docstring (missing-docstring)
C: 7, 0: Invalid constant name "tilefile" (invalid-name)
```

whereas the cleaned-up code results in

```
C: 18, 4: Invalid variable name "x" (invalid-name)
C: 19, 4: Invalid variable name "y" (invalid-name)
W: 25, 4: Redefining name 'tile_positions' from outer scope (line 36) (redefined-outer-name)
C: 26,27: Invalid variable name "f" (invalid-name)
C: 36, 4: Invalid constant name "tile_positions" (invalid-name)
```

All of these warnings point us to things that could be improved. Variable names with one character are discouraged, as is using a variable with the same name inside and outside a function. We *could* start renaming our variables (make them longer) and constants (to uppercase characters). However we will restrain ourselves for a moment and scroll to the bottom of the output.

Code Score

At the end the pylint output we find a score for our code of up to 10 points:

```
Global evaluation
-----------------
Your code has been rated at 7.73/10
```

Working with pylint is sometimes very rewarding. When we start fixing PEP8 issues, we can rerun pylint and see our score improve. This makes the PEP8 standard a bit treacherous. You may have noticed that after cleaning up our code, we have ***more*** PEP8 warnings than in the previous, messy code. This tells us that the warnings and the score pylint produces do not represent bigger changes in the code well. Focusing too much on style conformity distracts from more important issue. A Best Practice is to use pylint to conform with the PEP8 style guidelines, but don't try to push every Python file to a pylint score of 10.0. Usually a score around 7.0 is already good enough. It is OK to ignore warning messages you do not agree with. Use your reason. According to Python core developer Raymond Hettinger, "***PEP8 is a guideline, not a lawbook.***" Think of PEP8 as a layer of paint on our building (see Figure 14-3). It improves how our code looks, but it does not support the roof.

Figure 14-3. *Adhering to the PEP8 coding standard is like a good layer of paint: it looks beautiful and protects your code from bad weather.*

Make It Work, Make It Right, Make It Fast

When writing small programs that fit on one screen page, it was not much of a problem *how* exactly the code was written. We cared mostly about getting the program to run. But with growing size, the lack of readability will fall on our feet. We need to organize our code, or make it *right*. During our cleanup, we followed a guideline formulated by Stephen C. Johnson and Brian W. Kernighan: *"First make it work, then make it right, and, finally, make it fast."* This guideline has been attributed to different people, including Kent Beck (also see http://c2.com/cgi/wiki?MakeItWorkMakeItRightMakeItFast). It certainly applies to Python programs above 100 lines. Let's take a closer look at the three parts of the guideline.

Make It Work

Here, *work* means that the program finishes without Exceptions and that there are no semantic errors that we know of. In Part 1, we have already learned many debugging techniques to make a program work. In Part 2, we used **automated testing** to detect defects more thoroughly.

Make It Right

Making it right generally means **organizing** your code. In this chapter, we have already seen cleanup steps to make a program more **readable** and **well-structured** and to make the **logic** of execution transparent. However, these cleanup strategies are only the beginning. Keeping code well-organized becomes more important, as our programs grow further. Besides organizing functions and modules, designing **classes** and their interplay, building Python **packages,** and developing an **architecture** including all components of a system are topics where you can expect to find a lot of **refactoring**. These topics go beyond the scope of this book, though.

Make It Fast

When your program works correctly and is well-structured and readable, it is worth looking at its performance. Often at this stage, a program turns out to be *fast enough* already. If it is not, well-organized code is at least easier to tune for higher performance. There are many options to accelerate Python programs, ranging from adding computing power and compiling Python to faster programming languages and eliminating bottlenecks from the Python code itself. Performance optimization is not a topic of this book, but in Chapter 11 you find an example for writing **performance tests**.

Examples of Well-Organized Code

The transition from less than 100 to above 100 lines of Python code is interesting. When a program grows beyond 100 lines, there are *very many* possibilities to write the same program. Which is the right one? To give you some tentative answers, we look at the structures of programs written by some of the best Python programmers on the planet. In Table 14-2, the structures of seven Python projects by well-known programmers are summarized. Instead of their (mostly huge) main projects, I selected smaller everyday or pet projects for the comparison. The projects are

- **shirts** by **Joel Grus**, author of the book ***Data Science from Scratch* (O'Reilly, 2015)**. The program compares images of T-shirts using machine learning. (https://github.com/joelgrus/shirts)

- **pipsi** by **Armin Ronacher**, author of the web framework *Flask*. pipsi is a tool to make package installation into virtual environments easier. (`https://github.com/mitsuhiko/pipsi`)

- **crawler** by **Guido van Rossum**, the inventor of Python himself, is a fast web crawler to follow links in web pages in under 500 lines. (`https://github.com/gvanrossum/500lines/tree/master/crawler`)

- **move-out** by **Ola Sitarska**, one of two developers who ignited the **Djangogirls** movement, is a Django web application to share stuff when moving out. (`https://github.com/olasitarska/move-out`)

- **python-progressbar** by **Nilton Volpato** is a module to display progress bars on the command line. (`https://github.com/niltonvolpato/progressbar`)

- **gizeh** by **Zulko**, a serial author of graphics libraries for Python, is a package to create vector graphics in Python. (`https://github.com/Zulko/gizeh`)

Table 14-2. *Metrics for Seven Python Projects of Between 100–1000 Lines. The packages, modules, functions, and classes were counted with Unix command-line tools. The comments, blank, and code lines were counted with the **cloc** tool.*

Project	Packages	Modules	Funcs	Classes	Blank Lines	Comments	Code Lines
shirts	0	2	6	0	59	55	227
pipsi	0	5	40	2	123	22	486
crawler	0	3	30	5	91	90	531
move-out	3	23	35	25	170	34	599
python-progressbar	1	6	61	17	223	231	567
gizeh	1	14	57	5	230	242	614

When comparing the projects in Table 14-2, we see that all projects contain 10%–25% empty lines and up to 25% lines with comments. We also see that there are big differences in the structures of the code. The **shirts** project is essentially a cleaned and commented linear script for data analysis, while **pipsi** and **python-progressbar** are decomposed into 40+ smaller code units usable for different purposes. Classes are used by most but not all of the authors (e.g., **gizeh** places a stronger emphasis on functions, while **move-out** uses classes derived from the Django framework). We conclude that even among prominent programmers, there is apparently more than one way to do it right.

Best Practices

- There are infinite possibilities to implement the same functionality.

- Software Entropy is the phenomenon that code becomes unorganized over time.

- Unorganized code is less readable, less structured, or redundant or contains other design weaknesses.

- Cleaning up code is an everyday programming task.

- Place `import` statements at the beginning of a Python module.

- Place **constants** together, their names written in UPPER_CASE.

- Unnecessary lines need to be removed rigorously.

- Variables should have meaningful names.

- **Refactoring** a program into small, simple functions makes it easier to understand.

- Large programs should be split into modules of up to 400 lines.

- A __main__ block is not executed upon imports.

- **pylint** is a tool that checks adherence to the **PEP8** coding standard.

- Obey the central Dogma of Programming: Make it work, make it nice, make it fast.

CHAPTER 15

▓ ▓ ▓

Decomposing Programming Tasks

The programmer, like the poet, works only slightly removed from pure thought-stuff.
– Fred Brooks,

—The Mythical Man-Month

A crucial part of programming is to divide a problem into smaller parts. This **problem decomposition** is an essential skill of every programmer. No matter whether you want to write a program from scratch or add functionality to an existing problem, you need to decompose the programming problem first. Problem decomposition, also called **requirements analysis**, is a skill underestimated by inexperienced and experienced programmers alike. The former underestimate it because they are busy mastering the programming language itself, the latter because they think it is trivial and they have it figured out already (although they are often right). It is therefore not surprising that many programming projects run into problems because of lacking or bad decomposition of its functionality. As a result, products are brittle and suffer heavily from Software Entropy, they take longer than expected, or they fail completely. Such problems have been reported by individuals and big development teams, by teams using a traditional software engineering approach and by dynamic, Agile teams. This chapter is dedicated to decomposing programming tasks to help you write software that is less prone to this pitfall.

Decomposing Programming Tasks Is Difficult

But why is decomposing programming problems difficult? Let us consider an exemplary programming task: *We want to add a ghost to our game. The ghost shall move randomly through the maze, trying to eat the player.* How can we decompose this feature? Intuitively, dividing a problem into smaller pieces can be thought of hierarchically (see Figure 15-1). We first divide it into two smaller subproblems. Then we decompose each subproblem into even smaller ones. Finally, we implement all the smaller parts and we are done.

© Kristian Rother 2017
K. Rother, *Pro Python Best Practices*, DOI 10.1007/978-1-4842-2241-6_15

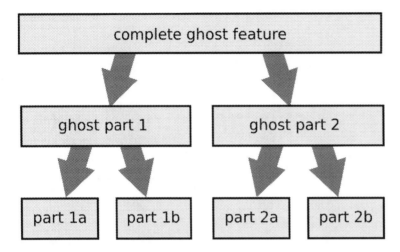

Figure 15-1. *Hierarchical decomposition of a programming problem. First, the problem is divided into two separate subproblems, which are divided further. Unfortunately, this approach rarely works in practice.*

This is a nice model. Unfortunately, it does not work for all but the most simple programs. The reason is that the smaller components in the majority of programs are highly interdependent. Most programming problems are *multidimensional*. There are multiple **problem dimensions** that we need to keep in mind:

- **the programming task itself**—what *exactly* is it that we are trying to program?

- **data**—what information do we need to store in the program and how is it structured?

- **control flow**—in what sequence does the program perform its tasks?

- **technologies**—what components (pythonic and non-pythonic) does the software consist of?

- **cost**—which features are affordable and which are not?

All of these dimensions (and others not mentioned here) depend on each other. Over the years, many books addressing decomposition have been written. They reach into very diverse fields like **Requirements Analysis**, **Universal Modeling Language (UML)**, and **Scrum**. All of these are very powerful techniques. In a (mostly corporate) environment where one of these methodologies is being applied in large projects they are certainly worth learning about. But for the average Python programmer they are not very helpful.

Is there anything that makes decomposing problems in Python special? There is: One key advantage of Python is its rapid speed of development. It is very tempting not to spend *any* time on planning and start programming right away. A good approach to decomposition needs to be *fast* as well, so that we do not jeopardize the advantage Python gives us. This is why this chapter describes a **lightweight decomposition process** that is applicable within minutes or a few hours. We are going to decompose the ghost feature in detail. Finally, we will start implementing it in this chapter.

A Process to Decompose Programming Tasks

Decomposing programming tasks is difficult, because we have to make design decisions in multiple dimensions (functionality, data, control flow, technologies, cost). To avoid premature design decisions, we need to deal with these dimensions more or less in parallel. What does that mean? Our initial view of a program feature resembles a cloud (see Figure 15-2). We have a rough idea what the program should do, but the functionality is too imprecise to implement it. During the design process, components start emerging from the cloud and take shape. Instead of fixing one dimension completely before starting the next, we will balance each dimension against the others in parallel, thus solving big design problems. Finally, the components have gained enough sharpness that an implementation is feasible. If the path from a feature to its implementation is clear, we can say that the feature is fully decomposed.

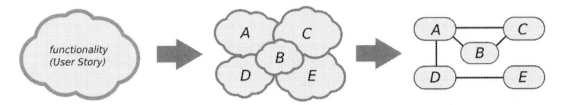

Figure 15-2. *A program feature is like a blurry cloud in the beginning. Only by decomposing it will details of the functionality and program components become apparent. When we finally arrive at sharply defined, implementable components, the decomposition is complete.*

In the following, we will decompose the ghost feature into smaller parts using a seven-step process:

1. Write a **User Story**, a simple description of the programming task

2. Add details to the description

3. Check nonfunctional requirements

4. Identify possible problems

5. Decide on an architecture that solves the main problems

6. Identify program components

7. Implement

This process reflects what many programmers do intuitively when implementing an *easy* piece of functionality. Going through the seven steps systematically, we can apply the same process to more *difficult* tasks as well. In the process, we make *conscious* design decisions to find components in the cloud that are implementable in Python. This is what we will do next.

Can we extend an existing program using this process? Yes! Very little software is developed *from scratch*. The process of decomposition does not differ fundamentally between starting from zero or extending an existing program. Of course when adding to existing software we need to take into account what we already have (in step 3 and beyond), because we shouldn't turn our design upside down every time we add a piece of functionality.

Write a User Story

The first step is to write down what we want to program. This description must be short enough to fit on a small piece of paper (A6 paper cards). The description also must be simple enough that a nonprogrammer is able to see value in it. Such descriptions are also called **User Stories**. For the ghost, the according User Story could be (also see Figure 15-3): *As a player, I want a ghost, so that I can run away from it through the maze.* The sentence structure of this User Stories is a standard Best Practice. For more clarity, many developers have agreed to use the structure "*As a (type of user), I want (some goal), so that (some reason).*" This structure of User Stories not only documents *what* program feature to implement but also *why* the feature was introduced. Also see https://www.mountaingoatsoftware.com/agile/user-stories. The value of our User Story is of course that the game with a ghost is more interesting than without. Although writing down the feature is a simple thing to do, it improves the work of a programmer in many ways:

- The task becomes *tangible*. User Stories are easy to manage in whatever project management approach is used. We can prioritize them, estimate or track the time to completion and, of course, check whether they are finished. A common Best Practice when writing User Stories is to keep them in a well-visible place. Surprisingly, paper cards or a board are often superior to electronic systems.

- The description helps us to *focus*. Including something in the description that users of the program will *see* or *do* helps us to develop a more useful program than if we would write "*implement a ghost module in Python.*"

- The description is ignorant of technical details. At this point, it is too early to decide *how* the functionality will be implemented.

- Most importantly, a User Story makes it apparent that our understanding of the functionality might be **incomplete**. We will need to think or communicate further to clarify the details we want to implement. Therefore User Stories have also been referred to as a "*promise of communication.*"

Figure 15-3. *User Story for adding a ghost to the game. A User Story is a short description of a program feature with an emphasis on the value the feature has for users.*

Whenever you start working on a new piece of program, writing down User Stories for all planned features is an easy first step to get organized.

Add Details to the Description

From the preceding simple description we can already see that the ghost will change our program considerably. Previously, we only needed to react to keys pressed by a user. Now, the ghost and the player will move simultaneously: there is *concurrency*. This is a very dangerous moment for a programmer. When encountering concepts like *"concurrency,"* interesting things happen. Less experienced but smart programmers raise their hands saying *"Wait! I have no idea how to do this."* More experienced, enthusiastic programmers tend to come up with their preferred solution immediately (e.g., *"Python threads are the ideal solution for that"* or *"Avoid threading in Python at all costs. The GIL will drive you crazy!"*). The resulting discussions among experienced programmers can be a bit intimidating for others. Also, it may be too early to decide on a technical solution. Whether you see many possible solutions or none at all it is worth collecting more information.

Acceptance Criteria

A constructive way to deal with the new situation is to gather details about the problem first. Many times, simply jotting down a list of **bullet points** is the best thing we can do. The bullet points for the ghost feature could look like this:

- The player and the ghost must move in parallel.

- The ghost moves in regular intervals (below one second per square).

- The ghost moves straight in one direction until it hits a wall. Then it changes the direction randomly.

- The ghost does not eat dots.

- When ghost and player are on the same square, the game terminates.

Such details of a feature are sometimes called **acceptance criteria** or **requirements**, depending on the project methodology. In an Agile project, the acceptance criteria fit on another A6 card. In big, traditional software projects, the requirements sometimes grow to documents with hundreds or thousands of pages. The latter is definitely **not** what we want to happen in an average Python project. For us it is sufficient to keep requirements in a small text file or on the back side of User Story cards. If a simple bullet-point list is not enough, we can add **textual descriptions** and **diagrams** describing the feature in even more detail. If such information already exists (e-mails with instructions, articles, examples, meeting minutes), it is a good idea to keep that information close to the other descriptions.

Use Case Descriptions

Unless we are writing a huge piece of software, I wouldn't start by writing a long textual description of features we are going to implement: they are probably going to change anyway. A faster pragmatic planning technique than writing text is to write down a sequence of events or **Use Case description**. A Use Case description is a list of events that are to happen in a certain order. For instance, we can describe the movement of the ghost like in Figure 15-4. The Use Case description is already much more similar to Python code than the User Story was. But still, there are no *technical terms* inside; we still do not need to decide whether the movement of the ghost will be handled by a single function (maybe), by ten different classes (maybe), or whether it will be better to implement it in the COBOL language (very improbable).

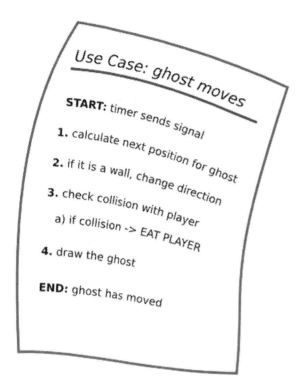

Figure 15-4. *Use Case for moving the ghost. The movement feature has been broken down into a chronological order of steps that make it easier to reason about it. This Use Case description is not exhaustively accurate, nor does it suggest how to implement the feature. The description simply helps us to gradually shift to higher precision while postponing technical decisions.*

The Use Case in Figure 15-4 contains a branch (in 3a) when the player gets eaten. A Use Case may, but doesn't have to, contain branches. If there are many different situations, it is usually sufficient to pick a few representative ones. Use Cases do not have to be complete. It still needs to fit on a slide or a piece of paper. Don't worry if there is more than one "*correct*" sequence, either. We will find out in the next steps. Descriptions of Use Cases are a tool that helps to break down the hard cases. Most of the time, a list of bullet points will add sufficient detail to proceed toward the implementation.

Check Nonfunctional Requirements

In the first two steps, we have described the *functionality* we want to implement in sufficient detail. In this step, we will pay attention to a more subtle part of development: the **nonfunctional requirements**. What is a nonfunctional requirement? In a nutshell, nonfunctional requirements are all constraints on the project that are not directly related to the *functionality* we are implementing. These include, for example, **technologies, development methods, platforms, performance and other technical parameters, and ethical and legal issues**. Safety and security also are part of the nonfunctional requirements, but as stated in Chapter 1 we won't discuss them in this book. Some of the nonfunctional requirements for the **MazeRun** game are as follows:

- The game needs to be written in Python because of the book title (technology).

- The game needs to have automated tests (development method).

- The game needs to be installable on Linux, Windows, and Mac, so that many developers can experiment with it (platforms).

- The source code needs to be less than 1000 lines long to fit in a book (technical parameter).

- There are between zero and ten ghosts moving in intervals of 0.1–1.0 seconds (technical parameter).

- The game needs to be suitable for six-year olds (ethical).

- The game needs to be publishable on GitHub under an open source license (legal).

Why are the nonfunctional requirements important? Imagine we added a nonfunctional requirement that, in addition to the preceding, **MazeRun** should run on Android and iOS phones and be able to handle 10,000 simultaneous ghosts chasing the player (to make sure even the most hyperactive mobile phone users don't get bored). The outcome would be a totally different program, and we would have to use different technologies than Python and SDL to get it running. Being wrong about nonfunctional requirements has the potential to make a program completely useless, so skipping this step is not optional.

On a deeper level, the nonfunctional requirements help us to determine *what kind of program* we are writing. The first working version of **MazeRun** (the one without the ghost from Chapter 7) could be developed into many different games: a chess-like strategy game with a efficient AI (not in this book), a fast-paced shooter game with lots of fancy graphics (not in this book either), or a small Pacman-like game built for the purpose of reasoning about Python Best Practices (precisely!). Having a clear direction expressed as a few technical parameters or other nonfunctional requirements makes later technical decisions a lot easier.

Like with the description of functionality, writing down the nonfunctional requirements is a good idea. Fortunately, the nonfunctional requirements usually do not change during a project (however, if they do you need to be very cautious).

Identify Problems

With the functional and nonfunctional description, we hopefully have a clear picture of what the ghost feature is about and what border conditions it needs to fit into. This is a good moment to look for potential problems. What is there that still seems *difficult*? Are there any User Stories conflicting with a nonfunctional requirement? Are any of the descriptions contradicting each other? Is there anything that even sounds *impossible*? In this section, we take a break to think about problems we will need to deal with.

░ **Tip**   **Take a break** is meant literally. After spending some time (anything between 10 minutes and a few hours) writing User Stories, Use Case descriptions, and nonfunctional requirements, it is a good moment to take a step back and look at the task from a new angle. Fresh air does help!

With the ghost feature, there is one main challenge: **concurrency.** The player and ghost have to move simultaneously. At the moment, we don't have a plan for how to implement that. Here we will analyze the concurrency problem in detail to see how to approach a problem from different angles. Typically, we can expect trouble from at least four different directions: incomplete information, domain expertise, changing existing code, and anticipating future change.

Incomplete Information

When you try to apply this process on your own, you most likely will get to a point where you realize that you do not have sufficient information to continue. The description of your feature contains assumptions or simply lacks details pertaining to what your supervisor/client really needs. *This is completely normal.* When facing incomplete information, you have two options. Either you create a (quick) prototypic implementation and see whether it lives up to the expectations, or you try to get more information first. When asking for more information it may happen that your supervisor/client won't know either, because they have never thought about that question before you decomposed it. Or they come up with bright ideas that sound good at first but turn out to be useless once they are implemented. Therefore, a good strategy responding to lack of information is to proceed in small steps.

With the ghost feature, we have no information on *how* to deal with concurrency. On the other hand, we have many liberties with the feature because its main purpose is to provide a learning experience. Any working ghost will be fine, so lack of information is not a problem here.

Domain Expertise

The opposite problem is having *overabundant information*, knowing that the problem we are solving is full of exceptions and special cases. A common symptom is that we are reasoning repeatedly about very special aspects of a feature like "*Yes, but in the tax law of Anhk-Morpork, if the employee is a ghost, the tax rate is 13% instead of 21% because it is a nonphysical entity.*" If you are unfamiliar with the problem domain (Ankh-Morporkian tax law in this case), such domain-specific details quickly become overwhelming. The solution to this kind of problem is to **simplify** first. Find a model that represents the problem domain concisely, but does not oversimplify. In a well-built model of the problem domain, the special cases can be included during the implementation. **Background knowledge about the problem domain is key.** Depending on whether you are a domain expert or not, this kind of problem can be solved over a cup of coffee or by going to the library and doing extensive background research. Fortunately, every one of us has played or at least seen computer games before. We know enough about games to understand the concurrency problem in **MazeRun** stated in the preceding. Our understanding helps us to enumerate a few situations that we need to take care of:

- What happens if the player moves on the ghost? This is not *explicitly* covered by the preceding Use Case description!

- Does it make a difference whether the player moves on the ghost or the ghost on the player?

- Can the player and the ghost theoretically move at the same time so that they swap positions?

- Will the moving ghost make the player move slower?

Collecting such questions will help us to evaluate our solution.

Changing Existing Code

Adding new features to a program can be challenging because they need to fit to the already existing code. Often, the existing code needs to be reorganized to make room for the new feature. The question is how to do that without creating a total mess. In a nutshell, you need to keep the concept of *Software Entropy* introduced in Chapter 14 in mind. When thinking about the existing code for **MazeRun** in light of the concurrency problem, which parts do we need to change? For sure, the *event loop* will have to change. So far, the implementation from Chapter 4 does nothing unless the player presses a key. We will have to take a closer look at that code.

Anticipating Future Change

Another aspect of Software Entropy is that we know our program is going to change in the future. The design decisions we take now will have long-lasting effects. Therefore, we not only need to take the *current* requirements to the program into account, but also *anticipate* how the program might evolve in the future. To create a stable design, we need to know which parts of our program are *least likely* to change and which parts will change *for sure*. These parts need to be separated. Of all possible problems, this is the most difficult one. To solve it, a combination of domain expertise, experience, and luck is necessary. Recalling the past decades writing and playing computer games, some things that are very likely to change in **MazeRun** are

- additional game elements (species of ghosts, special floor tiles)

- parameters (speed of ghosts, screen size)

- graphics and animations

One aspect that everyone who plays the game realizes immediately is *the lack of animation when moving the player*. The player figure simply jumps from one square to the next. Making the movement *smooth* would indeed be a nice improvement. At first sight, this looks like a harmless feature that we could implement as a stop-motion animation in a few lines:

```
import time

for offset in range(32):
    draw_map_without_player()
    draw_player(100 + offset, 100)  # starting point (x=100, y=100)
    pygame.display.update()
    time.sleep(0.05) # seconds
```

But wait! If we add the ghost, somehow the smooth movements of ghost and player need to be coordinated. It is a concurrency problem again. Without thinking this through any further, we can expect the concurrency problem to become **even more important** in the future. To summarize, we have collected three issues in this section, all related to concurrency:

1. At present, we have no solution how to deal with parallel movement of player and ghost.

2. To allow simultaneous movement, we will need to change the event loop.

3. In the future, there will be even more things happening simultaneously.

Such a list of possible problems can get quite long. What we need to do is to prioritize them and then focus on the worst problem. In our case, concurrency is the biggest challenge. In the rest of this chapter, we will focus on solving it.

Decide on an Architecture

We have identified **concurrency** as the hardest problem. In order to add a ghost to the game, any implementation needs to solve this problem properly. Now, if this sounds easy enough already, we could skip the next two sections and start writing code. But assuming we are doing this kind of thing for the first time, it is better to consider the **architecture** of our program first. To be honest, *architecture* is a bit of a pompous word for adding a ghost to a computer game. The term *software architecture* is also used to describe things consisting of hundreds of connected servers. But I prefer *architecture* to the more modest term **software design**, because *design* is often incorrectly associated with how things look. What we are really interested in here is to find a **program structure** that helps us solve the problem. Let's look at a few potential architectures.

In Figure 15-5 we find six common **architectural patterns** used in software. Four of them are useful. A **pipeline** describes a sequence of steps that depend on each other. We find pipeline structures in programs that perform calculations, data processing, and on the tools on the Unix command line. A **layer model** is useful to organize components that talk to each other in two ways. It is the classical model web servers are built upon. A **feedback loop** is a good structure for all kinds of regulatory processes and found, for example, in monitoring tools and sensory devices. Finally, the **mediator** model organizes communication between components that do not talk to each other directly. For instance, a drawing program is structured as a mediator; the canvas is the central mediator that all the different drawing tools interact with.

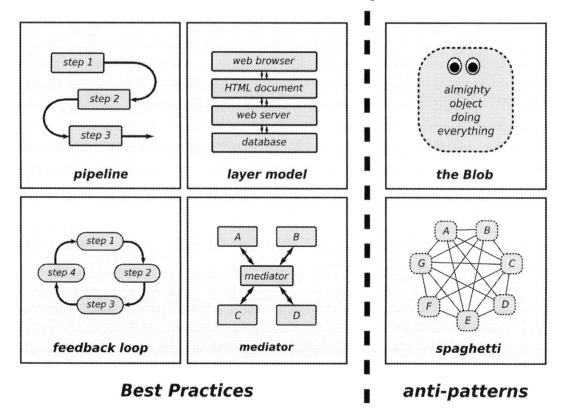

Figure 15-5. *Six frequent architectural patterns in software. The four on the left are useful patterns; the two on the right are **antipatterns** that should be avoided.*

The figure also contains two **antipatterns**, structures that should be avoided. The first one, **the Blob**, avoids decomposition by placing everything in one component. The result is a big messy nonstructure. The second one, the **spaghetti model**, has many components, but all of them talk freely to each other. The result is a chaotic nonstructure again.

There exist other basic architectural patterns not included in the figure. There are not too many, because there is a limited number of distinct topologies that are neither blobs nor spaghetti. We cannot mix two architectures, because the result will be a spaghetti-like structure again. However, architectures can be **nested**, that is, contain each other. For instance, the second layer of a layered architecture could internally consist of a pipeline.

How can we use this information to solve the concurrency problem? We need to make it possible that both player and ghost can move in parallel and take care of some background tasks in between (e.g., drawing the maze). Let us consider the two alternative structures in Figure 15-6.

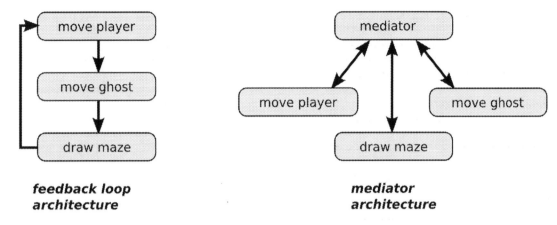

feedback loop architecture

mediator architecture

Figure 15-6. *Two alternatives for taking care of concurrency: a feedback loop architecture (left) and a mediator-based architecture (right)*

1. A simple **feedback loop**. We take care of everything in a single loop. First we move the player, next we move the ghost, and finally we draw the graphics.

2. We introduce a **mediator**, a component whose sole responsibility is to decide whose turn it is to do something. The player, ghost, and drawing part communicate over the same protocol with the mediator.

There may be even more possibilities to approach the problem, but we will stick to these two here. Which of the two architectures is the best in our case? The feedback loop is probably the easier one to implement. We could write it from scratch quickly, and it would work. The loop structure has a few significant drawbacks though. First, it is not easy to extend: every time we add a new game element, we will have to add it to the loop. Second, the slowest step in the loop will slow down all the others. In a game, adding a few more elements could easily result in noticeable delays. We could avoid that by eventually skipping one or more steps in the event loop, but then the architecture won't be so simple any more.

The mediator structure, on the other hand, is easy to extend. As long as the components use the same protocol to communicate with the mediator, it does not matter much how many elements are plugged in. The mediator only needs to have some kind of queue or other set of rules that decide which component's turn it is. The latter property is exactly what we need. We **know** that players' and ghosts' moves will follow very different rhythms. The mediator architecture is able to accommodate such differences. This is why we will continue toward our implementation with the mediator architecture.

Identify Program Components

We have decided to use a mediator architecture to implement the ghost. But so far, we have not decided what exactly the mediator and the components around them *are*. We still need to decide whether to use functions, classes, modules, or something else for the parts of the figure. We postponed this (obviously important) decision in order to solve the higher-order problems first. In this section, the last before the implementation, it is time to make such decisions. Generally, identifying components means drawing boundaries across the dimensions of a programming problem mentioned in the beginning (functionality, data, control flow, technologies). We now need to see a sharp structure emerging from the initial cloud that is easy to implement.

In Python, deciding whether to use a function, class, or module in a given place is not a very *hard* decision in itself. Because all of these are Python objects, it is generally possible to exchange one for the other easily. For instance, we could start by implementing a function, but exchange it for a class later if the program grows. Such decisions are a bit more difficult in other languages. The aim of this step is to bring the architecture from the previous step to life, not to create an exhaustive list of functions, classes, and modules. We will need the liberty to add or change some details during the implementation. It is enough to have an outline of the components our program will contain.

What components do we need for our mediator? Again, we face a design decision: *What exactly will we use as a mediator and how will it communicate to other components?* Again, we will consider two options. First, we could use **multithreading**. We run three subprocesses in parallel, one for the player, one for the ghost, one for drawing things. All three share the same data. In this case, the mediator is the threading engine built into Python. Multithreading is a mediator model found in games frequently. There exists plenty of documentation on implementing threads in Python and libraries for more sophisticated concurrency models (e.g., `asyncio`, `twisted,` or `gevent`). A multithreaded model is easy to extend. We can simply add more threads for more ghosts. On the other hand, threads are known to be challenging to debug, not only in Python. Also, performance optimization with threads in Python is not easy (because of the so-called Global Interpreter Lock or GIL).

Second, we could use communication built on Pygame events. As a mediator, we would have an event loop that collects events and distributes them to different functions, based on the event type. The good thing about the event model is that Pygame takes care of queuing up the events and that there are predefined event types. We basically need to make the event loop more general, so that we can plug in custom events (player and ghost moves and drawing). Like multithreading, debugging an event queue is not easy, and I do not dare to make assumptions about its performance. The decision whether to use threads or an event queue is much smaller than the previous decision about the architecture, because we now decide within the constraints of the architecture. If there isn't much speaking in favor of one or the other model, the programmers' experience and preference decide. Personally, I prefer the event loop model, mainly because I have done it before and for me threads are the bigger pain to debug. But I firmly believe the game could be successfully implemented in a number of different ways. You are free to try your own favorite approach.

With that question resolved, we can open our text editor and write an outline of the program. For the start, we will use functions for everything. To get the event loop working as a mediator, we will need the following components (see Figure 15-7 for an overview):

```python
def move_player(event):
    """moves when keys are pressed"""
    pass

def move_ghost(event):
    """Ghost moves randomly"""
    pass

def update_graphics(event):
    """Re-draws the game window"""
    pass

def event_loop():
    """a mediator using the Pygame event queue"""
    pass
```

Creating a skeleton structure like this is a good preparation for the implementation, no matter if you want to implement small or big components. The approach presented here is the same. There are practically an infinite number of possible components. To avoid getting lost in the details, Table 15-1 lists a few frequently occurring ones.

Table 15-1. *Some Frequently Occuring Components in Python programs*

Name	Purpose	Python Keyword or Module
data structures	separate data from code	any (CORRECT)
classes	modularize data + code	`class`
command-line interface	parse command-line options	`argparse`
logging	write information to log files	`logging`
configuration	set parameters or read them from a file	`configparser`
file I/O	read or write data files	many
database interface	access external data	module, depending on DB
C extension	speed up calculations	external module
HTML template	separate code from display	`jinja2 or django`

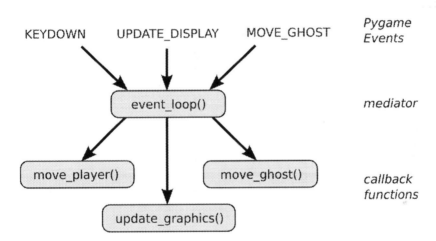

Figure 15-7. *A clear structure has emerged. We have decided to solve the problem of concurrency by using a mediator structure—the event loop. Other game components communicate with the mediator using pygame. event.Event objects, each of which is associated with a callback function. The decomposition is now ready for an implementation.*

With that, we have done enough dry practice. It is time to cast our planning work into working code.

Implement

Let's start implementing the ghost. The central component will be the event loop. The main responsibility of the event loop is to act as a mediator of concurrent events. We start our implementation from the skeleton functions in the previous section. The event loop will communicate with the other functions in Figure 15-7 via pygame.event.Event objects. It comes in handy that Pygame has the built-in integer USEREVENT for defining custom event types. We start by defining events for ghost moves, updating the screen, and exiting the game (for the player moves, we will use the already existing keyboard event KEYDOWN):

```
import pygame
from pygame.locals import USEREVENT, KEYDOWN
```

```
EXIT = USEREVENT
UPDATE_DISPLAY = USEREVENT + 1
MOVE_GHOST = USEREVENT + 2
```

Next, we create dummy procedures for the main events in the game (we will grow these into fully functional components over the next two chapters):

```
def move_player(event):
    """moves when keys are pressed"""
    print('player moves')

def move_ghost(event):
    """Ghost moves randomly"""
    print('ghost moves')

def update_graphics(event):
    """Re-draws the game window"""
    print('graphics updated')
```

We want to write the event loop in a way that allows us to plug in different components flexibly. For that, we associate the event types with our functions. Such functions are often referred to as **callbacks** in programmer jargon. A Python dictionary is the ideal structure for storing event types and callback functions:

```
callbacks = {
    KEYDOWN: move_player,
    MOVE_GHOST: move_ghost,
    UPDATE_DISPLAY: update_graphics,
}
```

But where do all the events come from? For the keyboard events, this is quite clear: Pygame generates these automatically, unless we omit initializing the display (like we did in Chapter 4). The remaining events need to be generated explicitly. For instance, we could send an EXIT event into Pygame's event queue with

```
# not part of the final program
exit = pygame.event.Event(EXIT)
pygame.event.post(exit)
```

Another possibility is to start a timer that generates an event every N milliseconds. For instance, a timer for moving the ghost every 0.3 seconds could be started with

```
pygame.time.set_timer(MOVE_GHOST, 300)
```

Now we can write the event loop itself. As our previous implementation, it collects events from the queue. But instead of interpreting them, it redirects them to a callback function. The only exception is the EXIT event, which terminates the loop:

```
def event_loop(callbacks, delay=10):
    """Processes events and updates callbacks."""
    running = True
```

```
while running:
    pygame.event.pump()
    event = pygame.event.poll()
    action = callbacks.get(event.type)
    if action:
        action(event)
    pygame.time.delay(delay)
    if event.type == EXIT:
        running = False
```

Finally, we can start the event loop. We need to set a few timers for moving the ghost and updating the screen in regular intervals. We also set a timer to trigger an EXIT event after five seconds:

```
if __name__ == '__main__':
    pygame.init()
    pygame.display.set_mode((10, 10))
    pygame.time.set_timer(UPDATE_DISPLAY, 1000)
    pygame.time.set_timer(MOVE_GHOST, 300)
    pygame.time.set_timer(EXIT, 5000)
    event_loop(callbacks)
```

If we start the program and hit a few keys the output looks like this:

```
player moves
player moves
ghost moves
ghost moves
player moves
player moves
ghost moves
graphics updated
ghost moves
..
```

What did we achieve so far? We have created a general structure, much more general than the ghost problem. We can use the same mechanism for **many** concurrent game elements. Note that the event loop does not care what we connect to it. We can plug in one or two players, one to many ghosts, or other things we might invent later. Of course there is a practical upper limit *how many* components we can plug in. But we are far from the area where we will have to be concerned about optimizing our architecture. In the next chapters, we will deal with implementing the rest of the ghost.

The seven-step planning process is an example how the decomposition of a problem can be approached. Although it is a Best Practice to have such a process, I rarely go through all the steps in full and sometimes vary the steps considerably. Most of the time, the solution points at itself halfway through the recipe (beeping *"implement me!"*). But whenever there is a problematic programming task to add, a slow and systematic process gives the best long-term results. For a complete implementation of the ghost, see http://github.com/krother/maze run.

Other Planning Tools

Planning is an essential skill in programming. Although it is distracting us from writing code, and a lot can be achieved by rigorous application of common sense, knowing a few planning tools saves your day when things get more complex. This is not a book about software project management, so we won't go into detail. However, I have a couple of favorite planning tools that are worth mentioning:

The One-Page Project Plan

In projects where there is no formal planning phase (and sometimes not even a formal project manager), writing a minimal plan is often sufficient to have everybody on the same page. The plans I have been using summarizes on a single A4 page:

- what is the project about?

- who is on the team (and how to contact them)?

- why are you writing the program?

- what is the main goal?

- what are the most important subgoals?

- is there a deadline?

- is there a budget?

In a small team having such a miniplan avoids many misunderstandings.

Issue Trackers

When you have identified programming tasks or decomposed them into smaller ones, where do you keep them? One possibility is to use an **issue tracker**. An issue tracker is a software that manages programming tasks, descriptions, and who is taking care of them. Using one helps tremendously against things getting forgotten. Popular issue trackers are **JIRA**, **Trac,** and the issue system on **GitHub**. But basically any project management system offers functionality to track issues.

Kanban

Originally invented by Toyota, **Kanban** is a method to manage stockpiles in lean manufacturing. The concept was applied to software development by *David Anderson*. A Kanban process limits the number of things to work on simultaneously and displays them on a well-visible board. I have had Kanban boards on my desk, on my browser, and in my kitchen—all of them worked well. Kanban is a pragmatic method to focus on improvement and getting things done that integrates easily with most existing practices in a work environment.

Best Practices

- Decomposing programming tasks resembles shapes slowly emerging from a cloud rather than a series of sharp cuts.

- A **User Story** is a short, nontechnical description of a programming task that makes it manageable.

- Details can be added to User Stories as **bullet points**, **text documents**, **diagrams**, and **Use Case descriptions**.

- **Nonfunctional requirements** are border conditions describing the environment in which a program will be used. Thinking of them early greatly reduces the risk of a program becoming difficult to maintain or useless.

- Based on a User Story, Use Case description and nonfunctional requirements, **contradictions**, and **other problems** can be identified.

- While decomposing a programming problem, **domain knowledge** is essential.

- Frequent sources of problems include lack of information, overabundant information, existing code, and future change.

- Choose an **architecture** that solves the main problem(s).

- Create a skeleton program after identifying program components (functions, classes, modules, etc.) for implementing the architecture.

- An **implementation** is the final step after a full decomposition.

- The seven-step process to decompose programming tasks is to be understood as a guideline.

CHAPTER 16

Static Typing in Python

Things as certain as death and taxes, can be more firmly believed.

—Daniel Defoe, *The Political History of the Devil*

Dynamic typing is one of the most praised features of Python. Praised because it allows for rapid development. But dynamic typing also has a dark side. Dynamic typing also means that there is no certainty of receiving a certain type of object—anywhere in the program. In this chapter we will examine why dynamic typing is a risk and how this risk can be mitigated. As an example let us consider that we want to add a **high score list** to our game. A simple high score list contains the scores of five top-scoring players and their names (see Table 16-1).

Table 16-1. *High Score List with Five Top-Scoring Players*

Player	Score
Ada	5500
Bob	4400
Charlie	3300
Dad	2200
Elle	1100

For simplicity, let's define each entry as a namedtuple:

```
from collections import namedtuple

Highscore = namedtuple('Highscore', ['score', 'name'])
```

Now we can generate entries as instances of Highscore:

```
entry = Highscore(5500, 'Ada')
```

In Python, nothing prevents us from swapping the order or parameters accidentally:

```
entry = Highscore('Ada', 5500)
```

© Kristian Rother 2017
K. Rother, *Pro Python Best Practices*, DOI 10.1007/978-1-4842-2241-6_16

Although obviously wrong, this command is executed and passes without errors. It produces an instance of Highscore, and the defect propagates, probably until we try to compare the score with that of another player (unless the order is swapped there as well). If we are unlucky, the defect does not produce an error at all and propagates until it has infested other parts of our data. The main reason is the permissive dynamic typing in Python. With earlier type control, the defect would not propagate. At this point we can already conclude that **dynamic typing makes it easier for defects to propagate**. If we want to limit error propagation because of dynamic types, we have to add it ourselves.

Weaknesses of Dynamic Typing

The weaknesses of dynamic typing manifest themselves in many different situations. In this chapter, we will look at four kinds of common type-related problems more closely:

Function Signatures

Like in the preceding high score example, Python does not care for types when assigning parameters to functions. It is easy to call functions with different types than they were designed for. As a consequence, we may end up having the same function do completely different things, as this classical example illustrates:

```
>>> def add(a, b): return a + b
...
>>> add(7, 7)
14
>>> add('7', '7')
'77'
```

Value Boundaries

Frequently, data contains hard boundaries (minimum and maximum values, sizes of lists, possible values, etc.). Python does not stop us from violating these boundaries, and the result is syntactically correct nonsense:

```
>>> year = -2016
>>> month = 13
>>> days = [day for day in range(1, 33)]
>>> weekday = "Cupcakeday"
```

(Of course, using the datetime module would catch a few of these issues in the case of dates. But we **still** could write expressions like date.day + 42 that push a value outside of the expected range.)

Semantic Meaning of Types

The same data may have different meanings. Imagine we were storing lengths in different units:

```
>>> cm = 183.0
>>> inches = 72.05
>>> cm - inches 110.95
```

Since both values have the type float, Python will never complain about the calculation that is obviously wrong. The same bug can happen with currencies instead of length units. If the exchange rates are close to each other, such a defect may be quite hard to spot. Having a program that gets a financial calculation wrong by a few percent is something most people will not find very amusing.

Composite Types

In Python, it is generally difficult to say *"I want a list that must not contain anything else than integer numbers."* The same is true for dictionaries, sets, tuples, and so on. As a result, it is easy to mix incompatible types together, like in the preceding example.

Is Stronger Typing Possible in Python?

These four problems have in common that they are related to *typing*. They are Python-specific problems. Taken together, despite all its advantages dynamic typing is a soft spot in the Python language. Let us see whether we can do anything to prevent these problems and make typing in our code *more strict*. In an ideal world, a construction similar to the following would be possible:

```
>>> Highscore = typedtuple(['int score', 'str name'],)
>>> entry = Highscore(5500, 'Ada')
```

and when we mess up the types accidentally, Python complains immediately:

```
>>> entry = Highscore('Charlie', 3300)

Traceback (most recent call last):
    Python expected type 'int' but got type 'str'
    in line ...
                Hey wait. This is not real Python code!
```

You might come to the same conclusion as the fictitious interpreter in the preceding: *"But Python is not a statically typed language. There is no static typing in Python."* And I agree. The title of this chapter is a bit of a teaser. Python is not a statically typed language, and this is not likely to change. Instead, we are looking at *workarounds*, strategies to enforce **stronger type control** in Python programs. Fortunately there exist a few type control strategies. In this chapter, we will examine pros and cons of several such type control strategies, and see whether they help us to get the worst errors out of the way.

Assertions

A first idea might be to simply check the type of a variable explicitly. For instance, we might create an assertion when adding high scores to a list:

```
from collections import namedtuple

Highscore = namedtuple('Highscore', ['score', 'name'])

highscores = []

def add(name, score):
```

233

```
assert type(name) is str
assert type(score) is int
hs = Highscore(score, name)
highscores.append(hs)
```

This strategy is called **defensive programming**. The idea behind defensive programming is that we *"never trust the code calling our function."* The two assertions explicitly state the expectations of the function to its parameters. If these expectations or *preconditions* are violated, the function won't do anything. This way, we catch a type-related defect before it propagates:

```
add('Ada', 5500)
add('Bob', 4400)
add(3300, 'Charlie')
```

The program exits cleanly with an `AssertionError`:

```
Traceback (most recent call last):
  File "highscores_assert.py", line 19, in <module>
    add(3300, 'Charlie')
  File "highscores_assert.py", line 9, in add
    assert type(name) is str
AssertionError
```

Using assertions, we can also check more complex conditions on our data. For instance, we can make sure the highscore list never has more than five elements:

```
def add(name, score):
    assert type(name) is str
    assert type(score) is int
    hs = Highscore(score, name)
    highscores.append(hs)
    highscores = highscores[:5]
    assert len(scores) < 5
```

The second kind of assertion is also called a **postcondition**. We deliberately introduce another point of failure to cut error propagation short. Since we can use any valid Python expression with `assert`, we can basically check anything we want. The good thing about pre- and postconditions (and defensive programming in general) is that they fail early and in a specific way. A welcome side effect is that the assertions spell out requirements explicitly and are thus more reliable than documentation. The assertion is like a ghost from the past that warns you *"If score is not an integer, bad things will happen!"*

▓ **Hint** In some languages, pre- and postconditions are powerful formal constructs that can be checked by an external tool before running the code. Not so in Python. We essentially replace one error with another.

But defensive programming also has a few serious disadvantages. First, **assertions inflate our program**. Of the six lines in the add function, three are assertions. More code means more space for bugs to hide. Second, **some assertions introduce redundancy**. The last two instructions of the function add both take care of the same, making sure the list never becomes longer than five. Third, assertions need computation time and make the code slower. If we were to call the preceding function a million times, the assertions would cost us about a second. If timing in our code is critical or we want to run it on a Raspberry Pi, assertions get in the way quickly. Taken together, defensive programming tends to make the code more *bulky* and more difficult to change rapidly.

Nevertheless, when dealing with a complex set of dependencies, defensive programming can reasonably reinforce our code. For instance, in a calculation pipeline consisting of many steps, assertions in the middle make sense. Depending on the calculation we could make sure that the numbers really are floats, that triangles really have three edges, and that the number of samples in the beginning and in the end is the same. In a long chain of events, cutting error propagation short by an `assert` statement might save our day. It has also been stated that defensive programming can be useful to prevent an aging program from falling apart (for some time). But I wouldn't go as far as recommending defensive programming as a Best Practice that helps to control type in general. For instance, in the previous high score example code, it surely would be overkill.

NumPy

As one of the most prominent Python libraries, **NumPy** deserves to be mentioned here. As the name implies, NumPy is designed as a library to handle large arrays and matrices of numerical values. Internally, NumPy maps data to data structures written in C. This has the welcome effect that all items of a NumPy array have the same type. Written in NumPy, our high score list could look like this:

```
import numpy as np

scores = np.array([5500, 4400, 3300, 2200, 1100], dtype=np.int64)
players = np.array(['Ada', 'Bob', 'Charlie', 'Dad', 'Elle'], dtype=np.str)
```

The type of an array is preserved rigorously. We can check that if we try to break an array with a mismatching type. Using a string where a number is expected fails immediately:

```
>>> scores[2] = "Charlie"
Traceback (most recent call last):
  File "<stdin>", line 1, in <module>
ValueError: invalid literal for long() with base 10: 'Charlie'
```

However, if we fit a number into a string array, it gets converted automatically:

```
>>> players[3] = 100
>>> players
array(['Ada', 'Bob', 'Charlie', '100', 'Elle'], dtype='|S6')
```

That means we effectively cannot type control strings very well, because every Python object has a string representation. Inserting a float into `scores` also results in a conversion. Thus, the types are not enforced *strictly in all directions*. The `dtype` parameter sets a type for an entire array. For many basic data types in Python, multiple options for the `dtype` parameter exist (integers and floats with various precision, etc.). More complex data types are represented by `dtype=np.object`. That means that NumPy cannot exert any type control on dictionaries, sets, or even custom types. The `'object'` type is not helpful for our purpose.

Another disadvantage is that the NumPy interface forces us to keep the names of players and scores in two separate arrays. In practice, this limits the usefulness of typing in NumPy for building type-controlled data structures—it simply *has not been built for that (unless we use numpy.recarray that mitigates the situation a bit)*. NumPy is much better at what was originally built for: arrays of numbers. The speed of numerical calculations in NumPy is legendary, and this is why most people use the library.

Taken together, the type system of NumPy introduces some rigor to list-like collections of objects of the same type, preferably numbers. Using a wrong type still fails, but earlier. This is nice but it does not give us a strong enough reason to use a NumPy array only for the sake of type control.

▧ **What about the pandas library?**   The **pandas** library is a luxury interface built on top of NumPy to facilitate analysis of tabular data. **pandas** infers types of data columns similar to NumPy. However, the type checks are more permissive: You may assign everything to a column in pandas, regardless of its type. If necessary, the column will automatically change its type. This leads to nasty type-related bugs; for instance reading a German spreadsheet with decimal places separated by commas (,) instead of dots (.) will result in a column of strings instead of floats.

Databases

Since we are mainly interesting in type controlling our data, we could delegate our data to an external tool (in contrast to delegating *everything* like with a C extension). There is a big family of tools built for exactly that purpose: **databases**. The main idea is: If we use a database for storing data, we can impose a rigid structure, including data types. As a consequence, every time we access our data, we have certainty that the data we obtain is exactly of the type we want. The good thing about this approach is that Python cooperates extremely well with almost all available database engines. Here we will use **PostgreSQL** as a database engine and **psycopg2** as the Python module that creates the database connection to implement the high score list. Depending on your system, the process for setting up the database may be a bit complicate. On Ubuntu, the following commands are sufficient:

```
sudo apt-get install postgresql
sudo /etc/init.d/postgresql start
createdb highscores
sudo pip install psycopg2
```

If you prefer to skip the installation and would like to concentrate on the code instead, here is how the highscore table would be stored to and read from the database:

```
import psycopg2

DB_SETUP = "'
CREATE TABLE IF NOT EXISTS scores (
    player VARCHAR(25),
    score INTEGER);
    "'

db = psycopg2.connect(host="127.0.0.1",
                      user="krother",
                      dbname="highscores")
cur = db.cursor()

# create the database
cur.execute(DB_SETUP)
```

```
# fill the database with entries
insert = "INSERT INTO scores VALUES (%s,%s);"
cur.execute(insert, 'Ada', 5500)
cur.execute(insert, 'Bob', 4400)

# retrieve the top five entries in descending order
query = 'SELECT player, score FROM scores ORDER BY score DESC LIMIT 5;' cur.execute(query)
for result in cur.fetchall():
    print(result)

db.close()
```

Executing the code results in:

```
('Ada', 5500L)
('Bob', 4400L)
```

The 'L' after the numbers specifies that these are long integers. If we add another call with swapped arguments (3300, 'Charlie'), we get the desired type error:

```
Traceback (most recent call last):
  File "highscores_postgres.py", line 20, in <module>
    cur.execute(insert, (3300, 'Charlie'))
psycopg2.DataError: invalid input syntax for integer: "Charlie"
LINE 1: INSERT INTO scores VALUES (3300,'Charlie');
```

Python modules for other SQL databases work in almost the same way. A more convenient way is to use an **Object-Relational Mapper (ORM)**, a set of classes that create SQL queries and convert the results to Python objects. Widely used ORMs are **SQLAlchemy** and the data models in **Django**. There are also Python interfaces for most NoSQL databases (MongoDB, Redis, etc.), but they differ too much to discuss their approach to typing here.

▓ **Warning**   The **SQLite** database is a full-featured SQL database interface that is installed with Python. However, SQLite is *dynamically typed* and thus does not contribute to type control at all.

Using a database has a couple of extra benefits: persistence (the data is safe even if our program crashes), interoperability (non-Python programmers can use them), and scalability (if a PostgreSQL database becomes too small, we can replace it by a dedicated database server (or an Oracle cluster) without fundamentally changing our code. Of course, databases are not a perfect solution, either. First, interacting with a SQL database produces a lot of overhead in terms of code size and speed. To manage as little as a single table, writing a helper module to build and interpret SQL queries is a good idea, if only to get the SQL code out of sight. With an ORM the code gets shorter, but creating data models in a helper module is still a good idea. Second, we can only use types offered by the database (e.g., there are no dictionaries in a SQL database). Third, we *still* do not get type control inside our program; we only move data management out of it.

Given these limitations, what do databases contribute to the type control problem? In a nutshell, we control the types of data where violations would hurt the most: We get a clear, persistent, strongly typed structure for our *"business data."* All other variables with a more local context inside our Python code stay as dynamic as ever, Databases offer a pragmatic partial solution to the type control problem. We don't get very close to *"real"* static typing, but it works.

Integrating C Code

Python is very good at interacting with code written in C/C++. Usually, this is done to speed up Python code. However, C code is unthinkable without static typing, which is why we take a closer look at this option. Writing **C extensions** in Python allows us to call C functions as if they were Python functions. The C header file Python.h provides functions to convert standard Python data types to C types and back. That means, we get full type control inside the C part of the program. An alternative to achieve the same is the **scipy.weave** package, which allows to execute C instructions as strings directly in Python modules.

However, in both cases we are responsible for catching all kinds of type errors during at the Python-C interface. This type checking can be done on the C side (with Python.h) or on the Python side (as assertions, with scipy.weave). Using a wrong type in C carries the risk of crashing the entire program with a segmentation fault. Generally, C-code gives us both flexibility and speed in addition to static typing. There are however, a few drawbacks:

- There is some overhead: We need to write the Python-C adapter, set up the C compiler, and integrate everything into whatever builds your program.

- On the Python side, nothing changes. Everything is as dynamic as ever.

- Compilation of C code means that our compiled code is not platform-independent any more.

- Strictly speaking, using C code is not Python any more. If we have good reasons to write code in a statically typed language, maybe converting the entire program to that language is worth a thought (replacing a Python prototype by a more rigid implementation is in a strongly typed language is a Best Practice pursued by many development teams).

When optimizing a program for speed or using an external C library, type control is a welcome side effect. I haven't seen anyone write a C extension for the sake of type control, though.

Cython

The **Cython** project has received a lot of attention (see http://docs.cython.org/en/latest/index.html). Cython is a tool that converts Python source code to C source code. Afterward, we can use a C compiler to build an executable program. The executable program can be used without a Python interpreter and is usually faster than a regular Python program. With very few exceptions, Cython interprets Python code in the same way as the standard Python interpreter. What is interesting for us is that we can add **type annotations** that Cython understands. The Cython version of the highscore implementation would be

```
cdef struct Highscore:
    char *name
    int score

cdef Highscore scores[5]

scores[0] = Highscore('Ada', 5500)
scores[1] = Highscore('Bob', 4400)

for i in range():
    print(scores[i].name, scores[i].score)
```

The **struct** is a C data structure similar to a `namedtuple`, but with static typing.

Given that **Cython** is installed, we can compile an executable and run it in the Unix shell:

```
cython --embed highscores_cython.pyx
gcc -Os -I /usr/include/python3.4m -o highscores.out highscores_cython.c -lpython3.4m
-lpthread
./highscores.out
```

Which results in

```
Bob              4400
Ada              5500
```

What happens if we try using an invalid type in the Python code?

```
scores[2] = Highscore(3300, 'Charlie')
```

When recompiling the program, a bunch of errors are raised in the first step (compilation with Cython):

```
highscores_cython.pyx:11:28: Only single-character string literals can be coerced into int

Error compiling Cython file:
------------------------------------------------------------
...

cdef Highscore scores[5]

scores[0] = Highscore('Ada', 5500)
scores[1] = Highscore('Bob', 4400)
scores[2] = Highscore(3300, 'Charlie')


------------------------------------------------------------
highscores_cython.pyx:11:22: Cannot assign type 'long' to 'char *'
```

Here we finally have real static typing: Types are checked and generate error messages before any code is executed! The price we pay is that the code itself is only partially similar to a Python program (the second half is, but the first half looks more like C). Fortunately, C-types are optional. We can run normal Python code via Cython, or add static types in a few critical places. A disadvantage of this approach is that the build process for Cython-annotated code changes completely. Cython code is not understood by the standard Python interpreter any more. Also, if we import Python modules inside Cython, they will require compilation as well.

Using Cython to compile an executable program is not the most orthodox way to use Cython. Its main field of application is to produce libraries. As with C extensions and NumPy, a common motivation for using Cython is speed. However, with the extra type annotations using Cython for type control is a viable option. If you don't worry about the extra compilation step (and know how to configure a C compiler), Cython gives you the best from both worlds.

Type Hints

Starting with Python 3.5, it is possible to annotate the types of variables and parameters. These **type hints** are a rapidly evolving feature of the language, and the example presented here requires Python 3.5 or above. The main idea behind type hints is that we write types into the Python code, so that other programmers know what type we *intend* a variable to have. Note that type hints are **hints**, not **checks**—at present, the Python interpreter ignores them. The type-annotated high score list looks like this:

```python
from typing import NamedTuple, List
import csv

Highscore = NamedTuple('Highscore', [('score', int), ('name', str)])

class HighscoreList:
    """A sorted list of top scores"""
    def __init__(self, places: int=10) -> None:
        self.scores = [] # type: List[Highscore]
        self.places = places

    def add(self, highscore: Highscore) -> None:
        self.scores.append(highscore)
        self.scores.sort()
        self.scores = self.scores[:self.places]

    def __repr__(self) -> str:
        return str(self.scores)

hs = HighscoreList()
hs.add(Highscore(5500, 'Ada'))
hs.add(Highscore(4400, 'Bob'))
```

In the code, type hints appear in several places:

- **Function signatures**—the function parameters have types (e.g., :int for an integer or :Highscore) for a Highscore object. The return values have types as well, for example, -> None or -> str.

- **Variable definitions**—when a variable is defined for the first time, a comment starting with # type: specifies its type.

- **Composite types**—We use the typing module to define scores as a list of Highscore objects.

- **Predefined types**—We define our own NamedTuple together with types for each field. Note that this is a different tuple than the common collections.namedtuple.

The typing offers more detailed and flexible ways to annotate types, for example, **Any** (the type does not matter), **Union** (one from a list of types), and **NewType** (distinct clones of existing types). You find a full description in the **PEP484** document and the documentation for the typing module (see https://docs.python.org/3.5/library/typing.html#module-typing). In itself, type hints help as documentation: other programmers know what we *meant*. The biggest disadvantage of this approach is that **type hints do nothing**. The Python interpreter ignores them, and the runtime failures resulting from wrong types do not change at all.

But we can use additional tools to interpret type hints. At the moment among these tools we find **pydoc** for generating documentation, the **PyCharm** IDE that warns you of type violations while writing code (see Figure 16-1), and **mypy**. Here, we will focus on **mypy**.

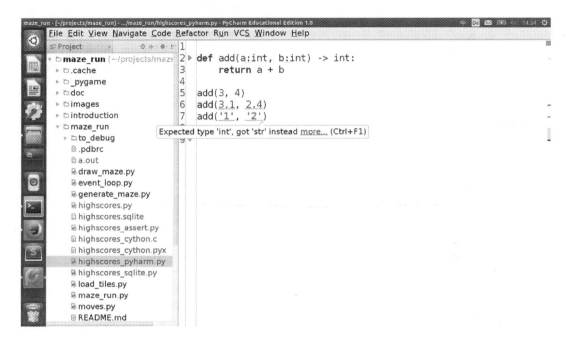

Figure 16-1. *Type checking in PyCharm for function calls. The checker needs to be activated by setting the 'Python – editor – Type checker' preferences to 'Error.' Also see* `https://www.jetbrains.com/help/pycharm/5.0/type-hinting-in-pycharm.html`*.*

mypy

mypy is a *static type checker* (see `http://mypy-lang.org/`). It examines Python code and checks whether the annotated types are used consistently. If they are not, mypy creates an error message before any code is executed. **mypy** can be installed with

```
> pip install mypy
```

Next, we invoke mypy from the command line by typing `mypy <filename.py>`:

```
> mypy highscores.py
```

If everything is consistent, the output of mypy is empty. Let's try adding a wrong type to the Python script.

```
add(3300, 'Charlie')
```

Rerunning mypy produces an error message:

```
> mypy highscores.py
highscores.py, line 37: Argument 1 to "Highscore" has incompatible type "str";
    expected "int"
highscores.py, line 37: Argument 2 to "Highscore" has incompatible type "int";
    expected "str"
```

This is finally the kind of error we would like to see with strict typing applied, and we did not have to distort our Python program too much. Yay! To apply type checks to objects created by third-party modules, mypy uses **stub files**. These contain type-annotated signatures of functions and variables in `.pyi` files that mypy interprets. Stubfiles for the Python standard library and many other modules can be found in the **typeshed** project at `https://github.com/python/typeshed/`.

Note that mypy does not find every single issue. For instance, if we would use `collections.namedtuple` instead of `typing.NamedTuple`, the types inside the tuples would be ignored. Like **pylint**, mypy adds an extra quality check that we can switch on and off. As such it can be integrated into a Continuous Integration platform like Jenkins, so that type checks are performed every time code is added to a repository. Currently, version 0.4.6 of **mypy** has been released (in November 2016). The tool is being developed very actively and probably going to change, like the type hints in Python themselves. Given their short history, I would not call the combination of type hints and mypy a Best Practice *yet*, but it is a very promising candidate and I hope to see more of mypy in the future.

Which Method of Type Control to Use?

We have seen six possible strategies to improve type control in Python. Do they help us to restrict types in our program, so that a majority of `TypeErrors` and/or `NameErrors` will never occur? Let's review the pros and cons of each method. For that, let's consider the four problems we stated in the beginning:

- **function signatures:** Can we force a function being called with or returning a specific type? (`9 + 9` vs. `'9'+ '9'`)

- **semantic types:** Can we define multiple nonsynonymous types? (keeping cm and inches separate)

- **value boundaries:** Can we restrict values to a certain range or selection? (players must have positive scores).

- **type composition:** Can we restrict the composition of complex types? (e.g., all items in the high score list must be `Highscore` objects).

Table 16-2 contains quick answers to these questions. Let us summarize each of the six strategies in detail.

Assertions and **Defensive Programming** add stricter type control to Python code itself. Assertions allow us to introduce any kind of constraint, fail early, and with a defined error message. This sounds like a perfect solution. In practice, assertions are expensive to maintain: they increase code size and make a program less flexible, less *pythonic*.

Table 16-2. *Strategies to Improve Type Control in Python*

Method	Assertions	NumPy	C code	Databases	Cython	Mypy
Function signatures	yes	no	yes	no	yes	Yes
Value boundaries	yes	no	no	yes	no	No
Type semantics	yes	no	yes	no	no	Yes
Composite types	yes	no	yes	tables	yes	Yes
Fails during	execution	execution	execution	execution	compilation	analysis
Overhead	high	low	high	medium	high	Low

But in a long calculation or a process stretching across dozens of modules, a single assert can save us many hours of debugging. Used sparingly, assert is a valuable tool.

NumPy gives us type control for integer and float numbers. A NumPy array of numbers stays an array of numbers, so we do not have to worry about typing while implementing calculations. With other types, it does not help us at all. It is an awesome, useful library, but type control is not what NumPy was built for.

Writing **C extensions** to control type looked like a good idea at first sight, but it turns out to be not worth the trouble. We have great ways to control type inside the C part, but the Python part remains completely unaffected. The overhead is high because we need to write *defensive code* to keep typing problems away from the C code. If you depend on the benefits of a strongly typed language, maybe Python is not the right choice for the problem. But, if we are planning to extend Python with C *anyway* (e.g., for speed), it is good to know that typing is easier.

Storing data in a strongly typed **database** is often a good idea. We delegate our core data to a dedicated, strictly typed engine. Type control is only one of many benefits of using a database. In fact, it is rather a side effect, and a database still does not fix type problems inside the Python program. Regardless whether we use an ORM or write SQL code into a Python module, a database produces some overhead in building, administrating, and interfacing with it. Nevertheless we get what we set out for: more control over our data.

Cython is the only strategy here that introduces real static typing to Python code. It also is the only method that refuses to execute badly typed code. That comes at a price: The result is a somewhat strange Python-C hybrid that combines the best of each. A nice aspect is that we can decide which parts of the program we want to have statically typed. The biggest drawback is that building Cython programs is very different. Some effort is required to configure the compilation of Cython-based libraries and executables. The closer your life is to C (or the more willing you are to learn it), the more useful Cython gets.

Our final competitor, the combination of **type hints** with **mypy** offers a powerful typing system that is part of Python itself (at least in the newest versions). Type hints document code, and mypy warns about many type violations at the earliest possible moment. Having the checks performed by mypy as a separate tool integrates well with the toolchain used by many software development teams. A good way to use mypy is to have code automatically checked for type violations, (e.g., after committing to a code repository). Type hints in Python are still a new feature and not a standard procedure yet, but we can expect to see more about type hints in the future.

Taken together, controlling types in Python is possible to some extent. All of the methods described in the preceding have side effects (both good and bad ones). Most notably, all but **Cython** and **mypy** control types at runtime only. With any type control strategy, our programs will still fail. But they will fail earlier, with clearer error messages so that defects can be found sooner. In a program growing to 1,000 lines and beyond, this is the kind of robustness that makes development less painful.

Best Practices

- **Dynamic typing** is a major source of defects in Python.

- **Type-related problems** include function signatures, value boundaries and semantics, and composite types.

- There are several strategies to improve **type control** in Python programs.

- **Assertions** can be used for checking types and other restrictions, but add a considerable overhead.

- **Defensive programming** is the systematic use of assertions to protect a function from inconsistent parameters.

- **NumPy** arrays have a set type that is strictly enforced for numbers only.

- **SQL Databases** help to move core data from a Python program into strictly type-controlled tables.

- **C extensions** use static typing, but the programmer is responsible for catching errors at the Python-C interface.

- **Cython** is a tool to generate C code from Python code. Cython uses type annotations that speed up the program.

- **Type hints** annotate Python code, but do not change how the code is executed.

- **mypy** is an independent tool that checks consistency of type hints without executing code.

CHAPTER 17

∎ ∎ ∎

Documentation

"But even the hacker who works alone," said Master Foo, "collaborates with others, and must constantly communicate clearly to them, lest his work become confused and lost."

"Of what others do you speak?" the Prodigy demanded.

Master Foo said: "All your future selves."

—Eric S. Raymond, "Master Foo and the Programming Prodigy"

When my parents refurbished the wooden panels on the house in the 1980s, my mother deposited a newspaper in between the wall and the new panels. When I wondered what my mom was doing, she explained: ***"This is our message into the future. Whoever will be the next to replace the panels, will find the newspaper and see how we saw the world today."*** Someone else, maybe a few decades later, would catch a glimpse of our life when the paneling was built (for instance that newspapers were considered to give testimony of history). Looking into the past is difficult. Of course, it is easier than looking into the future. There is some information: we can see the old, wooden panels, in their probably withered state. We can see what has been built, but not what our state of mind was, our hopes, our reasons, our intentions. Documenting software is similar.

When we write software, documentation is our message into the future. It helps future developers to understand how we came to build something and how it was built. Consider a statement like the following: ***"The program contains 7 classes and 23 functions."*** At best, this will be an accurate description of what you see in the code. More often, this kind of documentation will be wrong after a short time, as the program continues evolving. In contrast a statement like ***"We constructed mazes as the central data structure of the game and everything else around it"*** helps you to grasp an idea hard to see in the code. But the latter statement lacks technical detail: we need to find the right balance between describing ideas and technical detail. In this chapter, we will explore how to write useful, balanced documentation for a Python project.

Who Do We Write Documentation For?

In general, there are three groups of people for whom we write documentation: **developers, other team members**, and **users**. It is key to understand that a few months into the future you as a developer are the main beneficiary of the documentation you wrote earlier. This is why we will focus on developer-centered documentation here. To some extent, a good developer-oriented documentation also helps other participants in a project, for instance new team members joining a project or people reporting bugs in an open source project.

We will ignore documentation for nonprogrammer end users here. Writing a user manual or, for example, a project-related document matters of course, but it is a completely different kind of technical writing. It is the technical documentation that will save the program from an engineering point of view.

© Kristian Rother 2017
K. Rother, *Pro Python Best Practices*, DOI 10.1007/978-1-4842-2241-6_17

Sphinx: A Documentation Tool for Python

For quite some time, we have been able to comfortably document our program using a single README.md file in our main project directory, plus a LICENSE.TXT file for the legal stuff. There are many projects where the README file is more than enough. But as your program grows, it will eventually reach a size where a single file is not sufficient any more. Here are some symptoms that your program has grown out of the README file:

- The README file gets too long to browse comfortably.

- The file describes many special situations that are relevant for some people only.

- There are many code examples, and it is difficult to keep them up to date.

- You cannot verify automatically whether the code examples in the documentation are correct.

When we find one or more of the preceding apply, it is time to switch to a larger documentation tool. We will still keep the README file, if only to point to the bigger documentation. In this chapter, we will document mazes (the generate maze module) from our project using **Sphinx**, a standard documentation tool available for Python. Many big and small Python projects are documented with **Sphinx**, including Python itself.

In a nutshell, **Sphinx** combines documentation files written by us plus the Python source code we are documenting. Sphinx then compiles these files to HTML, PDF, and EPUB documents (see Figure 17-1). The documentation files are written in the **ReStructuredText** (.rst format that may contain automatically generated tables of contents, hyperlinks, and even automated tests). In this chapter, we will take a tour of all these features before returning to the question of what makes *good* documentation.

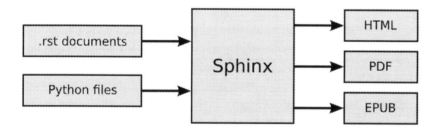

Figure 17-1. *Workflow for creating documentation with Sphinx*

Setting Up Sphinx

First, we need to install Sphinx. This can be done using pip:

```
pip    install   Sphinx
```

Sphinx uses a lot of other Python packages. Most notably, it uses the pygments library to create syntax-highlighted source code in text documents.

We will add the documentation in the docs/ folder of our project. If you used pyscaffold to set up your project, it should be there already. If not, simply create an empty docs/ directory:

```
cd docs
```

Next, we run `sphinx-quickstart` to initialize the documentation:

```
sphinx-quickstart
```

Sphinx asks you a lot of questions. In most cases, the defaults will be fine, but I recommend changing a few values. For the first questions, it is fine to use the default settings:

```
> Root path for the documentation [.]:
..
> Separate source and build directories (y/n) [n]:
..
> Name prefix for templates and static dir [_]:
```

For the project name, authors, and version number, you can insert whatever you prefer:

```
>  Project  name:
..
>  Author  name(s):
..
>  Project  version:
```

With the next three questions, the defaults are fine:

```
> Project release [1]:
> Source file suffix [.rst]:
>  Name  of your master  document  (without suffix) [index]:
```

Now we have reached the interesting part. **Stop accepting defaults** when the program asks about building documentation in the **epub** format. This is a very useful thing to have, so we say *'yes'* to that one.

```
Sphinx can also add configuration for epub output:
> Do you want to use the epub builder (y/n) [n]: y
```

Next come the extensions. I strongly recommend *changing* the default values for a few very useful ones like `autodoc`, `doctest`, `todo`, `ifconfig`, and `viewcode`.

```
Please indicate if you want to use one of the following Sphinx extensions:
> autodoc: automatically insert docstrings from modules (y/n) [n]: y
> doctest: automatically test code snippets in doctest blocks (y/n) [n]: y
> intersphinx: link between Sphinx documentation of different projects (y/n) [n]:
> todo: write "todo" entries that can be shown or hidden on build (y/n) [n]: y
> coverage: checks for documentation coverage (y/n) [n]:
> pngmath: include math, rendered as PNG images (y/n) [n]:
> mathjax: include math, rendered in the browser by MathJax (y/n) [n]:
> ifconfig: conditional  inclusion  of  content  based  on  config  values  (y/n) [n]: y
> viewcode: include links to the source code of documented Python objects (y/n) [n]: y
```

Finally, Sphinx asks about script creation. You can press enter twice to complete the configuration.

```
> Create Makefile? (y/n) [y]:
> Create Windows command file? (y/n) [y]:
```

We will use most of these features later on.

Files Created by Sphinx

Sphinx creates the following files in the doc/ folder:

```
_build      conf.py      index.rst   Makefile    _static     _templates
```

The file index.rst is the main file of your documentation. The _build/ directory will contain the compiled documentation. The file conf.py contains the settings we chose in the sphinx-quickstart configuration script, so that we can edit them later. We don't need to worry about the other files for now.

Building the Documentation

To create documentation, we need the make tool and LaTeX on our system. On Ubuntu, we can do this with

```
sudo apt-get install make
sudo apt-get install texlive-full
```

Note that the LaTeX packages are huge (1.8 GB)!

Building HTML Documentation

We can now compile the documentation to HTML by typing

```
make html
```

When we open the file _build/html/index.html in a web browser, we see a default page. The page does not contain much yet, because we haven't written any documentation (you weren't expecting all the documentation to write itself, were you?). Also see Figure 17-2.

***Figure 17-2.** Barebones HTML documentation generated by Sphinx*

Building PDF Documentation

Alternatively, we can compile PDF documents. This requires installing **LaTeX** and the **pdflatex** package.

```
make latexpdf
```

The PDF is available in the _build/latex directory.

■ **Warning** At time of writing, Sphinx reported it was unable to find the file iftex.sty. I solved the problem by downloading the file manually and pasting the ***full path*** to the file several times whenever Sphinx asked for it. I assume the issue will be resolved by the time this book is published.

Building EPUB Documentation

You can build the EPUB e-book format as well:

```
make epub
```

And open the documentation from _build/epub using your favorite e-book reader.

By pressing make [TAB] you see a list of other options for building documentation. Internally, make uses the sphinx-build program. A more verbose way of building HTML documentation is

```
sphinx-build -b html . _build/html
```

Where . is the directory with all source files and _build/html the directory to which the built documentation is written.

Writing Documentation

Sphinx uses reStructuredText as a markup format. Generally, documentation is written in text files with the suffix .rst. The ReST file tile grid.rst for documenting the generate maze module could contain the following text:

```
The Maze Generator
------------------

The module "maze_run.generate_maze" is responsible for generating mazes. It creates a
**two-dimensional list** with a *fixed size* that can be used to create a graphical
representation in Pygame.
```

The maze consists of corridors represented by dots and walls represented by hashes. The algorithm leaves a circular path close to the border.

Some special characters are used to indicate formatting. For instance, underlining a line is a heading, while double apostrophes create fixed-width font for code, shell commands, and so on. Likewise, you can make italic and bold text, images, and many more. See Table 17-1 for some examples. The full ReST format is explained at www.sphinx-doc.org/en/stable/rest.html.

Table 17-1. *Markup in the ReStructuredText Format*

Function	ReST Markup
Bold	*text*
Italic	**text**
fixed-width (code)	"code"
Hyperlink	'link name <http://academis.eu/>'
bulleted list	* first bullet
Enumeration	1. first item
heading 1	underline with '--------', same length as text
heading 2	underline with '========', same length as text
heading 3	underline with '++++++++', same length as text

Directives

Directives are a special kind of markup. Directives are rules that determine how **Sphinx** generates documents: Most of the ***interesting*** features of Sphinx like linking documents together, writing Python code, and including Python docstrings require the use of directives. All directives start with .. and end with ::, so, for example, the directive to include an image in the document is

```
.. image:: example_maze.png
```

Organizing Documents

A central directive is toctree. It creates a tree-like table of contents. In Sphinx, all documents are organized by tables of contents or **toctrees**. A toctree directive could look like this:

```
.. toctree::
   mazes.rst
   tile_grid.rst
   sprite.rst
   :maxdepth:  2
```

Here, the documents mazes.rst and tile grid.rst have been added to the table of contents. The instruction :maxdepth: 2 tells Sphinx to not only include the documents listed here, but also to ***recursively*** include whatever documents are listed in the toctree statements in the respective documents. When writing a toctree directive, we can use absolute and relative paths, and have multiple toctree statements in a single document. Sphinx will automatically create the navigation and indices from all toctrees in the entire document, using the headings inside the files as titles.

▨ **Warning**   The space after the two dots in a directive is crucial! If you forget it and write, for example, ..toctree:: instead of .. toctree::, Sphinx will treat that line as regular text and won't complain about it.

Code Examples

One of the most important things when documenting software is code itself. To include Python code in a
.rst file, we simply need to set a double colon (::) and introduce an indented paragraph:

```
Using the "generate_maze" module::

    >>> from maze_run.generate_maze import create_maze
    >>> maze = create_maze(14, 7)
    >>> print(maze)
    ##############
    #...........#
    #.#.#..#.###.#
    #.#...##.#...#
    #...#....#..##
    #.#....#.....#
    ##############
```

The Python code will be rendered to syntax-highlighted text, no matter whether it contains the prompt
symbols (>>>) or not. The rendering is done by the **pygments** library. This option is sufficient to write a
cookbook containing many code examples (see Figure 17-3).

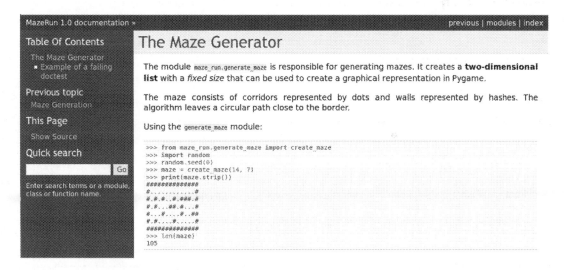

Figure 17-3. *HTML output with source code rendered by Sphinx*

Generating Documentation from Docstrings

If we have installed the autodoc extension when setting up Sphinx, we can generate documentation from
docstrings for functions, classes, or entire modules. In the autofunction directive we can reference a
function from our program:

```
.. autofunction:: maze_run.generate_maze.create_maze
```

In the documentation, the signature of that function appears with the documentation. If you included
the viewcode extension as well, you also get a link to the source code automatically.

▒ **Hint**   You need to set the PYTHONPATH variable to the directory with the maze_run package, so that Sphinx can import it. You might have done that already in one of the previous chapters (or used pip with the -e option). To make the modules available for import, I occasionally add the correct import path to sys.path in conf.py if it is not found in the PYTHONPATH variable by default.

Entire modules can be discovered with the automodule directive as well:

```
.. automodule:: maze_run.generate_maze
   :members:
```

Sphinx collects all functions and classes *having a docstring* and the module-level docstring and compiles the according documentation. If you don't see a function description generated by autodoc this doesn't mean that such a function does not exist, only that it has no docstring.

Note that Sphinx completes building the documentation even if the import fails. With the exception of few very serious errors, Sphinx will always attempt to complete the build instead of terminating with an error. Look out for error messages in the generated documentation (see Figure 17-4).

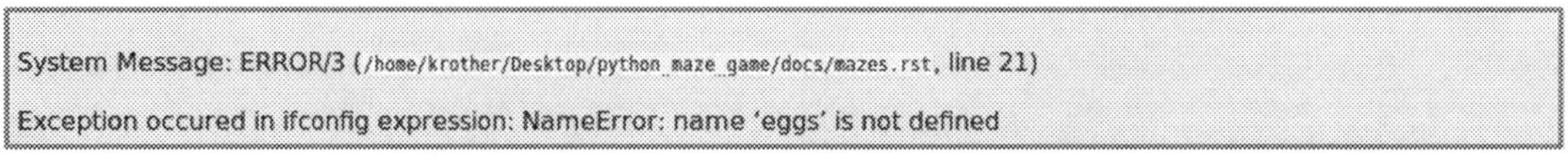

System Message: ERROR/3 (/home/krother/Desktop/python_maze_game/docs/mazes.rst, line 21)

Exception occured in ifconfig expression: NameError: name 'eggs' is not defined

Figure 17-4. *Error messages generated by Python appear in the documentation generated by Sphinx*

▒ **Warning**   Both autofunction and automodule import the module in the same way as Python programs do. Code being executed in the body of the function may have side effects (e.g., if it creates or deletes files).

Doctests

Documentation tests or **doctests** are an efficient way to combine documentation with automated testing. strongdoctests consist of Python shell sessions inside your Sphinx documents. When executing the tests, Sphinx executes the commands from these sessions and matches their output with the output from the documentation. That way, we can effectively provide documentation that is ***proven to be correct***.

To write a doctest, we need to have the doctest extension activated in Sphinx (as described in the preceding initial configuration). Then we copy a Python shell session into a .rst file and place it under the doctest directive. A doctest for producing a maze from a set of corridor positions would look like this:

```
.. doctest::

    >>> from maze_run.generate_maze import create_grid_string
    >>> dots = [(1,1), (1, 2), (2,2), (2,3), (3,3)]
    >>> maze = create_grid_string(dots, 5, 5)
```

```
>>> print(maze.strip())
#####
#.###
#..##
##..#
#####
```

To execute the tests, write

```
make doctest
```

In the output, we obtain an overview of passing and failing tests for each `.rst` document and a summary at the end. Each Python line is interpreted as a separate test (because each line could fail individually):

```
Document: tile_grid
-------------------
1 items passed all tests:
   4 tests in default
4 tests in 1 items.
4 passed and 0 failed.
Test passed.

Doctest summary
===============
    4 tests
    0  failures  in  tests
    0 failures in setup code
    0 failures in cleanup code
build succeeded.
```

In contrast, if we write a failing test:

```
.. doctest::

   >>> 1 + 2
   2
```

In this case the output of `make doctest` contains a failure message indicating the line in the documentation file:

```
**********************************************************************
File "tile_grid.rst", line 21, in default
Failed   example:
    1 + 2
Expected:
    2
Got:
    3
**********************************************************************
```

░ **Are doctests a replacement for Unit Tests and other kinds of automated testing?** To some extent, we can replace automated tests like the ones created with **pytest** in Chapter 8 by doctests. Especially, if we are testing the user-centric side of a Python library—its interface—doctests are very valuable. However, they are not so great to test detailed functionality of smaller units of code. When we try to cover many *border cases* or a series of test scenarios by doctests, the amount of code will quickly skyrocket. Also, doctests lack many options such as test parametrization or running tests selectively. Therefore, a Best Practice is to use doctests for creating tested, human-readable documentation rather than an exhaustive test set.

Configuring Sphinx

Todo Entries

We can mark entries in the documentation as TODO items. For instance, we could mark planned features in the documentation using the todo directive. The following two features have not been implemented yet:

```
.. todo::
```

```
Adding caching to the function drawing mazes could accelerate graphics a lot.
```

```
.. todo::
```

```
Describe how to move an element of a maze.
```

Creating a Todo-List

The todolist directive shows us all TODO items defined so far:

```
TODOs in the MazeRun project
++++++++++++++++++++++++++++++
.. todolist::
```

With the todo extension (configurable when starting the Sphinx project) we can switch the TODO items on and off in the final documentation. A configuration variable in conf.py is used to toggle the TODO items (by default it is set to True:

```
todo_include_todos  =  True
```

Alternatively, we can override the configuration setting using a command-line option:

```
sphinx-build -b html -D todo_include_todos=1 . _build/html
sphinx-build -b html -D todo_include_todos=0 . _build/html
```

Conditional Building

Similarly, we can add our own variables (e.g., to compile documentation for different operating systems, processor architectures, or simply a long and a short version). Let's assume we want to build a long documentation for developers and a shorter one as an appetizer for a website.

This requires the ifconfig extension to be switched on (this should have happened when starting the project, but we can add it later in conf.py). To create our own switch, we need to define a new configuration variable size at the end of conf.py. This can be done in a few lines:

```
size = "long"

def setup(app):
    app.add_config_value('size', '', 'env')
```

Next, we add the optional text inside an ifconfig directive in the .rst file. We add a small text for the short version, and for the long version we link to an extra document.

```
.. ifconfig:: size == "short"

Magic Methods in MazeRun
++++++++++++++++++++++++
Some classes in MazeRun contain examples for reusable object-oriented design. It uses
several magic methods and properties to make it easy to access the data.

.. ifconfig:: size == "long"

   .. include('magic_methods.rst')
```

ifconfig evaluates the Python expression size == "short". If it evaluates to True, the extra text in the paragraph will be rendered. We can build both the long and short version of our documentation with

```
sphinx-build -b html -D size=long . _build/long_html
sphinx-build -b html -D size=short . _build/short_html
```

To use multiple configurations in parallel, we might edit the Makefile to include them, or create a second copy of the configuration file conf.py and switch between them using the -c option when building documentation.

Changing the Look and Feel

To style your documentation or give it a corporate look and feel, we may want to change the templates Sphinx is using. Sphinx comes with several built-in themes. We can configure them by changing the html theme variable in the conf.py file:

```
html_theme = 'classic'
```

Possible names include 'alabaster', 'classic', 'sphinxdoc', 'sphinx rtd theme', 'scrolls', 'agogo', 'traditional', 'nature', 'haiku', 'pyramid', and 'bizstyle'.

For more detailed or customized changes, we can create our own templates in the templates directory. Internally, Sphinx uses **Jinja** as a templating engine. This means we can replace only a part of the default templates by our own or edit only the CSS files to change how the site looks. See more information at www.sphinx-doc.org/en/stable/templating.html.

How to Write Good Documentation?

Writing good documentation is different from writing a novel or a technical book. Readers approach them with many different intentions. Some readers want to understand the basics of our program, some are looking for very detailed answers, and others just want to look up something quickly. Because of these intentions, good documentation needs to be easily accessible, accurate, and actionable. Making everybody happy all the time is very difficult, and probably not even desirable. But there are **typical text sections** that occur frequently in many projects.

Text Sections in Technical Documentation

We will consider the following typical text sections as Best Practices for documenting software.

Summary

Good documentation starts with answering the *why*. Why would we want to use the software? Why did we build it in the first place? What is the *single problem* that it solves? A good summary needs to be short.

Prerequisites and Installation

A necessary aspect of software is getting it to work. Our documentation needs to cover that, even if it only contains nothing more than a single `pip install` command. In other cases you may need to include step-by-step instructions. Mentioning the available and/or tested platforms is also worthwhile. If we think the program should work on a particular platform, but we haven't tested it, this is a good thing to write in the installation section as well.

Getting Started

This section is to describe the intended primary use of the software. In many cases, this can be phrased as a *"Hello world"*-like example. Depending on our program this example may include Python code, a step-by-step recipe or both. If our program does more than one thing, we can include a small tour of features in this section.

Cookbook

A cookbook is a set of recipes illustrating the use of our program, including code examples. The examples must be complete and accurate, which is where doctests have their moment of glory. Cookbook-style documentation works for basic and advanced features.

Case Studies

An even more practical way than cookbooks is to document **case studies**, examples of how we actually *used* the software in practice. It will help users to get a better feeling of what is possible with the software and what is not.

Technical Reference

A technical reference is typically an enumeration of parts: the description of an input format, a table of parameters, and a list of functions in our program (possibly automatically generated). This is the part for readers who want to look up things. Sphinx having a search function by default comes in handy.

Design Documentation

The most advanced readers (those that want to work with our source code) will be interested in details of the program design. Here, the *why* becomes important again. Why did we build the program the way it is? What were our main design considerations? Can we provide a visual overview of our software? Whether we should document our program design or not depends a lot on the kind of software. In a complex server architecture this might even be the most important part of the documentation.

Legal Aspects

The documentation should say who is the author, point to a license, and contain a legal disclaimer (which could be in the LICENSE file). If you wish to be contacted, don't forget your e-mail address.

Examples of Good Documentation

There are many Python projects with great documentation. This documentation has in common that it contains instructive headings and short sections and avoids complicated vocabulary. If the use of domain-specific language cannot be avoided, they are at least used consistently.

Some examples of well-documented Python projects are:

- **gizeh** by zulko (http://github.com/Zulko/gizeh): gizeh is a library for creating vector graphics built on top of **cairo**. The documentation fits on a single web page, yet the library is very powerful. This is an example that documentation does not have to be long.

- **py.test** by **Holger Krekel** (http://pytest.org/latest/contents.html): The documentation of the test framework used in this book finds the right balance between documenting basic and advanced features. On the front page, there is a detailed but clearly structured table of contents. The first two sections cover the basics and are sufficient for basic usage. The remainder (about two-thirds) describes special use cases. By focusing on concrete examples, the authors avoid explaining every possible special case.

- **scikit-learn** (http://scikit-learn.org): The number one library for Machine Learning in Python (*Learning scikit-learn: Machine Learning in Python,* **Raúl Garreta and Guillermo Moncecchi, JMLR 12, pp. 2825–2830, Packt Publishing, 2011.**) has to balance two challenges:

First, the library itself is huge, and second, the underlying concepts are complex. The resulting documentation is vast and there are many good things to find in there. I would like to point out the use of images to illustrate different methods (e.g., http://scikit-learn.org/stable/auto_examples/classification/plot_classifier_comparison.html).

■ **Tip** You can view the Pygame documentation in a browser with:

```
python -m pygame.docs
```

Like writing software, writing documentation is an iterative process. Don't expect to clean up the documentation *"once and for all."* The ideal Best Practice is to maintain documentation and code in parallel. That does not mean we need to update the documentation every time we change something in the code. Aim at documenting things that **do not change frequently**. For frequently changing parts, comments in our source code or the source code itself are a better place. Using Sphinx in combination with doctests makes our life a lot easier, because we can check which parts of your documentation are correct.

Other Documentation Tools

There are many other tools that help maintain documentation for Python projects worth mentioning. Some of them are thought as possible replacements for Sphinx, but the majority rather complement the functionality Sphinx provides:

MkDocs

Compared to Sphinx, **MkDocs** is a lightweight documentation tool. It renders documents in the **Markdown** format to HTML with a number of templates available. It has a preview functionality; that is, we can see the rendered documentation as we write. At this moment, **MkDocs** does not have any functionality to include Python docstrings directly like Sphinx does. See `www.mkdocs.org/`.

Jupyter Notebooks

Jupyter notebooks offer a unique mixture of text and executable code. They serve the purpose of documenting work, especially in rapidly evolving projects. When writing code for data analyses that we want to share together with results, diagrams, and text describing whatever went through our mind, notebooks are a widely accepted tool. See `http://jupyter.org/`. Jupyter notebooks can be combined with **reveal.js** to convert a notebook to a slide presentation (`http://lab.hakim.se/reveal-js/`).

Gitbook

Gitbook is a program to create documents in multiple e-book formats (PDF, EPUB, MOBI, and HTML). It is also a web portal that builds and hosts the resulting e-books. Gitbook uses the **Markdown** format as a markup language. **Gitbook** is a good choice for tutorials and guides where the integration with source code is not as tight as with Sphinx. In more recent versions, Gitbook supports multilanguage documents. See `www.gitbook.io`.

Read the Docs

Read the Docs offers free hosting of documentation built with Sphinx and **MkDocs**. The service allows using **git web-hooks** so that the documentation is rebuilt automatically as soon as we push changes to the **git repository** containing our documentation. See `http://readthedocs.org/`.

pydoc

The `pydoc` tool displays documentation for any importable module in the console. For instance if we are in the directory with the `maze run.py` file:

```
pydoc maze_run
```

pydoc also allows searching documentation, creating HTML documents, and starting a local web server to browse documentation. `pydoc` is installed with Python by default. See `pydoc   --help` for details.

S5

The **S5** layout, established by **Eric A. Meyer,** is a standard for HTML5 templates useful for slide presentations. They allow writing a presentation in the *Markdown* format and compiling it to a slideshow. See `http://meyerweb.com/eric/tools/s5/`.

pygments

`pygments` is the Python library Sphinx uses to render Python code to syntax-highlighted representations. `pygments` can create HTML representations for most programming languages on this planet. If we want to display Python code on our own Python-based website, `pygments` is the tool of choice. See `http://pygments.org/`.

doctest

The `doctest` module from the Python Standard Library can be used independently of Sphinx. We can write doctests directly into our docstrings and execute them with

```
python  -m  doctest  my program.py
```

See `http://docs.python.org/3/library/doctest.html`.

PyPDF2

The Python library `PyPDF2` allows splitting and merging PDF documents with a few lines of Python code. I find it highly useful for postprocessing PDFs (e.g., adding a cover). See `http://github.com/mstamy2/PyPDF2`.

pandoc

With **pandoc** you can quickly convert a variety of markup formats into each other and generate Word or PDF documents. It is very handy to keep a diverse set of documents under control. See `http://pandoc.org/`.

Best Practices

1. **Sphinx** is a tool to build documentation for Python projects.

2. Sphinx builds documentation as HTML, PDF, or EPUB documents.

3. It uses the **ReStructuredText** format as a markup language.

4. **Directives** link multiple `.rst` documents, include images, or trigger other special functions of Sphinx.

5. Python code in the documentation is rendered with syntax highlighting via **pygments**.

6. Documentation for Python functions and modules can be autogenerated from **docstrings**.

7. **doctests** are shell sessions written into your documentation. They can be executed by Sphinx, effectively verifying whether your documentation is correct.

8. Parts of your documentation may be toggled on and off using **configuration variables**.

9. Good documentation covers both the **why** and **how** of a piece of software, both for technical and nontechnical readers.

Index

© Kristian Rother 2017
K. Rother, *Pro Python Best Practices*, DOI 10.1007/978-1-4842-2241-6

Get the eBook for only $4.99!

Why limit yourself?

Now you can take the weightless companion with you wherever you go and access your content on your PC, phone, tablet, or reader.

Since you've purchased this print book, we are happy to offer you the eBook for just $4.99.

Convenient and fully searchable, the PDF version enables you to easily find and copy code—or perform examples by quickly toggling between instructions and applications.

To learn more, go to http://www.apress.com/us/shop/companion or contact support@apress.com.

Printed in the United States
By Bookmasters